*Ling-yuh W. (Miko) Pattie, MSLS*
*Bonnie Jean Cox, MA, MSLS*
*Editors*

# Electronic Resources: Selection and Bibliographic Control

*Pre-publication*
*REVIEWS,*
*COMMENTARIES,*
*EVALUATIONS . . .*

"Miko Pattie and Bonnie Cox have put together a timely, informative look at the rapidly changing world of electronic resources and libraries. Libraries are struggling to come to terms with new methods of access and new forms of information which are changing even as procedures and workflows are being discussed. New methods of applying traditional principles in the context of these new technologies are explored in this thought provoking volume. This compilation will be of interest to librarians in all areas interested in taking advantage of new and developing technologies to connect the user information needed. . . ."

**Barry B. Baker, MLS**
*Assistant Director*
*for Technical Services*
*University of Georgia Libraries*

*More pre-publication*
*REVIEWS, COMMENTARIES, EVALUATIONS . . .*

"In a succinct statement of intent, editors Miko Pattie and Bonnie Jean Cox clearly recognized that discussions on the selection and bibliographic control of electronic resources bear some resemblance to "nailing Jell-O® to a tree" while simultaneously recognizing the urgency underlying the need that these conversations occur. Toward that end, they have compiled an outstanding set of chapters from leaders in the field addressing conceptual and practical issues regarding electronic resources. The articles on the principles for selection and bibliographic control and the relationship between library online catalogs and the World Wide Web build a fundamental background for the following detailed examinations of ground breaking projects, including works in progress for creating access to electronic resources at the University of Virginia, Stanford University, North Carolina State University, Library of Congress and OCLC.

The impact of using standards and tools relatively new to the world of library cataloging, such as TEI, SGML and the Dublin Core, is described together with assessments of their potential for future use. The international arena is considered as well with descriptions of innovative work in Australia and Scotland, the latter utilizing a subject tree approach for access to Internet-accessible resources.

Written for a general audience who are themselves grappling with these issues, the articles are uniformly well written and informative. While it is difficult to open a journal today without seeing mention of electronic resources, this volume should prove to be a resource for librarians and others on this topic for years to come. It is an excellent compendium of issues and progress to date in defining workable solutions which will be equally useful to practitioners seeking answers as well as researchers probing the historical record."

**Jennifer Younger, PhD**
*Assistant Director*
*for Technical Services*
*University Libraries*
*The Ohio State University*

# Electronic Resources: Selection and Bibliographic Control

# Electronic Resources: Selection and Bibliographic Control

Ling-yuh W. Pattie, MSLS
Bonnie Jean Cox, MA, MSLS
Editors

The Haworth Press, Inc.
New York • London

*Electronic Resources: Selection and Bibliographic Control* has also been published as *Cataloging & Classification Quarterly*, Volume 22, Numbers 3/4 1996.



The Haworth Press, Inc., 10 Alice Street, Binghamton, NY 13904-1580 USA

**Library of Congress Cataloging-in-Publication Data**

Electronic resources : selection and bibliographic control / Ling-yuh W. Pattie, Bonnie Jean Cox, editors.

p. cm.

Includes bibliographical references and index.

ISBN 1-56024-847-5 (alk. paper)

1. Cataloging of databases. 2. Cataloging of databases–United States. 3. Database selection. 4. Database selection–United States. I. Pattie, Ling-yuh W. II. Cox, Bonnie Jean.

Z695.615.E44 1996 96-27556

025.04–dc20 CIP

# INDEXING & ABSTRACTING

Contributions to this publication are selectively indexed or abstracted in print, electronic, online, or CD-ROM version(s) of the reference tools and information services listed below. This list is current as of the copyright date of this publication. See the end of this section for additional notes.

- ***CNPIEC Reference Guide: Chinese National Directory of Foreign Periodicals,*** P.O. Box 88, Beijing, Peoples Republic of China
- ***Computing Reviews,*** Association for Computing Machinery, 1515 Broadway, 17th Floor, New York, NY 10036
- ***Current Awareness Bulletin***, Association for Information Management, Information House, 20-24 Old Street, London EC1V 9AP, England
- ***IBZ International Bibliography of Periodical Literature,*** Zeller Verlag GmbH & Co., P.O.B. 1949, D-49009 Osnabruck, Germany
- ***Index to Periodical Articles Related to Law***, University of Texas, 727 East 26th Street, Austin, TX 78705
- ***Information Science Abstracts***, Plenum Publishing Company, 233 Spring Street, New York, NY 10013-1578
- ***Informed Librarian, The,*** Infosources Publishing, 140 Norma Road, Teaneck, NJ 07666
- ***INSPEC Information Services,*** Institution of Electrical Engineers, Michael Faraday House, Six Hills Way, Stevenage, Herts SG1 2AY, England
- ***INTERNET ACCESS (& additional networks) Bulletin Board for Libraries ("BUBL"), coverage of information resources on INTERNET, JANET, and other networks.***
  - JANET X.29:UK.AC.BATH.BUBL or 00006012101300
  - TELNET: BUBL.BATH.AC.UK or 138.38.32.45 login 'bubl'
  - Gopher: BUBL.BATH.AC.UK (138.32.32.45). Port 7070
  - World Wide Web: http: //www. bubl.bath.ac.uk./BUBL/ home.html
  - NISSWAIS: telnetniss.ac.uk (for the NISS gateway)

  The Andersonian Library, Curran Building, 101 St. James Road, Glasgow G4 ONS, Scotland
- ***Konyvtari Figyelo-Library Review,*** National Szechenyi Library, Centre for Library and Information Science, H-1827 Budapest, Hungary
- ***Library & Information Science Abstracts (LISA),*** Bowker-Saur Limited, Maypole House, Maypole Road, East Grinstead, West Sussex RH19 1HH, England
- ***Library Hi Tech News***, Pierian Press, P. O. Box 1808, Ann Arbor, MI 48106
- ***Library Literature,*** The H.W. Wilson Company, 950 University Avenue, Bronx, NY 10452

(continued)

- ***National Clearinghouse for Primary Care information (NCPCI),*** 8201 Greensboro Drive, Suite 600, McLean, VA 22102
- ***Newsletter of Library and Information Services,*** China Sci-Tech Book Review, Library of Academia Sinica, 8 Kexueyuan Nanlu, Zhongguancun, Beijing 100080, People's Republic of China
- ***Periodica Islamica,*** Berita Publishing, 22 Jalan Liku, 59100 Kuala Lumpur, Malaysia
- ***Referativnyi Zhurnal (Abstracts Journal of the Institute of Scientific Information of the Republic of Russia),*** The Institute of Scientific Information, Baltijskaja ul., 14, Moscow A-219, Republic of Russia

## SPECIAL BIBLIOGRAPHIC NOTES

*related to special journal issues (separates) and indexing/abstracting*

- ❑ indexing/abstracting services in this list will also cover material in any "separate" that is co-published simultaneously with Haworth's special thematic journal issue or DocuSerial. Indexing/abstracting usually covers material at the article/chapter level.
- ❑ monographic co-editions are intended for either non-subscribers or libraries which intend to purchase a second copy for their circulating collections.
- ❑ monographic co-editions are reported to all jobbers/wholesalers/approval plans. The source journal is listed as the "series" to assist the prevention of duplicate purchasing in the same manner utilized for books-in-series.
- ❑ to facilitate user/access services all indexing/abstracting services are encouraged to utilize the co-indexing entry note indicated at the bottom of the first page of each article/chapter/contribution.
- ❑ this is intended to assist a library user of any reference tool (whether print, electronic, online, or CD-ROM) to locate the monographic version if the library has purchased this version but not a subscription to the source journal.
- ❑ individual articles/chapters in any Haworth publication are also available through the Haworth Document Delivery Services (HDDS).

# Electronic Resources: Selection and Bibliographic Control

CONTENTS

∞ ALL HAWORTH BOOKS AND JOURNALS ARE PRINTED ON CERTIFIED ACID-FREE PAPER

## ABOUT THE EDITORS

**Ling-yuh W. (Miko) Pattie, MSLS,** is Assistant Director for Technical Services at the University of Kentucky Libraries and Adjunct Professor in the University's School of Library and Information Science. Ms. Pattie is an OCLC Users Council delegate, a library automation consultant, and has served as a cataloger and an automation librarian at other academic libraries in Kentucky.

**Bonnie Jean Cox, MA, MSLS,** is Assistant Director for Collection Development for the University of Kentucky Libraries and is a member of the library team overseeing electronic resources. She is Chair of the Collection Development and Electronic Media Committee of the Association for Library Collections and Technical Services' Collection Management and Development Section and is Chair-Elect of the Women's Studies Section of the Association of College and Research Libraries. Ms. Cox served as Director of Women's Studies in the College of Arts and Sciences at the University of Kentucky for three years.

# Foreword

Rapid and explosive developments in the generation and delivery of information in the electronic environment have made it necessary for library professionals to rethink traditional concepts and practices in acquisition and cataloging. Because information packaging is no longer tangible, and resources are no longer contained in specific locations, traditional methods for selection and bibliographical control are becoming increasingly inadequate, particularly for the resources that are available on the Internet.

Because information resources are now "accessed" rather than "acquired" and "owned," the very notions of "selection" and "collection development" have taken on different meanings. Furthermore, the concept of "location," in particular, is undergoing fundamental changes, because electronic information is distributed rather than centralized. In the search for viable methods in the handling of electronic information, traditional cataloging concerns must be reconsidered. An important issue in the ongoing re-examination is the relevance and the applicability of traditional concepts and practices to the digital environment. Such concepts include the principles of collocation and differentiation, and the practices include object identification, coding, and subject access. Also pertinent is the relationship of various mechanisms for accessing electronic resources and library catalogs. A further consideration is the relationship between electronic resources and whatever print counterparts exit. These relationships must be clearly understood, defined, and delineated if access to remote electronic resources is to be integrated with other access provisions in exiting library catalogs and if necessary user services connected with those resources are to be provided.

---

[Haworth co-indexing entry note]: "Foreword." Chan, Lois Mai. Co-published simultaneously in *Cataloging & Classification Quarterly* (The Haworth Press, Inc.) Vol. 22, No. 3/4, 1996, pp. xi-xii; and: *Electronic Resources: Selection and Bibliographic Control* (ed: Ling-yuh W. Pattie, and Bonnie Jean Cox) The Haworth Press, Inc., 1996, pp. xi-xii. Single or multiple copies of this article are available from The Haworth Document Delivery Service [1-800-342-9678, 9:00 a.m. - 5:00 p.m. (EST). E-mail address: getinfo@haworth.com].

 

Library professionals have already made advances in the field of selection and bibliographic control of electronic resources. At the same time, the digital environment itself is evolving at a rapid pace. Thus, devising effective and efficient means for handling electronic information is an ongoing process, and the end is nowhere in sight. At this midpoint of the decade, between the time when the Internet and the World Wide Web took off at the beginning of the decade and the looming new millennium, it is perhaps an opportune moment to pause and ponder where we have been and where we are heading by reviewing some of the advancements made thus far. This collection of essays on various aspects of the topic reports on several recent efforts and reflects some of the best thinking at this particular point in time.

*Lois Mai Chan*
*University of Kentucky*
*Lexington, KY*

# Introduction

Ling-yuh W. (Miko) Pattie
Bonnie Jean Cox

The stunning growth and the democratization of the Internet usage during this past year when this collection was conceived has further validated the need for honest and provocative discussions among information professionals as to where we fit into what Clifford Stoll called the "unreal universe."[1] It almost seems that overnight we have awakened from a well-defined print world to this electronic universe and, though dazed and incredulous, are struggling to make some sense of it. The struggles to define, select, and control electronic resources in our own institution convinced us that an attempt such as this would help provide a common ground for deliberations and decision-making in libraries and information centers. We sincerely hope so.

It is our intention to address both conceptual and pragmatic aspects of selection and bibliographic control of electronic resources. We want to engage the thinkers and doers in the field in constructive and productive dialogues as to where we are going and how we are going to get there from here. Keeping our own struggles in mind, we also want this volume to be broad-in-scope in the sense that historical context is properly presented against innovative thinkings and doings. We know we are dealing with a moving target. We know we are nailing Jell-O® to a tree. Nevertheless, we hope this contributes to the ongoing process of defining the role of information professionals in this brave new world of electronic resources.

---

[Haworth co-indexing entry note]: "Introduction." Pattie, Ling-yuh W. (Miko), and Bonnie Jean Cox. Co-published simultaneously in *Cataloging & Classification Quarterly* (The Haworth Press, Inc.) Vol. 22, No. 3/4, 1996, pp. 1-8; and: *Electronic Resources: Selection and Bibliographic Control* (ed: Ling-yuh W. Pattie, and Bonnie Jean Cox) The Haworth Press, Inc., 1996, pp. 1-8. Single or multiple copies of this article are available from The Haworth Document Delivery Service [1-800-342-9678, 9:00 a.m. - 5:00 p.m. (EST). E-mail address: getinfo@haworth.com].

 

The universe of electronic resources is indeed diverse, expanding, intimidating and unstructured compared to the finite, pre-packaged print world upon which the information delivery infrastructure has been constructed. It ranges from magnetic disks accompanying books, magnetic tapes housed in computing centers, CD-ROMs, either single-stationed or networked, and in-house full-text centers to an array of remotely-accessible information resources, such as commercially-available abstracting and indexing or full-text files, and Internet resources. These papers give us a general overview of the universe and remind us of the distinctive nature inherent in traditional and electronic formats. As information technology shapes alternative forms of scholarly communication, libraries have found their entire traditional infrastructure in need of an overhaul, from organizational structure, selection, acquisitions, bibliographic control, processing, preservation, to user services. Even more significantly, they are scrambling to define their role against the backdrop of the information-glutted Internet. Information at our fingertips looks more like a reality than it really is as we, along with our users, surf and hunt for meaningful bytes. We must, however, keep in mind that the content, value-added, is what we are about. The container, conduit, or wiring should be put in its own proper context as we attempt to integrate electronic resources into our collection and services. As Ann Ockerson so aptly stated " . . . one must not underestimate the difficulties involved in anticipating a reconfiguration, nor the important role traditional print media are likely to retain far into the future."[2] The reconfiguration of that value-added content for which we provide stewardship begins with selection of electronic resources.

As selection of electronic resources begins to encompass networked-accessible information, either via campus, state or regional consortium, or Internet, source files and selection tools have evolved and brought us to the unfamiliar world of legal, technical and economic fronts. No longer is it sufficient for us to know what's out there (if we really can), we also need to possess some basic knowledge and skill to evaluate access methods in order to deliver needed information in a timely and cost-effective manner. A formal, collaborative working relationship with the computing and communications units becomes a necessity, so does the internal group of staff from systems, acquisitions, cataloging, preservation, and user services. Still central to this issue is meeting user needs. Instead of being provided with traditional information storage and retrieval tools, i.e., book stacks, card catalogs, journal indexes, interlibrary loans, or even mediated database searching, our users are now confronted with issues such as connectivity, unfriendly or dissimilar user interfaces, and information overload. Their need for value-added content is still the same, yet the container and the conduit have added a layer of complexity. Selection with user access capability foremost in mind will make integrating electronic resources into the collection easier on users and library staff alike. Peggy Johnson provides us a succinct overview of these issues, their implications on our existing services, and how we are to formulate selection policies and procedures. Not to be overlooked is her decision-making matrix model that gives us a pragmatic lead to implement an effective selection process.

For establishing a full-text service, David Seaman strongly advocates the adoption of Standard Generalized Markup Language (SGML) as a critical selection criterion for purchasing commercially available e-texts or creating in-house ones. The benefits of such a commitment are not to be underestimated, whether in user training, system configuration, transportability or in resource sharing. The Internet presents another new challenge for selectors. What are the selection tools? How do we include these resources in our collection? The participants in the OCLC Internet Cataloging Project are asking these questions on their listserv, INTERCAT, and are sharing their local solutions. The consensus seems to be that selection policies remain the same as those for other formats and that better local control is to be provided through mirroring the files in local World Wide Web homepages or policing the validity of the linking Uniform Resource Locator (URL). We are pleased to see that Mann Library at Cornell University has come up with a workable implementation scheme to mainstream Internet resources into their collection.[3]

The follow-up process of organizing selected electronic resources warrants ongoing discussions and investigations from both conceptual and pragmatic standpoints. Carol Mandel and Robert Wolven provide an overview of how we traditionally create intellectual access to our collection and what new approaches can be applied to organize electronic resources. The concept of reconfiguring bibliographic control by layering OPAC with other tools challenges us to think about how best to use what we know to do what needs to be done. Crucial to this undertaking is defining the relationship between OPAC and the Net as Diane Hillmann does for these "parallel universes." For most of us who are still struggling to include all electronic resources that we own, be it electronic serials or networked CD-ROMs, in our OPACs, the task of cataloging the Net resources is daunting. Based on the postings on INTERCAT, not only do we ask how but more often than not we also ask why. We know that underpinnings of bibliographic control elude the Net tools and thus render them ineffective and unreliable for more sophisticated surfing. When we saw an ad for a cataloger's position from Yahoo, one of the most popular Net tools, we were vindicated. However, can AACR2 and MARC do the job? Judy Brugger explores the Core Language and Information Bus central to the Stanford University Integrated Digital Library Project and how they relate to AACR2 and MARC. She speculates that the Text Encoding Initiative (TEI) header appears to have more potential value in accommodating the type of data digital libraries need to have to manage and control their resources. While a traditional cataloging record is a type of metadata, Priscilla Caplan and Rebecca Guenther bring us another type called "Dublin core metadata" which purports to serve as a discovery and retrieval tool for network-accessible information resources. The mapping of this elements set to USMARC reveals some predictable problems; it also raises a fundamental question of how best to offer simplified access with effective retrieval capabilities. The prescriptive nature of AACR2 and MARC is now confronted with syntax-independent TEI headers and Dublin core metadata. And the dilemma is born. The involvement of catalogers in the creation and modification of TEI headers at UVa's E-Text Center and VPI's E-Theses Project gives us a glimmer of hope that somehow we may yet strike a balance between simplified access and effective retrieval.

Amid this chaotic yet vital environment we are able to pin down some of the people involved with cutting-edge projects that create, select, and provide access to electronic resources. Given the ever-changing nature of this type of information, these projects may have opted for different approaches by the time this goes to print. It is, nevertheless, the underpinnings that support these undertakings that may, we hope, serve as references or models for other trailblazers to come.

The CATRIONA Project from the United Kingdom presents a pragmatic approach to designing an Internet discovery and retrieval system. A distributed MARC-based Z39.50-compliant catalog is aimed to provide systematic and effective access to Internet resources via the MARC 856 field and the system's capability to activate a Web client for patrons' retrieval. It is interesting to note that Nicholson and Steele deem it essential to provide one single tool for both traditional and electronic resources after their involvement with BUBL, a UDC-based subject tree tool for Internet resources. We anticipate significant findings to be forthcoming from their extended follow-up project.

Eric Morgan's ALCUIN Project, though informal and experimental, gives us a glance at how a traditional infrastructure is able to accommodate Internet resources in selection, acquisitions, cataloging, database maintenance, and patron access with some modifications. It is through his close collaboration with Hunter Monroe of Alex Catalog and Tim Kambitsch that this project takes its present shape. Coupled with his Mr. Serials project, Morgan is someone we look to for new and exciting doings in managing electronic resources.

Along with the Center for Electronic Texts in the Humanities (CETH), the Electronic Text Center at the University of Virginia has made some important strides in the electronic texts arena. The deliberate and systematic approach in selecting, creating, and cataloging e-texts at UVa reveals to us that a viable, strategized operation is possible to integrate e-texts into library collections. David Seaman and his team will no doubt continue to be at the forefront in this area. Not to be outdone is the Virginia Polytechnic Institute and State University's Electronic Theses and Dissertations Project. It addresses the total processing of e-theses, including the moving of files from the Graduate School to cataloging, patron access, in-house archiving via CD-ROM, and even sending files to UMI for microfilming process. One is certain to note, from Gail McMillan's article, the vital role the library plays in the electronic publishing chain.

Beth Davis-Brown and David Williamson give us a general overview of the Library of Congress' leadership role in the bibliographic control of digital materials through myriad projects and activities. Prominent among these are the National Digital Library Program (NDLP) and the electronic CIP project. From the NDLP initiative, one visible end result is the Encoded Archival Description (EAD) standard which will allow full text searching of archival materials across systems. With the integration of bibliographic workstations and the On the MARC program, the electronic CIP project demonstrates that it is possible to derive MARC records directly from electronic texts. It represents an alternative and viable strategy to tap the capabilities of the electronic medium in facilitating the cataloging process.

In a more pragmatic vein is Giles Martin's overview of Australia's systematic control of Internet resources. His snapshot seems to indicate a more structured approach than we have here. Yet the issues and deliberations inevitably remain the same.

The OCLC Internet Cataloging Project has generated much enthusiasm and anticipation for its unique ability to gather empirical data on how the traditional cataloging tools are capable of describing and providing effective access to Internet resources. Still immersed in the middle of this project, Martin Dillon and Eric Jul give a thorough overview of what types of resources are out there in the Net, how they differ from print materials, and what issues are to be addressed in providing the same level of intellectual access to Internet resources. Even though there appear to be quite a few obstacles to overcome, we are glad that OCLC is rolling up its sleeves and trying to see if this works. What can be gleaned from this project will definitely affect the course of things to come.

For information professionals the Web's wide acceptance and phenomenal growth on the Net calls for urgent measures to be taken before it is too late. The ease of publishing via homepages further gluts the Net with noise and congestion. Though one is tempted to side with Clifford Stoll's claim that this is nothing but silicon snake oil, we nevertheless have to face the sink-or-swim decision. It is with this sense of urgency that we extract the following issues from these papers for further deliberations and investigations:

1. The issue of having one single tool for both traditional and electronic resources seems to be one that warrants more discussions and experiments. Both the CATRIONA Project and the OCLC Internet Cataloging Project have not only used this as their premise but have also set out to validate if a decentralized cataloging cooperative will offer us universal bibliographic control and access to Internet resources. On the other hand, Mandel and Wolven propose a layering of linking tools including OPACs while Brugger reaches out to something new like the Information Bus.
2. Standards for creating record surrogates for item description, access and use are rapidly taking hold in the creation and delivery of electronic resources. SGML, HTML, the TEI header, and Dublin core metadata have joined the ranks of AACR2/MARC as standards for us to learn and use. The recent announcement on the Internet by Kluwer Academic Publishers of its collaborative arrangement with Pica in delivering SGML headers of journal articles containing bibliographical data and abstracts for its full text services reveals the potential role these standards play in the information delivery arena. The need to train information professionals in the use of these standards and the need to define the relationship between AACR2/MARC and the others are not to be taken lightly.
3. A librarian's role has evolved from that of safekeeping (or gatekeeping if so preferred) in the print world to that of an active player in the electronic environment as evidenced from the VPI's E-Theses Project, UVa's E-Text Center, and LC's National Digital Library Project. Whether it is a newly-created electronic thesis or a digitized and marked-up text the librarian has become an integral part in the creation, the packaging, and the delivery of these information resources. This transformation calls for alternative strategies in educating future information professionals and reconfiguring our traditional infrastructure for providing user services.

We urge all the thinkers in the field to come and take part in this debate as we march towards the next millennium. Michael Gorman, one of the most articulate among us, has given us his five new laws of librarianship:

1. libraries serve humanity;
2. respect all forms by which knowledge is communicated;
3. use technology intelligently to enhance services;
4. protect free access to knowledge; and,
5. honor the past and create the future.[4]

This revised version of Ranganathan's Five Laws of Library Science gives us the grounding for our profession just as the 1931 original did. How we embrace and integrate these into our day-to-day operations is yet to be sorted out. One thing we know for sure is that constant interchanges between those who select and catalog and those who serve users are critical at this juncture. It is our hope that librarians in public services will participate, just as Thomas Mann of LC has been doing, in this debate on how best to select and organize electronic resources to meet the needs of our users.

We want to thank the following for making this collection possible: Paul A. Willis, Director, University of Kentucky Libraries, for his support in including this project as a part of Miko Pattie's sabbatical leave; Benita Clarke, Technical Services, for her assistance in keeping us on track and assembling this final product; and these authors for sharing our vision of defining our role in this electronic universe.

## REFERENCES

1. Clifford Stoll, Silicon Snake Oil: Second Thoughts on the Information Highway (New York: Doubleday, 1995), p. 4.

2. Anthony M. Cummings et al., University Libraries and Scholarly Communication: A Study Prepared for The Andrew W. Mellon Foundation (Washington, D.C.: The Association of Research Libraries, 1992), p. xxv.

3. Samuel Demas et al., "The Internet and Collection Development: Mainstreaming Selection of Internet Resources," Library Resources & Technical Services 39, no. 3 (July 1995): 275-290.

4. Michael Gorman, "Five new laws of librarianship," American Libraries 26, no. 8 ( Sept. 1995): 784-785.

# Selecting Electronic Resources: Developing a Local Decision-Making Matrix

Peggy Johnson

**SUMMARY.** Selecting electronic resources requires both a policy statement to guide collection development and management and procedures to manage the process of selecting and handling these resources. Both policy and procedures must be crafted in response to local priorities, resources, limitations, and organizational structure. This paper examines issues that should be addressed when developing local procedures. Particular emphasis is given to preparing a mechanism to guide selection. One possible model–a decision-making matrix to guide selection between various media and modes of information delivery–is explored. *[Article copies available from The Haworth Document Delivery Service: 1-800-342-9678. E-mail address: getinfo@haworth.com]*

## *INTRODUCTION*

Selecting electronic resources for a library continues to be troubling for many librarians. While issues in making a selection decision are similar whatever the format, many differences separate the process of selecting electronic resources from selecting

---

Peggy Johnson, BA, MA, MBA, is Strategic Planning Officer, University of Minnesota Libraries and Assistant Director, St. Paul Campus Libraries, University of Minnesota, 1984 Buford Avenue, St. Paul, MN 55108.

[Haworth co-indexing entry note]: "Selecting Electronic Resources: Developing a Local Decision-Making Matrix." Johnson, Peggy. Co-published simultaneously in *Cataloging & Classification Quarterly* (The Haworth Press, Inc.) Vol. 22, No. 3/4, 1996, pp. 9-24; and: *Electronic Resources: Selection and Bibliographic Control* (ed: Ling-yuh W. Pattie, and Bonnie Jean Cox) The Haworth Press, Inc., 1996, pp. 9-24. Single or multiple copies of this article are available from The Haworth Document Delivery Service [1-800-342-9678, 9:00 a.m. - 5:00 p.m. (EST)]. E-mail address: getinfo@haworth.com].

 

traditional print and microform resources. Eventually, the process of making decisions about electronic resources and implementing these decisions will be familiar, comfortable, and even routine. However, few libraries are at this point. Choosing among formats, identifying what is available, analyzing costs, understanding licenses and other legal concerns, interpreting service implications, considering preservation, preparing equipment and facilities, and developing local approaches for acquiring, cataloging, and processing electronic resources introduce new challenges. Consequently, libraries are seeking to develop policies and procedures that will guide practice and ensure that all relevant aspects of the selection process are considered. Both policy and procedures must be crafted in response to local priorities, resources, limitations, and organizational structure.

This paper examines issues that should be addressed when developing local policy and procedures to manage the selection of electronic resources. Particular emphasis is given to preparing a mechanism to guide selection. One possible model–a decision-making matrix to guide selection between various media and modes of information delivery–is presented.

## *UNIQUE ASPECTS OF SELECTING ELECTRONIC RESOURCES*

Selecting electronic resources, developing the procedures for making these decisions, and deciding how to process the resources present librarians with new problems and new service implications. Being alert to these potential problems is a first step in dealing with them effectively. Important as intrinsic quality and local appropriateness are, selecting a particular electronic product or one format over another involves more. Each selection decision has consequences far beyond the cost of the product and the space required to house it. The challenges associated with selecting and managing electronic resources are both unique and unfamiliar.

The issue that must be confronted first is the unruliness of the medium. The universe of electronic information is not as well managed as that of print resources. Keeping informed about new commercial, government, and noncommercial electronic files can seem like a full time task, yet it is one that each selector should pursue. The routine reviewing infrastructure that handles print, audio, and video publications does not yet exist for electronic formats. Selectors must consult catalogs, journals, publication announcements, faculty, library colleagues, and various electronic resources including the Internet simply to identify what is available. Often the only way to gain information to evaluate a product is to see a demonstration at a conference or ask for a demo disk.

The higher relative costs and greater financial risk of electronic materials suggest extra care in selecting and handing. The high costs of electronic resources themselves, initial investments in hardware, software, special furniture, wiring, and telecommunication lines, and continuing costs of service and training mandate careful consideration of benefit and value. In addition, committing large sums of money to a technology that may be outdated quickly, a product that may be replaced by a better alternative, or a producer that may disappear increases the financial risk in choosing one resource over another. The total cost of a wrong decision can be intimidating.

Service implications when choosing electronic resources are more extensive than when choosing print or other familiar formats. The issues to be considered include what skills the user needs, how they will be taught, and who will teach them. Normally, this means that a selector must consult with those staff members who will be providing user service for the resource. Documentation, user manuals, and online help screens supplied by producers and vendors are considerations. Ease of use, access, and instruction are key decision components when selecting electronic resources. Such concerns are not usually an issue when considering print publications.

The need to evaluate licenses, contracts, and pricing structures as part of a selection decision is a new phenomenon. The surprising feature in this arena is that most contractual issues are negotiable. Each library must decide who is empowered to handle negotiations and who is authorized to make an institutional commitment. Usual license or purchase agreements address limitations on access (numbers and categories of users), ownership of electronic files when superseded or when the purchase arrangement is terminated, restrictions on downloading and other use of electronic data, responsibilities for monitoring use and potential copyright violation, restrictions on duplicating product documentation, liability for patron use of information, and other legal clauses that hold the publisher harmless in potential law suits. Because of legal ramifications, the selection of electronic resources frequently involves consultation with the library's legal advisor.

Both initial and continuing support costs for electronic resources are different from those associated with more traditional information sources. Electronic resources have unique equipment and facilities consequences. Consideration must be given to availability of appropriate space, hardware, workstation furniture, wiring, telecommunication lines, and technical support. Compatibility and interoperability can have significant effects on support costs for accessing and maintaining electronic information. Involving staff members with responsibilities for facilities and equipment and being knowledgeable about systems already in place becomes essential.

Current technical services operations do not always accommodate electronic resources. Decisions about selecting these information tools require consultation with staff members responsible for the units and procedures that handle ordering, receipting, claiming, cataloging, marking, circulating, housing, preserving, and updating library materials. Both placing an order and bursting the shrink wrap on a package may constitute contract agreement. Decisions must be made on claiming electronic journal issues. Libraries must decide if they will catalog all electronic resources. For example, a library cancels a print subscription to an index and provides gateway access to a remote file through an online menu choice. Should this new form of access to familiar information be reflected in a bibliographic entry in the online catalog? Circulating electronic resources, processing them through electronic security systems, and dealing with possibilities of virus introduction require new procedures. Finally, preserving and archiving electronic resources present different problems for libraries. All must be considered when making selection decisions.

Because the realm of electronic resources is still so new for most libraries, selection of these resources requires regular checking how each possible addition fits within the institutional vision. Most selectors understand and make selection decisions for traditional resources within the general mission of the library. They have internalized this image of their library and collection development occurs nearly automatically within it. The newness of electronic resources means that librarians must consciously stop and consider how this decision to acquire or access a particular resource fits into the library's general plan. They must take care not to be swayed by promotional promises, individual faculty member demands, or the immediate appeal of a new product. Developing such a vision of the library's plan for electronic resources is one important reason to develop an electronic resources collection development policy.

## *DEVELOPING AN ELECTRONIC RESOURCES POLICY STATEMENT*

Adding electronic information resources is easier when libraries have both a policy statement to guide collection development and procedures to manage selecting and handling these resources. Policies serve to guide the selection process within a systematic framework. Many policies contain procedures, which describe how decisions are made and who is involved. Both policies and procedures are developed within the local library context. This paper focuses on policies and guidelines for making decisions about electronic resources and briefly identifies procedural issues that should be addressed.

Paul Mosher writes that collection development is a process that "should constitute a rational documented program guided by written policies and protocols and should reflect, in a sense, a contract between library users and library staff as to what will be acquired, for whom and at what level."[1] Mosher makes important points–libraries need formal, written policies that guide the systematic, rational, and timely selection and deselection of library materials in response to user need. This is particularly critical as librarians work through the complex issues surrounding electronic resources, yet libraries face difficulties in crafting policies.[2]

A collection policy for electronic resources should follow the model of other collection development policies in place at the institution. It must be crafted within the context of existing collection policies. It should be systematic, comprehensive, and detailed. The policy should describe the library's objectives in developing its electronic resources and map plans for future development in terms of formats and subjects.

The electronic resources collection policy begins with a section that introduces the policy and sets the framework for decision making. Typical components in this portion are common to all selection policies. They typically include the following:

- Introduction, stating the purpose of the policy and the audience to whom it is directed. The intended audience may include library staff, users, administrators, governing board (regents, trustees, etc.), and librarians at other libraries.
- Description of the community served, types of users (undergraduates, graduate and special students, faculty, public, business community), and users' needs. This section describes academic programs or other subject needs and addresses the library's responsibility to the off-campus community and other constituencies.
- Statement of library priorities, related to user community.
- Identification of limitations affecting electronic resources selection. These may be financial, technical, legal, or institutional. It is here that the library may wish to speak to ideas about the imminence of a paperless society. The limits imposed by selective retrospective digital conversion and present publishing practices mean that libraries must select and maintain a mix of media formats.
- Overview of existing collection (both on site and remote) of electronic resources and future goals. This section identifies subject areas and formats that are emphasized, de-emphasized, or excluded and any general principles guiding selection. For example, the library may favor remote access to files instead of locally mounted resources because local technical support is limited. The library may be moving toward local area networks and the policy will encourage selection of CD-ROMs with licenses that permit networking.
- Description of library collection development organization. The location of responsibility (legal or delegated) for selec-

tion decisions is identified here. This component is critical in managing electronic information because of the consultative nature of selecting these resources. In many libraries, policies mandate a shared decision making structure and specify involving individuals who can speak to technical issues, services issues, and user concerns as well as evaluative criteria.

- Information on existing cooperative collection development agreements (networks, consortia, etc.). Commitments to resource sharing and size of total user community are pertinent when negotiating licenses.
- Identification of institutional priorities for cataloging and preserving electronic resources.
- Statement of the library's policy on use of funds for materials, equipment, and software needed to support electronic information resources. Some institutions require separate budget lines for acquisition of information resources and hardware, software, and technical support.
- Statement of the institution's policy or policies relating the responsibilities of the library, computing center, and campus network in acquiring and providing access to digitized information. Clarifying these responsibilities early can prevent later confusion and conflict.

The central component of an electronic resources policy details the principles guiding selection and explains the library's priorities when deciding which materials are added and to which materials access is provided. This section details the criteria for selection. These criteria usually begin with those relevant to all materials, though issues associated with electronic resources may be highlighted. Typical selection criteria are:

- relevance of material to program needs
- scope of treatment (refers to depth and breadth of the material)
- ability to fill gaps
- uniqueness of content or treatment
- quality of scholarship
- quality of physical product
- currency of information and frequency of updating
- accessibility of information (how it is organized and retrieved)

- language
- cost (immediate and continuing)
- reputation of author/reliability of publisher
- special features

The nature of electronic resources suggests additional criteria that should be considered in the selection process. These are the features that are unique to electronic information resources. They are particularly important because many electronic information resources are available in various delivery formats that must be compared and contrasted with each other and with paper versions. A policy guiding selection will identify the following considerations when evaluating and choosing between electronic resources:

- network, hardware, and software compatibility
- availability of network, hardware, and software resources
- availability of electrical and telecommunication lines
- quality of interface (ease of use for library users and staff)
- quality of retrieval/search engine
- training implications
- potential use (size of user community and frequency of use)
- reliability of vendor and availability of vendor support
- availability of documentation
- licensing considerations
- treatment of graphics, formula, and other nonstandard characters

When preparing an electronic resources collection policy, it is important to remember what a policy is not. It is not a static document. To remain meaningful, a policy must be reviewed and revised regularly. It is not general, vague, or overly simple. Conversely, it is not idealistic and it does not use flowery language. A policy must be a useful document, providing clear guidelines but not detailed to the point it becomes unworkable.

Most important, a collection policy is not a substitute for selection. It defines a framework and provides parameters, but cannot select specific titles. A policy is not prescriptive to the point of eliminating human decision. No matter how detailed the collection development policy statement may be, individual judgment still needs to be applied. Collection development policies can substitute for neither intelligent discernment nor an awareness of and sensitivity to the changing needs of the library's community. The most effective decisions are rational, based on explicit criteria, and linked to library objectives.

## *IMPORTANCE OF LOCAL INSTITUTIONAL CONTEXT*

The importance of responding to local needs, priorities, and constraints may seem self-evident, but frequently is given insufficient attention in the rush to move forward toward the electronic library. Decisions are too often made because an opportunity presents itself without considering how this resource fits within the library's mission. Much of the literature on selecting electronic resources concentrates on evaluating and costing technical aspects of the resource and negotiating purchase and lease agreements, while ignoring the central issues of quality and utility. User and programmatic needs are always the prime consideration. The first questions to ask are "Do we want this information resource for our library?" and "Is it the right resource for our users?" Only after these critical questions are answered affirmatively should the librarian go on to explore evaluative criteria and compare and contrast delivery options.

Moving too quickly or without careful regard to the library's collection development policies and library's mission creates feeling of chaos and lack of direction for staff and users. One librarian remarked that local faculty thought the library had joined the database of the month club because of the frequency with which new and sometimes surprising resources were being offered. Librarians must monitor user needs and priorities and keep knowledgeable about academic initiatives. This is the only way to keep electronic collection development objectives relevant. All selection criteria must be developed and evaluated against these objectives. Library objectives, crafted in response to the user community, must be implicit in the selection policies for all formats of information resources.

The useful *Guide to Selecting and Acquiring CD-ROMs, Soft-*

*ware, and Other Electronic Publications*[3] suggests several ways in which libraries can involve their user communities in the selection process. A library can acquire preview copies for staff members and library users to use and review. Librarians can encourage their faculty contacts to check with colleagues at other institutions and participate in relevant electronic discussion groups. An additional possibility is to volunteer the library as a beta test site for field testing a new product.

If an electronic resource is considered particularly valuable, other considerations follow. If the library's long range plan endorses a movement toward electronic provision of information, supporting this direction becomes a priority for budget allocation. Funds can be reallocated to acquire, access, and support electronic resources and staff members will support these priorities.

Decisions to eliminate an electronic resource also should be made within the local context and through consultation. Libraries usually seek to consult with users when beginning a serials cancellation project. Deselecting electronic resources is an equally important decision. Faculty members have said they are changing their methods of instruction and expectations for student performance as a consequence of the information provided through electronic resources. Decisions to cancel or withdraw and electronic information resource must be made against the backdrop of these changing user priorities.

## *DEVELOPING LOCAL PROCEDURES*

Each library will identify certain aspects of selecting electronic resources that will require special documented procedures. The following paragraphs look at four areas that may be considered for local approaches.

Developing a planning cycle with specified actions to occur at regular intervals can improve the selection and management of electronic resources. Libraries need to review products currently acquired or accessed. Continuing relevance to institutional priorities and programs should be evaluated. Owned, leased, and accessed resources should be compared and contrasted with new products, which may provide different pricing and licensing structures, expanded scope, and new modes of information delivery. Selectors normally carry on these tasks, but the greater cost of electronic resources suggests the importance of a specified review calendar. The planning cycle should match the library's budgeting cycle and consider renewal dates for subscriptions and contracts. Sufficient time should be allowed for careful review of alternatives and wide consultation both within the library and with users. A planning cycle document will lay out a calendar noting when various actions and decisions must be completed. If the OCLC First-Search contract is signed in late June, then selectors will spend several months in the spring reviewing files and considering alternatives. Having a prescribed schedule helps the library capitalize on opportunities to improve information access and make the best use of available funds.

Licenses, contracts, and purchase agreements already have been identified as a problem area when selecting electronic resources. Libraries often develop a procedures document that states who in the library is responsible for reviewing and negotiating these agreements and who has signing authority. Other issues that may need attention include specified responsibility for monitoring compliance and a designated single location where all agreements are retained. The legally binding nature of these documents should not be disregarded. A set of procedures can help a library gain control.

Budgeting and cost considerations involve both policies and procedures. Since few libraries receive additional funding for acquiring and accessing electronic information, costs are covered through reallocation and redirection of available money. Funding issues are second only to the actual selection decision in importance. Local decisions that should be documented include:

- Are all purchases of and subscriptions to electronic resources considered within the materials budget?
- Are some electronic resources funded "off the top" of the materials budget? What types or categories?
- Do individual selectors have total discretion over their own subject budget lines and can they use these funds to acquire, access, and subscribe to electronic resources?

- Can materials budget funds be used to purchase hardware and software and to preprocess electronic files to make them accessible?
- Is there a set ratio (as many libraries have for serials and monographs) for expenditures for electronic resources compared to expenditures for traditional publications?

Closely related to funding decisions are questions of selection authority and responsibility. Libraries often stumble in deciding who has what level of decision making power. The dilemma faced by many libraries is a desire to mainstream electronic resources selection–to make selectors responsible for resources in their subject areas–and the need to insure consultation with all affected parties. Some decisions (purchasing a data file on a floppy disk) may have little impact on the library's services. Others may have small or no initial cost, but have large staff costs to develop a local interface. The importance of coordination and consultation often results in a formal procedure that mandates wide review. This may be either through consideration by a committee or use of a sign-off sheet tracking wide assessment of the proposed resource and its cost, processing, and service implications. The important constant is to ensure that all decisions are made by or in consultation with knowledgeable staff members.

## *ONE MODEL FOR SELECTION DECISIONS*

Developing selection criteria requires deciding which features of a resource or format are worth noting for a given comparison. Successful selection considers the unique features of each type of resource, both electronic and print. The importance of each feature depends on the local environment and how these are addressed in policies, procedures, and priorities. Many models have been and continue to be developed to assist in selecting electronic resources. Some follow a text-based approach in which the selector answers questions about a particular electronic product. The matrix model presented in this paper proposes one possible set of criteria and seeks to present them in a way that facilitates comparison. Each library will review and revise this list according to its own priorities.

This model contains two segments. The first (Table 1) is a vehicle for evaluating non-cost criteria. Most of these look at use factors, which include value to the user and additional burden to the library for providing these resources. Each consideration, identified in the left column, will be addressed with comments under the type of resource (listed across the top of the form) being considered and compared. If this model is used, columns are necessary only for those formats being evaluated. More space should be provided in each box to accommodate comments. The form presented in Table 1 should be completed first since here are answered the questions "Do we want this information resource for our library?" and "Is it the right resource for our users?"

The second segment (Table 2) of the matrix is offered as one approach to conducting a cost comparison of various delivery formats. The left column suggests several cost considerations; a library may expand or reduce this list depending on the local situation. Many formats have one-time or start-up costs and continuing annual costs. Both should be reflected in information provided on the form and in the total costs calculated at the bottom. Of course, the lowest cost is not necessarily the best resource. Each library will decide how to balance cost with a resource's or format's utility or local value (Table 1).

## *CONCLUSION*

Providing seamless and easy access to information, whatever the format, is frequently a stated library goal. Libraries move toward this goal as librarians select more resources in electronic format, yet selecting electronic information resources is not yet routine. Much is still too unfamiliar or unique about the resources and the process of making selection decisions. This paper has sought to identify some of the more complex issues and suggested the importance of developing local policies and procedures that can guide libraries through them. One model has been offered as a possible approach to making informed selection decisions. In all cases, librarians should recognize the importance of tailoring both the policies and processes to the library's needs and priorities.

TABLE 1. Electronic Resources Decision-Making Matrix: Evaluation

| | Paper | Remote Online | Local Online | CD-ROM | Floppy Disks | On-Demand Magnetic Tape |
|---|---|---|---|---|---|---|
| Resource name: | | | | | | |
| Vendor/publisher name & address | | | | | | |
| Vendor support: telephone # 24 hr. service? onsite service? onsite training? | | | | | | |
| Coverage & currency: dates of coverage update frequency cumulative or supplements? | | | | | | |
| Audience: undergrad., grad., researcher, discipline | | | | | | |
| Quality: Sample, demonstration, or review copy? Beta test or trial period? Reviews available? (attach reviews) | | | | | | |
| Licensing considerations: limitations & restrictions | | | | | | |
| Unique features: | | | | | | |
| Skills needed: (patrons & staff) | | | | | | |
| Patron training needed: | | | | | | |
| Staff training needed: | | | | | | |
| Local needs for: acquisitions cataloging preservation archiving | | | | | | |

TABLE 2. Electronic Resources Decision-Making Matrix: Cost Analysis

| | Paper | Remote Online | Local Online | CD-ROM | Floppy Disks | On-Demand Magnetic Tape |
|---|---|---|---|---|---|---|
| Resource name: | | | | | | |
| Equipment:<br>microcomputer,<br>terminal, modem,<br>mainframe, disc storage,<br>printer,<br>CD-ROM player | | | | | | |
| Telecommunication:<br>telephone line,<br>Ethernet connection,<br>local area network | | | | | | |
| Electrical wiring: | | | | | | |
| Software:<br>comes with resource?<br>search software,<br>applications software,<br>data extraction software | | | | | | |
| Cost of Resource:<br>purchase, pay per use,<br>subscription,<br>acct. with vendor | | | | | | |
| Staff costs:<br>training,<br>programming,<br>maintenance | | | | | | |
| Other costs: | | | | | | |
| Skills needed:<br>(patrons & staff) | | | | | | |
| TOTAL COSTS: | | | | | | |
| Initial | | | | | | |
| Annual | | | | | | |

## REFERENCES

1. Paul H. Mosher, "Fighting Back: From Growth to Management in Academic Library Collection Development." (Paper delivered at the Pilot Collection Management and Development Institute at Stanford University, July 6-10, 1981), p. 4.

2. Elizabeth Parang and Laverna Saunders, *Electronic Journals in ARL Libraries: Policies and Procedures*, SPEC Kit 201 (Washington, D.C.: Office of Management Services, Association of Research Libraries, 1994), p. 5. An ARL survey conducted in early 1994 discovered that only 14% of thirty-five acquiring electronic journals had a collection development policy addressing their selection.

3. Stephen Bosch, Patricia Promis, and Chris Sugnet, *Guide to Selecting and Acquiring CD-ROMs, Software, and Other Electronic Publications*, Acquisition Guidelines no. 9 (Chicago: Publication Committee of the Acquisition of Library Materials Section, Association for Library Collections & Technical Services, American Library Association, 1994), pp. 19-20.

# Intellectual Access to Digital Documents: Joining Proven Principles with New Technologies

Carol A. Mandel
Robert Wolven

**SUMMARY.** This paper considers the relevance of Charles Ami Cutter's principles of bibliographic access to the universe of Internet accessible digital objects and explores new methods for applying these principles in the context of new information technologies. The paper examines the value for retrieval of collocating authors' names, identifying authors' roles, collocating works and versions, and providing subject access through classification and controlled vocabularies for digital resources available through the World Wide Web. The authors identify emerging techniques and technologies that can be used in lieu of or as a supplement to traditional cataloging to achieve these functions in organizing access to Internet resources. *[Article copies available from The Haworth Document Delivery Service: 1-800-342-9678. E-mail address: getinfo@haworth.com]*

---

Carol A. Mandel is Deputy University Librarian at Columbia University and Robert Wolven is Director, Bibliographic Control and Processing at Columbia University Libraries. They can be reached at mandel@columbia.edu and wolv-en@columbia.edu.

The authors wish to thank their colleagues David Millman, Stephen Davis, and especially Judith Klavans for their advice and comments during preparation of this paper.

[Haworth co-indexing entry note]: "Intellectual Access to Digital Documents: Joining Proven Principles with New Technologies." Mandel, Carol A., and Robert Wolven. Co-published simultaneously in *Cataloging & Classification Quarterly* (The Haworth Press, Inc.) Vol. 22, No. 3/4, 1996, pp. 25-42; and: *Electronic Resources: Selection and Bibliographic Control* (ed: Ling-yuh W. Pattie, and Bonnie Jean Cox) The Haworth Press, Inc., 1996, pp. 25-42. Single or multiple copies of this article are available from The Haworth Document Delivery Service [1-800-342-9678, 9:00 a.m. - 5:00 p.m. (EST). E-mail address: getinfo@haworth.com].

 

## *WEBS AND CATALOGS: THE CHALLENGE*

Information on the World Wide Web (WWW) could be likened to a library in which authors shelve their own books, haphazardly, rewrite them overnight, and move them from place to place without warning. This comparison captures something of the volatility and mutability of electronic information resources, but it only begins to capture the difficulty of providing coherent intellectual access to this vast and motley corpus of material. A better image might be that of a grab bag in which the prizes all have cryptic labels, misleading sizes, shapes and wrappings, and contents ranging from blurry family photographs to whole art museums, from the slightest vanity press outpourings to the greatest poetry and novels, from Uncle Harry's chili recipe to Abraham Lincoln's personal correspondence. Any attempt to give organization to this grab bag must at first seem disheartening. Yet, if the attempt is not made, information seekers are doomed to countless hours of rummaging through the sack, happening on a promising package now and then and marking its place (hoping that it does not move), and never knowing of the far better prizes hidden elsewhere.

Any object can be cataloged, whether material or digital. And thus, any collection of objects can be brought under intellectual control by a catalog, including that collection of digital objects we know as the World Wide Web. But objects on the Web–hyperlinked, dynamic and almost infinitely diverse–present challenges to intellectual organization barely imaginable even a few years ago, and certainly outside the scope of the world of information imagined by Charles Ami Cutter, the father of the modern library catalog. This paper considers the relevance of Cutter's principles of bibliographic access to the universe of digital objects and explores new methods for applying these principles in the context of new information technologies.

## *UNIVERSAL BIBLIOGRAPHIC CONTROL AND THE WWW UNIVERSE*

Before facing up to the challenge of the World Wide Web as an information universe, it is instructive to look realistically at the non-digital world, and to consider the ways in which access is provided to "traditional" forms of information objects. The most striking point is that there is no single, overarching system of intellectual access to the world of information. Any given library catalog aims to control only a highly selected subset of that world, typically materials collected by a parent institution, and even then controls them with varying degrees of success. The traditional catalog is well designed for selected collections of books and periodicals, commercial films and recordings and musical scores; it serves rather less well for collections of slides and photographs, for manuscripts and archival materials, original artworks and museum objects. For these latter groups, specialized tools and approaches have been developed: different cataloging guidelines, specialized finding aids, etc. This panoply of access methods has developed not from one unified theoretical construct, but from a variety of overlapping needs and conventions.

To some extent, appropriate modes of description and access are determined by the ways in which intellectual and artistic works are created and disseminated. Most books, for example, are now given fixed form and distribution by a relatively small group of publishers, in standard formats and with identifying features brought out on title pages and covers. The object of catalog description is largely one of recording these standard marks of identification (author, title, publisher, date, etc.) in recognizable form. Producers of other forms of commercially distributed material–videos, musical recordings, maps–have adopted similar techniques. Standardized formats enable standardized descriptions. Non-standardized formats, such as those of archives and realia, require more flexible approaches.

By convention and pragmatic necessity, the indexing provided by the library catalog is only at the level of the object itself: for example, books, rather than chapters; CDs, rather than tracks. The exceptions to this rule–"in analytics," author/title added entries–merely serve to demonstrate the inadequacy of any single access tool to cover all needs, and to point to other possibilities. The commercial and specialized marketplace has stepped in to fill part of this void: with abstracting and indexing services for periodicals and conference publications; with poetry, short story, and essay indexes for anthologies; with concordances for textual analysis; with song and performer indexes for the world of music. To the extent that the ideal of "universal" bibliographic access can be achieved, it requires a complex system of interrelated, and not always interlocking, access tools.

Not all of these separate access tools are consistent with each other, nor have they been linked, except in very partial and rudimentary fashion. Users must choose the most appropriate tool(s) for their purpose and move sequentially from one to another, employing a different search strategy for each. Many of these indexes lack any form of name authority control; some employ thesauri and controlled vocabularies, but the particular terms chosen vary from one index to another. Forms of citation are also inconsistent. In electronic format, some periodical indexes have been linked, imperfectly, to individual library online catalogs, usually based on some common standard identifier such as an ISSN. At another level, separate services have been developed to direct a search to the most appropriate database(s) available, but the inconsistencies among the indexes themselves make this cross-database searching less than fully effective.

Such inconsistency and complexity can also be expected to characterize coverage of the digital information universe. For many of the electronic resources now available, standardized forms of presentation and distribution have not yet developed, and may never develop. Materials are made available by their creators, or others, with little attempt to document their content. Even when the creator provides some description and organization, there are as yet no commonly accepted methods for doing so. Experimentation and creativity reign, with opportunities for ever-better techniques to arise, but with very mixed and unpredictable results. In this respect, the universe of resources connected to the Internet is more akin to the world of museums and archives. (Although one should note that those institutions have had hundreds of years to learn to cope with relatively few and stable types of objects; digitization has reproduced most of these forms in just a few years, and continues to cast up new hybrids.) This world has developed its own conventions for describing form and content, with less emphasis on uniform descriptions of known objects. These conventions are driven somewhat by form, but also by the expectations, needs and habits of particular groups of users.

The Web, too, has quickly developed conventions of access compatible with the nature of its information resources and with the needs and search styles of its user community. Powerful, inventive network resource discovery tools such as Yahoo!,[1] Lycos[2] and Excite[3] traverse the Internet, scanning digital objects for textual clues to their content and responding to keywords input by searchers with a rich, if unpredictable, array of electronic resources. These systems offer a degree of universal access, both intellectual and actual, unthinkable in the non-digital universe. Covering millions of items and attracting millions of searches each week,[4] these tools use a new arsenal of techniques for gathering Web resources and processing their contents to match queries. Dynamic and continually refreshed, they are designed to track and keep up with continually shifting digital resources. They employ search engines that leave library online catalogs in the dust in any competition for retrieval power. With the arrival of these new tools, it is tempting to think that we have been liberated from the need to catalog digital resources, to expect that traditional principles and problems of cataloging can be confined to the non-digital realm. However these exciting new tools lack some important access features that have proven valuable to users of traditional access systems, such as classified arrangements, predictable author identification, selective coverage, controlled vocabulary searching. Rather than dismiss these features as unfeasible to apply in the realm of digital information, we need to determine their relevance in the context of networked digital information, and seek ways to apply what is relevant in an access system that can span both physical and virtual information resources.

## *THE MISSING PRINCIPLES*

While recognizing that traditional library cataloging is not the only solution to providing access to the entire diverse world of information resources, it is still useful to look at the basic purposes library catalogs were designed to serve. For this, there is no better summary than Charles Cutter's in his *Rules for a Dictionary Catalog*.[5] Cutter explains that the catalog should serve the following basic objectives:

1. To enable a person to find a book of which either

    (A) the author
    (B) the title
    (C) the subject

    is known.

2. To show what the library has

    (D) by a given author
    (E) on a given subject
    (F) in a given kind of literature.

3. To assist in the choice of a book

    (G) as to its edition (bibliographically)
    (H) as to its character (literary or topical).

These objectives have guided library cataloging for more than a century. They form the foundation for cataloging rules, authority files and shared databases. Those seeking information in electronic form are pursuing the same objectives as searchers in the non-digital universe, and Cutter's principles can still apply. In extending that application to the World Wide Web, however, it is important to distinguish these goals from the traditional means used to achieve them.

Libraries have developed a variety of tools to support Cutter's objectives, mechanisms that have evolved as catalogs have grown in complexity and changed in form. The most essential tools are access points for author, title, genre, and subject, generated from information specified in bibliographic records. To make these access points effective, rules have been developed for standardizing both the choice and form of index terms; controlled vocabularies such as *Library of Congress Subject Headings* and the *Art and Architecture Thesaurus* have been employed for subject access; and authority records with cross references and scope notes have been devised to guide users to the correct terms. To assist in identifying editions, catalog rules and interpretations have elaborated guidelines for recording publishers, dates, physical characteristics and series, and for tracing bibliographic history. Each of these mechanisms deserves closer examination in relation to the electronic information universe.

## *COLLOCATING NAMES AND IDENTIFYING ROLES*

Collocating works by a particular author and separating them from works by others with similar names is a basic function of library catalogs. The principle is simple, but its achievement requires far more than creating a field in which to record the author's name(s) as found in a work. Name authority control requires rules for choosing among different forms of a name, for distinguishing similar names, for referencing between variant forms and between related names. Arguably, this function also requires defining the concept of authorship in such a way that it may be applied to entities other than persons and that the role of author can be distinguished from other aspects of creation and dissemination. The more extensive the universe of names in use and the less standardized their appearance, the more complex these rules need to be. The World Wide Web, at least in future potential, provides possibly the worst imaginable universe for applying name authority control. The providers of Internet resources may or may not be responsible for their intellectual content; they are free to identify themselves in any form they choose, or not at all; they may or may not provide additional cues to identity to distinguish them from others; and the ease of electronic "publication" ensures a body of authors larger and more varied than that of book publication.

Simply collocating the forms of names found in such a large and diverse resource as the World Wide Web may not be sufficient. Identifying the role played by an individual or organization in the creation and dissemination of a resource may be equally important. Although Cutter does not attempt to define the term "author" in setting forth his objectives, cataloging rules have additionally recognized a need to distinguish among the roles played by authors, editors, translators, performers, book designers, typesetters and others. For those roles deemed most important, the rules prescribe controlled access points. The concept of main entry has served to highlight those "authors" most directly responsible for the intellectual creation of a work. Relator terms have been added to some name headings, describing in succinct and controlled form the role played by an individual in relation to a specific work. Other names are relegated to the descriptive portion of the catalog record, while still others are considered not worthy of mention.

This limited hierarchy of "authors" has become blurred in the online catalog. Online catalogs have not used the concept of main entry in retrieval or in the name index displays that result from a search. Relator terms are not usually an element of search strategy, and often not included in index displays. Even names that the cataloging rules do not designate as retrieval points can be used for retrieval when searched by keyword from the body of the text.

It may be time to take a fresh look at this increasingly confused concept of "author" in an access system for World Wide Web resources. As noted earlier, the resources accessible on the Web are likely to be more diverse than those hitherto found in library catalogs. The names included within them, and in metadata describing them, will include all the roles appropriate to books, videos, music, art objects, and other formats, as well as new functions: the organization responsible for scanning, the person who added textual mark-up, and many others. Particularly when researchers must scan and manipulate large result sets, the ability to distinguish among different roles or to limit search results to those performing a specific function may be an important element in effective retrieval.

## *COLLOCATING WORKS AND VERSIONS*

Titles pose a different problem in the world of electronic resources–or rather, a problem inherited from the world of archives and art objects. Many electronic documents, and even more images, do not have recognizable titles. Those wishing to catalog them for purposes of retrieval or citation must supply a title, generally a phrase descriptive of the content. This feature is not terribly significant in itself; Cutter, after all, demands only access to a work "the title of which is known," and a work may become very well known indeed by a supplied title (witness *The Bible* or *Whistler's Mother*). The more acute problem arises in linking works converted into electronic form without an obvious title with the descriptions of their non-digital forms–for example, in linking the description of a holograph letter with an ASCII text or digital image, particularly when those three formats are created and maintained independently.

This problem of linking and relating descriptions for different versions of a work leads directly to the electronic analog of Cutter's third principle: "To assist in the choice of a book . . . as to its edition." In the digital world, the provenance of a work–the edition used in scanning a literary text, the source of a slide or photograph used to produce a digital image, for example–may be an important element in evaluating the usefulness of the resource. Equally important may be characteristics of the digital item: the scanning resolution, the format(s) in which images are stored, the extent of markup. The same intellectual work may exist in multiple formats, at one or many sites, may be recopied and altered, refreshed or reformatted. A reader seeking a particular edition of Whitman's *Leaves of Grass* on the shelves of libraries may locate many copies scattered at different sites. Setting aside details of physical condition and possible annotations, however, each of those copies should afford access to the same text, formatted in the same way, and should be equally suitable for most uses. The reader seeking that same work on the Internet will, eventually, be faced with many choices, with no assurance, unless appropriate metadata are supplied, that the contents are identical or the formats equally useful. Those seeking digital reproductions of, say, the *Mona Lisa* will face a similar array of choices, with different but equally important distinctions among them. Access mechanisms must provide enough of the salient details to allow users to make purposeful choices.

## *SUBJECT ACCESS*

Perhaps the greatest challenge for World Wide Web organization arises from the third basic form of search Cutter identified: finding resources by subject. At least in these early, inchoate stages, Internet searchers are unlikely to be looking for "that new book by X" and even less likely to look for a known title. Most often, they will be seeking information on a topic, and facilitating those searches is no simple matter. Keyword searching can be a highly satisfactory means of retrieval, as many applications have shown, but keywords must come from somewhere. At present, access by Internet browsing tools is often limited to a search of brief, and frequently uninformative, file names–a process somewhat similar to browsing book titles in hope that a relevant word will appear. Full text searching offers a much richer base, but has significant limitations. The most sophisticated full-text searches cannot provide effective subject access to multi-language files or non-textual resources. And, even English language text is full of unpredictable vocabulary that may, or may not match a searcher's terms with relevant language. While controlled vocabulary searching alone has significant limitations, over years of experience with databases of abstracts and full text, the added value of classification and controlled vocabulary have been well documented.[6] Databases of textual and non-textual digital objects differ only in their degree of need for enhancement with controlled descriptors. In textual databases, this enhancement may become possible through advanced software tools that analyze and match natural language text to controlled thesauri. At present, and in the case of non-textual data for the foreseeable future, this enrichment requires human intellectual processing, ranging from the assignment of descriptors by authors to thesaurus headings or classification notation supplied by trained catalogers and indexers.

## *GENRE AND OBJECT TYPE*

The last of Cutter's objectives is, "To assist in the choice of a book . . . as to its character (literary or topical)." For the most part, libraries have not found it necessary to achieve this objective by adding explicit guidance in catalog records. Occasional notes may be added to identify a work as poetry, short stories or drama, but most literary works have been distinguished in more subtle ways. Catalog users are expected to recognize literary works by knowing something of the author's output, or by the absence of subject headings. These expectations worked well enough in card catalogs, when literary works would usually be located only through a deliberate search for an author or title. The addition of keyword searching in on-line catalogs makes it more difficult to distinguish literary from topical works, but little consideration has been given to this change. To date, perhaps the most effective device in separating literary and topical works has been classification. Library users have often been able to identify fiction through a segregated classification scheme, or even by separate shelving. But even classification has traditionally merged all "literature," including fiction, criticism, biography or belles-lettres. Cutter's "fact or fiction" principle has not been given rigorous implementation in library catalogs.

In the digital world, the distinction between literary and topical works may become more important. A single search of the World Wide Web may well turn up a list of titles that mixes both types of works, and it will be important to distinguish informational works from novels, art objects and entertainment without examining the actual content of each item. Indeed, the distinction between "literary" and "topical" may need to be expanded to allow a more precise identification of the character of the information object. A single search of the Web could retrieve citations to a digital text, map, painting, numerical data set or a multi-media object containing several of these and more. A simple listing of titles will not necessarily make plain the nature of these different objects. Given the substantive differences inherent in these different formats, as well as the often wide variations in skills, software and hardware needed to take advantage of the content they hold, an explicit metadata element such as "genre" takes on increasing importance for digital resources.

## *WEBS AND CATALOGS: THE EMERGING MODEL*

Is it possible to retain the benefits of Cutter's principles in a feasible system of access to Web resources? The challenges are daunting. But the technologies that have spawned the chaos that is the World Wide Web also offer the promise of assistance and enhancement to catalog creation and information retrieval. The next step is to demonstrate how Cutter-based cataloging principles and approaches can take advantage of current technology–and the more powerful generation of technology that is sure to succeed it–to organize access to networked electronic resources.

Perhaps the most intriguing route to cataloging the world of electronic resources is to exploit the content of the document itself as a means for access. Even without the explicit addition of metadata, many digital objects inherently contain information that can be used for retrieval. Full text itself is an obvious, but challenging, resource. Menu text, introductory pages, "about" explanations, abstracts and captions provide content information that can be effectively indexed for retrieval. As noted earlier, the new generation of Web crawling tools employs powerful search engines that enable many textual digital documents to be self-indexing. New research in natural language processing will further enhance the usability and relevance of retrieval results, improving matching and weighing for retrieval and supplying computer-formulated summaries and presentations for browsing and selection. Research systems have incorporated thesauri along with natural language access to add controlled vocabulary automatically. Researchers are also pushing into new frontiers of multi-media access, experimenting with non-verbal search and retrieval techniques for still images, video and sound.

Even the most optimistic expectations for such systems, however, leaves lacking aspects of the key elements identified earlier in this paper as traditional requirements for a useful access system: author identification, controlled subject vocabulary or classification, version control, and genre identification. These represent the most labor and intellect intensive aspects of cataloging, and software has not replaced them. However, software tools and new technologies hold promise for assisting and approximating some of these functions.

To achieve this, one needs to move from the current online library catalog model, which is alive and still quite well in most libraries, to a model in which metadata and the objects they describe are fully integrated. Key features of this new model are those that characterize the Web itself, interoperability and linkage. The concepts of interoperability and linkage extend to systems of access: a variety of access methods can operate together in a complementary fashion to guide searchers to the information they seek. As described earlier, this is the same kind of imperfect but functional interconnecting model that provides access to the universe of non-digital information. Readers search specialized indexes for subject access and then must move, automatically or physically, to the library catalog for a first step toward physical access. The library catalog search points to a call number that serves as a link to a classified, shelf-based access system. The index, the catalog and the ordered shelf are linked, complementary, interoperating systems. When both the search tools and the items "on the shelf" are digital, the potential for designing and streamlining interacting systems of access expands considerably.

There are tools and protocols that already begin to take advantage of this potential. Z39.50 clients have been merged into Web browsers, providing a single interface that can point both to records in library catalogs and to Web-based resources. A link from a record to the digital object it describes can be achieved by carrying the internet address of the object, its Universal Resource Locator (URL), in the MARC record; MARC tag 856 has been designed for this purpose.

In its most basic implementation, the method is limited by the content of the catalog record and its indexing in the online catalog, sometimes diluted by a poorly designed lowest-common-denominator Z39.50 application. Each digital object must be represented by a concomitant catalog record–a model that may not be scaleable given the speed with which digital objects proliferate. A more practical extension of this model relies on a collection level catalog record with a URL pointing not directly to the target resource but to an additional, Web-based, access layer, which in turn can be hyperlinked to the digital resource. The best-known current application of this expanded model is the design of an SGML-formatted archival finding aid, currently under development at the University of California, Berkeley Library.[7] Standardized General Mark-up Language (SGML) is a content-based, or "intelligent," encoding scheme for text that lends itself well to the carefully differentiated content fields in bibliographic access data. Work at Berkeley is producing a standard SGML content description, or Document Type Definition (DTD), that enables manipulation and searching of archival finding aids. Following and enhancing the paper-based model for access to archival materials, the user moves from an

AMC (Archival and Manuscripts Control) catalog record, to the SGML formatted finding aid, to digitized archival items.

Another variant of this model is in operation at Columbia University Libraries, where it is currently being used for access to digital image collections.[8] Following USMARC format fields, the cataloger creates a standard collection-level catalog record as an SGML document, adding to the document brief item records that can be used as links to, and captions for, individual digital images. The narrative form of the SGML document is more flexible than MARC, enabling the incorporation of subsets of items and sub-records for more than one version of an item–a very workable solution to two of cataloging's most thorny problems. A subset of the SGML record is mapped to standard MARC for loading into the library's online catalog. The full record is programmatically mapped to HTML–an interim approach awaiting further development and wider use of SGML-aware browsers–and merged with the matching image files to create a fully indexed, Web-based digital image library.

Another approach to facilitating the cataloging of electronic resources is to assume that less-than-full bibliographic descriptions provide sufficient access to resources that are readily available for browsing with the tap of a key. For example, when the title page and table of contents of a digitized book can be quickly browsed online, efforts to create a full bibliographic description in the access record may be redundant and unnecessary. As described earlier, new techniques in natural language processing can, in many cases, provide a high degree of subject access that can supplement less-than-full subject indexing. The ability to draw on the resources of the digital object itself enables us to limit the effort of cataloging by employing collection-level, minimal or user-created catalog records without making the trade-offs in bibliographic control that these kinds of records have required in the past.

OCLC is testing a version of this model in its NetFirst database, a catalog of records for Internet resources created by OCLC staff who work from information culled directly from Internet resources by an automated process. NetFirst records include a limited set of up to fifteen data elements. These include such standard terms as author, title, publisher and subject heading, but also some fields that help address special needs of Internet cataloging discussed earlier. For example, "Author Title" serves to identify the role played by an individual who may or may not be the actual creator of a resource's intellectual content. "Resource Type" describes the nature of the object, such as home page, gopher, or map. Subject terms are supplemented by one or more Dewey class numbers, helping to create a unified, hierarchical organization. While they follow no standard set of cataloging rules, NetFirst records are intended to provide a large amount of structured information for retrieval and identification.[9]

If a subset of standard cataloging data can suffice for access to many electronic resources, another promising route is to enlist the aid of document creators in providing metadata in their digital documents. An already established, although less-than-widely implemented, practice is the document header recommended by the *Guidelines* of the Text Encoding Initiative (TEI).[10] The role of the TEI header as an access enhancement was explored at a 1994 conference sponsored by the Center for Electronic Texts in the Humanities,[11] where participants put forth recommendations toward bringing the header into closer conformance to library practices and to MARC records. Conference participants also acknowledged, however, that relatively few text editors feel they have the time and expertise to create TEI-conformant headers, a task they believe is more easily handled by trained librarians.

What then are realistic expectations for useful metadata that can be supplied by document creators? Anyone who creates a Web page linked to other resources is in effect building his own personal library of electronic resources. The Web is a maze of idiosyncratically designed libraries, enthusiastically, albeit often ineptly, created by resource providers. Several efforts to harness and direct this enthusiasm are underway. The March 1995 MetaData Workshop in Dublin, Ohio, sponsored by OCLC and the National Center for Supercomputing Applications (NCSA), sought to develop a simple set of metadata elements that would be broadly applicable to, in conference parlance, "document-like objects." This set should be simple enough to enable untrained "authors and publishers to provide metadata, in a form that automated resource discovery tools could collect, when they make data available."[12] The data elements could also "serve as the basis for a more detailed cataloging record if the need arises." The "Dublin core" constitutes a (very) preliminary identification of those elements. The major achievement of the workshop and its online discussions and Web-published results has been to begin to build common cause and a shared language among librarians, computer scientists and Internet architects to work together to supply useful document descriptions.

A similar set of "core" data elements will be tested with the Internet community through OCLC's Spectrum Project.[13] Spectrum is essentially a Web page that serves as an input form, coaching resource authors through the process of creating a metadata record that can be mapped both into MARC and SGML. The results of this experiment should help to gauge the extent of the gap between useful records and an untrained individual's ability to create them.

All of these core sets of data elements begin to address the emerging need for better genre identification, as seen, for example, in the inclusion of "Resource Type" in NetFirst. Discussions at the March 1995 MetaData Workshop focused on use of a new term, "object type," to identify the broad character of a resource, distinct from its physical–or virtual–form. This concept begins to address the kinds of genre distinctions needed for digital information.

It is unlikely that metadata supplied by untrained resource providers will carry all the attributes necessary to achieve name collocation, subject access, version control and genre identification. To gain these, an overlay of cataloging effort is inevitable. But what we can work toward in the digital environment is the development of tools that multiply the effects of a feasible investment of human intellectual effort by supplementing it with software aimed at achieving the principles of good access. For example, post-creation processing or filtering of names based on algorithmic matches to authority files and internal cues in document content could provide collocation of name forms, to distinguish, e.g., John Smith, the 20th century chemist from John Smith, the 17th century adventurer. Class numbers, most likely human-supplied, could serve as links to indexes of controlled vocabulary that take advantage of machine-readable files of classification schemes and thesauri currently under development. And, as noted earlier, SGML and HTML provide far more flexible formats for identifying and linking multiple versions than does MARC. The long-awaited, unfortunately not yet imminent, development of the Universal Resource Name/Characteristic/Code (URN/URC)–a scheme for uniquely naming digital objects and tracking changes of address–will add some much-needed relative stability and reliability to Internet locator systems.

## *CONCLUSION*

The challenge of providing intellectual access to the World Wide Web of digital resources can be met by applying well proven principles and employing new methods to achieve them. New formats and protocols for encoding, indexing and linking metadata can offer far more flexibility and retrieval potential than MARC records without necessarily losing the well understood benefits of current modes of cataloging. New techniques of natural language processing can replace–and even far outpace–some aspects of catalog searching. And the immediate availability of digital objects for examination can reduce some of the need for a catalog record to provide a descriptive substitute. Successful solutions to providing access to digital resources will enhance a minimal investment of human intellectual work by exploiting new methodologies to supplement cataloging effort and achieve an optimal level of name collocation, subject access, version control and genre identification. While these access principles are well-established, techniques for achieving them need not be the same as those that have been employed in the cataloging of non-digital documents. The examples described in the preceding section demonstrate a variety of emerging mechanisms. The immediate challenge is to employ these tools in new systems of intellectual access that continue to aim at the benefits Cutter's principles sought to gain.

## REFERENCES

1. Yahoo! is an Internet search service offered by Yahoo! Corporation. Its URL is http://www.yahoo.com.

2. Lycos is an Internet search service developed at Carnegie Mellon University and offered by Lycos, Inc. Its URL is http://www.lycos.com.

3. Excite is an Internet search service offered by Architext Software. Its URL is http://www.excite.com.

4. The Yahoo! site alone averages 500,000 visits each day. "Making Searches Easier in the Web's Sea of Data." *New York Times*, October 5, 1995, Late City Edition, p. D5.

5. Charles Ami Cutter. *Rules for a Dictionary Catalog*. 4th ed. (Washington: Government Printing Office, 1904).

6. Jennifer Rowley. "The Controlled Versus Natural Indexing Languages Debate Revisited: A Perspective on Information Retrieval Practice and Research." *Journal of Information Science* 20, no. 2: 108-119 (1994).

7. The Berkeley Finding Aid Project is directed by Daniel Pitti, Advanced Technologies Projects Librarian at the University of California Berkeley Libraries.

8. Stephen Paul Davis. "Digital Image Collections: Cataloging Data Model and Network Access" in Patricia A. McClung, ed., *RLG Digital Image Access Project: Proceedings from an RLG Symposium held March 31 and April 1, 1995, Palo Alto, California*. (Palo Alto, CA: Research Libraries Group, 1995), pp. 45-61.

9. NetFirst is described in its World Wide Web site at URL http://www.oclc.org/oclc/netfirst.

10. C.M. Sperberg-McQueen and Lou Burnard, eds. *Guidelines for Electronic Text Encoding and Interchange*. (Chicago and Oxford: Text Encoding Initiative, 1994).

11. Lisa R. Horowitz, ed. *CETH Workshop on Documenting Electronic Texts, May 16-18, 1994*. (New Brunswick, NJ: Center for Electronic Texts in the Humanities, 1994).

12. Stuart Weibel et al. *OCLC/NCSA Metadata Workshop Report*. Available at URL http://www.oclc.org:5046/conferences/metadata.

13. "Office of Research Project Develops Tools for Describing and Accessing Internet Resources." *OCLC Newsletter*, no. 213: 13-16 (January/February 1995).

# Metadata for Internet Resources: The Dublin Core Metadata Elements Set and Its Mapping to USMARC

Priscilla Caplan
Rebecca Guenther

**SUMMARY.** This paper discusses the goals and outcome of the OCLC/NCSA Metadata Workshop held March 1-3, 1995 in Dublin Ohio. The resulting proposed "Dublin Core" Metadata Elements Set is described briefly. An attempt is made to map the Dublin Core data elements to USMARC; problems and outstanding questions are noted. *[Article copies available from The Haworth Document Delivery Service: 1-800-342-9678. E-mail address: getinfo@haworth.com]*

## *INTRODUCTION*

The last year has seen explosive growth in the cataloging of Internet resources. It has become widely accepted that at least some remote, network-accessible resources deserve the same level of cataloging as materials more tangibly in our libraries' collections. Since the definition of the USMARC 856 field for electronic locations

---

Priscilla Caplan is Assistant Director for Library Systems, University of Chicago Library. Rebecca Guenther is affiliated with Network Development and MARC Standards Office, Library of Congress.

[Haworth co-indexing entry note]: "Metadata for Internet Resources: The Dublin Core Metadata Elements Set and Its Mapping to USMARC." Caplan, Priscilla, and Rebecca Guenther. Co-published simultaneously in *Cataloging & Classification Quarterly* (The Haworth Press, Inc.) Vol. 22, No. 3/4, 1996, pp. 43-58; and: *Electronic Resources: Selection and Bibliographic Control* (ed: Ling-yuh W. Pattie, and Bonnie Jean Cox) The Haworth Press, Inc., 1996, pp. 43-58. Single or multiple copies of this article are available from The Haworth Document Delivery Service [1-800-342-9678, 9:00 a.m. - 5:00 p.m. (EST). E-mail address: getinfo@haworth.com].

 

there has been a proliferation of cataloging experiments, and guidelines for cataloging Internet resources are starting to appear. The Library of Congress' guidelines for the use of the 856 field[1] and Nancy Olson's *Cataloging Internet resources: A manual and practical guide*[2] were both published in early 1995. More recently, CONSER, the Cooperative Online Serials Program, added a module for electronic serials to its cataloging manual.[3] OCLC's NSF-funded Internet Cataloging Project had, as of July 27, 1995, enrolled 183 participants from 43 U.S. states and nine participants from seven other countries and, even more impressively, boasted over 1200 subscribers to the INTERCAT discussion list.

It is hard to remember that even a couple of years ago many doubted both the utility and the practicality of cataloging Internet resources. Some felt that these resources were too protean and/or ephemeral for cataloging, while others questioned the importance of such materials to library collections. It was probably the proliferation and legitimization of e-journals that more than anything else made it clear that bibliographic control of network-accessible resources was both possible and necessary. Few could argue that the electronic *Chicago Journal of Theoretical Computer Science*, published by MIT Press and paid for by annual subscription, was any less a part of a library's collection than a print journal on the shelves. In any case, serials librarians were quick to realize both the potential and the problems inherent in electronic access, and they have been in the forefront of efforts to adapt USMARC to remote resources.

At the same time, in our zeal to gain bibliographic control over an important class of materials, we should not forget that the vast majority of network-accessible resources completely lack descriptive data of any sort. Only a very small proportion of data resources warrant library cataloging, although a much larger proportion is of potential interest to our patrons. Library cataloging is not the only source of metadata, of course. Any number of specific data element sets and rules for encoding them have been established by various communities, from the TEI header defined by the Text Encoding Initiative to the GILS (Government Information Locator Service) record defined by the federal government. Nonetheless, most Internet-accessible resources are accessible only if you already know how to access them. Descriptive metadata suitable for general use in discovery and retrieval simply doesn't exist.

Every community, of course, can provide its own examples of resources of interest that are difficult if not impossible to find. Academic libraries will be facing a particular problem if a number of current initiatives aimed at campus support for faculty electronic publishing succeed, as we hope they do. As faculty are encouraged to make their own publications available on campus and departmental Web and FTP servers, control of material at the individual article or unit level becomes increasingly problematic.

## *OCLC/NCSA METADATA WORKSHOP*

The OCLC/NCSA Metadata Workshop, held in Dublin, Ohio on March 1-3, 1995, was organized to address the problem of providing metadata for a larger proportion of network-accessible materials. The original intent was to recognize various "stakeholder" communities with an interest in the search and retrieval of Internet resources, to understand the uses descriptive metadata would serve for these communities, and to achieve if possible some consensus on a limited data element set for identifying these resources. Workshop participants included librarians and archivists, researchers, computer and information scientists, software developers, publishers, and members of the Internet Engineering Task Force (IETF) Uniform Resource Identifiers (URI) Working Group. Within these constituencies there was tremendous diversity of approach. Some participants were concerned with electronic data resources in general while others focused on particular types of materials, like humanities texts or geospatial metadata. Some were interested in network services and protocols, others represented authors or publishers, while others took the point of view of end-users or of people who assist end-users.

One thing that united the majority of participants was a belief that nearly any standard metadata would be better than none. Nonetheless, early in the course of the workshop it became evident that no single data element set whether limited or unlimited would satisfy the widely divergent and highly specific needs of the various stakeholders. The emphasis therefore shifted to something that was perceived as both useful and feasible: the definition of a simple data element set that could be used by information providers to describe their own resources. Would it be possible to draft a single sheet of instructions that an author or publisher mounting a document on a network server would be able to follow without excessive effort or specialized knowledge?

Such a data element set, if it were to become an official or *de facto* standard, would have at least four different uses. It would encourage authors and publishers to provide metadata along with their data. It would allow the developers of authoring and network publishing tools to include templates for this information directly in their software, thereby making it even easier for the information providers to supply it. Metadata created by the information providers could serve as a basis for more detailed cataloging or description when warranted by specific communities. And finally, the standard would ensure that a common core set of elements could be understood across communities, even if more specific information was required within a particular interest group.

In order to make the task more manageable, some limitations on scope were imposed. First, the universe of materials to be described was limited to document-like objects, or DLOs. The universe of document-like objects itself was left undefined, but intuitively this would seem to include certain things like electronic texts and to exclude others like human beings and computer services. Second, the data elements themselves were limited to those supporting discovery and retrieval of the DLO; that is, to ascertaining that an object exists and obtaining a copy of it. Enough description should be included to allow a searcher to confirm that the DLO in question is actually the desired object, but not necessarily all of the information one would need to support other valid purposes like security, authentication, purchase or use.

The metadata element set that emerged is documented in the *OCLC/NCSA Metadata Workshop Report.*[4] It includes thirteen data elements referred to as the "Core Metadata Elements Set" or more informally as the "Dublin Core." These can be grouped roughly into three categories: access points (Title, Subject, Identifier, Author, Other Agent), information to facilitate identification (Publisher, Date, Object Type, Form, Language, Coverage), and information to relate the object being described to other objects (Relation, Source).

Rules for use are simple. All elements are optional, and all are repeatable. All elements may have a Scheme sub-element identifying the scheme or authority used in supplying the data. For example, the Subject element could have a Scheme sub-element to identify LCSH as the authority. Some elements have additional sub-elements defined. For example, Other Agent includes the Role sub-element to identify the relation of the Other Agent to the object, like translator or editor.

The Core Metadata Elements set is a core set in the sense that it consists of a small number of elements, judged to have general applicability, that will be universally understood if the standard is followed. It is not a core data element set in the sense of being a minimum number of required elements. The assumption is that while the information provider is encouraged to supply all of these elements, information that is not applicable or not readily available can be omitted. It is also not a core data element set in the sense of being the minimum number of elements adequate to describe an object. Many specific types of objects will require additional data for discovery and retrieval, and nearly all objects will require additional data to support other purposes (e.g., cost and restrictions on access).

Awareness of these limitations led to the principle of extensibility, essentially the rule that anyone can add anything anywhere. Elements outside the core data element set can be defined by individuals or by communities with the understanding that there is no guarantee these will be universally understood. Any software written to search, parse, or otherwise process metadata compliant with the Core Metadata Elements must be designed so that it does not fail when unrecognized elements or sub-elements are encountered.

The Workshop can be best viewed as a beginning in defining the data element problem as it relates to networked information resources and sketching out possible solutions. Accomplishments made need further refinement and standardization, and both the data elements and the assumptions used may change. The workshop report identifies unresolved issues and proposes a number of steps required for further progress. Relevant stakeholder communities will need to be involved in future efforts, including further workshops to address aspects of the problem. One of the most important steps that can be taken to further acceptance and adoption of the Dublin Core will be to establish a standard mapping to USMARC.

## *MARC MAPPING ISSUES*

An important thing to note about the Dublin Core is that it is syntax-independent, meaning that the definition and content of the elements are described independent of any particular way of encoding them. An imperfect but commonly known parallel would be AACR2, which prescribes what data must be supplied and how it should be formulated but not how it must be encoded, which is in turn the function of the USMARC standard. Other syntaxes, for example, SGML or HTML, could be used to represent the same data if guidelines for consistent encoding were developed.

In actual fact, AACR2 itself is not syntax independent, as data elements are actually defined in the syntax of the catalog card, with its various areas and connectors between them. The Core Metadata Elements set, however, is truly syntax-independent, defined with no necessary relation to any particular transport syntax. The intent is that the Core set can be mapped to any desired syntax.

Interestingly, just as data element sets like AACR2 can have dependencies to particular syntaxes, syntaxes like USMARC can have dependencies to particular data element sets. Although we have used the MARC structure (Z39.2) to describe everything from subject classifications to community information, the bibliographic formats are closely tied to the cataloging rules. USMARC does not, for example, have a field for author, or even for personal author. Instead, there are two different fields for representing personal author as main entry and as added entry (100 and 700). The concepts of main and added entry, of course, are defined in the cataloging rules, or more specifically, in AACR and AACR2. The Core Metadata Elements set, which contains the concept of author but lacks the concept of main and added entry, cannot easily be mapped to USMARC as it currently exists. The best we can do at present is to assume all responsible agents are added entries and encode them as such.

The Network Development and MARC Standards Office prepared a paper that was discussed at a meeting of the USMARC Advisory Group during the American Library Association conference in June 1995 in Chicago. "Discussion Paper No. 86: Mapping the Dublin Core Metadata Elements to USMARC" provided a mapping of the Dublin core elements to content designators in the USMARC bibliographic format.[5] The proposed mapping is presented below with problems indicated where appropriate and results of the ALA discussion noted.

## *SUBJECT*

Subject is defined in the Dublin Core as "the topic addressed by the work." According to the Workshop Report, "The Subject element can be qualified by a scheme, which specifies adherence to a known classification scheme . . . "

Subject could be represented in USMARC in field 653 (Index Term–Uncontrolled) or in field 650 (Subject Added Entry–Topical Term). Field 650 would be appropriate when the Scheme sub-element identified LCSH or some other controlled vocabulary. The indicator would be set according to the Scheme. However, there may be cases of incorrect mapping, such as when a geographic name (which should be coded as 651) or a personal name (which should be coded as 600) is used as subject. The Dublin core element set does not distinguish these.

Field 653, an uncontrolled field for subject terms, can be used if Scheme is not present. However, terms that were controlled by an unspecified authoritative list might be misrepresented, since the implication of the 653 is that the headings are uncontrolled. As a result of this potential problem, The USMARC Advisory Group wondered whether there might be a need for a generic subject field in USMARC similar to the generic author field discussed below. This would allow a subject term to be encoded with no indication of whether or not it is controlled by a thesaurus and no need to specify the type of name.

## *TITLE*

This is described as "the name of the object." In USMARC, it would be represented in the 245 (Title Statement). However, US-

MARC distinguishes between title and subtitle(s), while the Dublin Core does not. Either all data would have to be mapped to 245 $a, or the conversion would have to attempt to use punctuation for parsing the data into subfields. However, it is not likely that authors and publishers will use consistent punctuation in providing title information.

## *AUTHOR*

This is defined as "the person(s) primarily responsible for the intellectual content of the work." Using current MARC bibliographic specifications, a number of fields could be appropriate, including field 100 (Main Entry–Personal Name), 110 (Main Entry–Corporate Name), 700 (Added Entry–Personal Name), and 710 (Added Entry–Corporate Name).

Problems are presented by both the concept of main entry and by the division of different types of names into different fields. The 1XX fields are not entirely applicable, since main entry is an AACR concept, and there is no assumption that the object is being described according to library cataloging rules. Also, Author is repeatable, but 1XX fields are not.

The need to identify a name as either personal or corporate in USMARC causes another difficulty for mapping. This same problem has arisen before with the MARC mapping for the Government Information Locator Service (GILS) core elements. The GILS profile mapped the element to field 710 because for that project, the majority of authors would be government agencies and under AACR2 would probably not be entered as main entry. With more generic metadata, however, it would be impossible to predict whether an author might be personal or corporate. To resolve this issue the USMARC Advisory Group considered a second paper at the June meetings proposing the definition of a generic author field, i.e., an author that is undistinguished by type ("Discussion Paper No. 88: Defining a Generic Author Field in USMARC"[6]). Group discussion revealed a general desirability for a generic author field, and a proposal will be written to add a new field 720 to the USMARC bibliographic format for discussion at the USMARC Advisory Group Midwinter meetings in 1996. The field would probably contain only subfield $a for a name and subfield $e for a relator.

## *OTHER-AGENT*

According to the Workshop Report, "The OtherAgent element is intended to describe less common roles [than author], such as editor, illustrator, compiler, convener, photographer, or any secondary but significant role of content responsibility."

If a generic author field is defined in USMARC for Author, it could also be used for OtherAgent. One could identify the OtherAgent from Author by the data in subfield $e (which would include the Role sub-element). Either all those identified as an author could use that data in subfield $e or alternatively, the absence of data in $e could signify an author.

The USMARC Advisory Group preferred to have Author and OtherAgent merged. The request will be forwarded to groups considering further refinement of the Dublin Core.

## *PUBLISHER*

This is defined as the name of the entity responsible for making the object available. In USMARC it would clearly be the 260$b (Name of publisher, distributor, etc.). A one-to-one mapping can be provided.

## *DATE*

This is described in the Metadata Elements Set as "the date the object became available in its current form." In USMARC, it maps best to 260 $c (Date of publication, distribution, etc.).

Many types of dates are defined in the USMARC bibliographic format. The only one considered a core element in the Dublin set is the publication date. Note that in the MARC record the publication date is also given in 008/07-10 in a standardized form and the date in 260 $c could include other elements in addition to date of publication. The extensibility mechanism would be needed in many cases, where other types of dates are particularly important (e.g., date of an original for digitized texts). However, if the definition for the Date element in the Dublin Core is refined to specify the same type of dates as in 260 $c, then a one-to-one mapping can be provided and any other types of dates will be handled by the extensibility mechanism.

## *IDENTIFIER*

The identifier is "a string or number used to uniquely identify an object." There are many types of identifiers in MARC. Most likely to be needed are 010 (LC Control Number), 020 (ISBN), 022 (ISSN), 024 (Other Standard Identifier), and 856 $u (Uniform Resource Locator). Since all elements are repeatable and a Scheme sub-element is allowed, this element can in theory be mapped to various USMARC fields. The Scheme sub-element would be needed to provide a correct mapping.

## *OBJECT-TYPE*

ObjectType is described as "the category or genre of the object." In USMARC, the Leader/06 (Type of record) might come closest to representing this information content.

Specific object types would convert to an equivalent value in Leader/06. For instance the object type "book" would convert to code "a" for language material; "map" to code "e" for cartographic material. (Note that the definition of this value was changed in June 1995 with Proposal No. 95-16.) When more than one value is available in the Leader/06, such as for sound recordings (nonmusical sound recording and musical sound recording), it may not be possible to make a distinction, but one unambiguous conversion will need to be supplied.

In some cases, using Leader/06 may not be specific enough, when something similar to a Specific Material Designator (SMD) may be used. In those cases, a code in the appropriate 008 character position might be more appropriate, but how to map these to US-

MARC is unclear. Essentially, there is not one data element in MARC but many that give object type information. The use of this element within the Dublin Core needs to be clarified.

## *FORM*

Described in the Metadata element set as "the data representation of the object" this element seems to map to USMARC field 538 (System Details Note). Examples might be "TIFF ver. 2.3.4.5.6" or "SGML / TEI P3-1994." Some applications (e.g., CONSER) have combined form information with type of computer file information in field 516, although this practice is likely to change in the future.

## *RELATION*

Relation is intended to describe important known relationship to other objects. In USMARC there are a variety of fields for recording such relationships, including fields 772 (Parent Record Entry), 773 (Host Item Entry), 775 (Other Edition Entry), 776 (Additional Physical Form Entry), 780 (Preceding Entry), 785 (Succeeding Entry) and 787 (Nonspecific Relationship Entry).

In the Dublin Core, the Type sub-element indicates the relationship being expressed, and is thus necessary to indicate the appropriate field to be used. The Scheme sub-element might indicate a URL or a record control number. In order to accommodate a URL in one of the linking entry fields, "Discussion Paper No. 87: Addition of Subfield $l in Linking Entry Fields 76X-78X in the USMARC Bibliographic Format" was presented in June to the USMARC Advisory Group.[5] However, the proposal was not approved for both practical and theoretical reasons. The practical fear was that URLs are so changeable that allowing them throughout the MARC record would create an untenable maintenance problem. The theoretical objection was that linking fields in fact point to bibliographic records for related items and not the items themselves (they contain, for example, no call number.) The group felt the linking entry field could point by standard means to the related bibliographic record, which could in turn contain the URL of the related object in its 856 field. The question will no doubt arise again, as possible uses of the URL in other fields are suggested.

## *LANGUAGE*

Language indicates the "language of the intellectual content." Scheme can be used to identify the source of a language code.

If the Scheme sub-element identified the USMARC Code List for Languages, USMARC field 041 (Language code) could be used. Alternatively, field 546 could be used for a textual note. Language is also given in USMARC in coded form in 008/35-37. Although there are several possible mappings, it is desirable to choose one. How the data might be supplied would determine which field is the most appropriate.

## *SOURCE*

Source is defined as "the object from which the object being described was derived" and may contain a nested object description. This might be accommodated in USMARC fields 786 (Data Source Entry) or 776 (Additional Physical Form Entry). A linking entry field is appropriate for a nested description, with the separate data elements of the nested description in defined subfields. Field 786 was recently defined for Data Source Entry. However, the following elements are not available in the linking entry fields: subject, object type, URL. Solutions need to be determined for accommodating these sub-elements.

## *COVERAGE*

Coverage "describes the spatial and temporal characteristics of the object and is the key element for supporting spatial or temporal range searching on document-like objects." Coverage can be modified by the qualifiers "spatial" and "temporal."

In USMARC, for spatial data either 034 (Coded Cartographic Mathematical Data) or 255 (Cartographic Mathematical Data) could be appropriate, depending on whether the data is recorded in a coded or textual form. The Coverage element was added to the Dublin Core after the March Workshop was held and it was not fully discussed. Presumably bounding coordinates would be recorded here. In USMARC field 034 coordinates are recorded in separate subfields (westernmost, easternmost, etc.); in field 255 they are recorded in a textual form in subfield $c. The Content Standards for Digital Geospatial Metadata (CSDGM), recently approved as a mandatory standard for communicating digital geospatial metadata, was mapped to USMARC fields before the Dublin Workshop; this crosswalk provides both fields depending upon whether the data is coded or textual.

Similarly, temporal data maps to USMARC fields 045 (Time Period of Content) or 513 (Type of Report and Period Covered Note). Again the data may be recorded in a formatted form as yyyymmddhh in field 045 or in a textual form in 513$b. The USMARC and CSDGM crosswalk uses field 045 for this data. The Government Information Locator Service (GILS) mapping also contains this element which is mapped to both fields, depending on whether the data is coded or textual.

Participants at the USMARC Advisory Group meeting recommended changing the name of this element (Coverage), because it was considered too general a term for an element with very specific meaning. Some also questioned whether Coverage ought to appear in the Core Elements Set at all, being relatively specific to a narrow community.

## *OTHER ISSUES*

*Versioning.* One of the elements considered for the core set was "Edition," defined as a free text identification of the version. Because of the difficulty in distinguishing between the concept of edition and version, this element was later left out of the final list, and it was considered an area that needed further discussion. Certainly the library world has different definitions for each concept. How to adequately handle versions of a bibliographic item has historically been problematic in bibliographic control; it becomes even more complex in the electronic world because of the ease with which a new version can be created. Whether or not an object is another version (same intellectual content in a different physical form) or an edition (changed intellectual content) can determine whether a separate record would be created. There is not yet any consensus on how to deal with this issue in the electronic world. Certainly the definitions of edition and version need to be separated to begin any analysis of the issue.

*Extensibility.* Many needs are not satisfied with the small number of elements defined in the Dublin Core. The extensibility mechanism allows for further elements to be added for specific purposes, and certainly libraries will desire many more. In having what is essentially a metadata standard that has been in use for a long time (MARC), the library community may have an advantage in extending the core element set. Other interest groups are developing metadata standards (e.g., in the fields of geography and biology) that provide exhaustive lists of elements needed to adequately provide information about information resources. All parties need to consider whether those elements in their individual metadata lists that are part of the Dublin Core are consistently defined.

*Dublin Core records in library catalogs.* There are many circumstances where bibliographic data is created and encoded in MARC with no reference to formal cataloging standards. Within the MARC community there has been much discussion on the desirability of identifying these as less than standard library catalog records. Some participants in the USMARC Advisory Group meetings wanted to go even further, and identify the origin of the non-standard record. The community needs to consider further the uses of such information and the best places in the record to store it.

In conclusion, we could revisit the question of whether a mechanical mapping from the Metadata Elements Set to USMARC is necessary at all. If a library wants to catalog an Internet resource and Dublin Core metadata exists for that resource, it seems reasonable to assume that the metadata would be helpful to the cataloger in describing the object. However in this case items would be cataloged one by one, and human judgment would be applied in the cataloging. Is machine mapping really necessary? Will we have large collections of metadata that we will want to convert wholesale from non-MARC representations? Is it likely, or even possible, that enough Scheme and other qualifying information would be provided in the metadata to allow even minimally acceptable translations to be performed?

These questions are impossible to answer without some experience. The library community has an immense existing infrastructure of MARC-based storage and retrieval systems, and on the surface it only makes sense to want to fold as much data of potential interest into these systems as possible. If this means mapping metadata for Internet resources from other description schemes, then we should at least attempt to do so. The fundamental challenge, however, is translating from a simple descriptive scheme to a complex one. Mapping will be imperfect unless additional qualifying information is added to the simple scheme (thereby complicating it) or more generic fields are added to the complex scheme (thereby simplifying it). There are reasons why AACR2 and USMARC are so complex, many of which have to do with the quality of information retrieval this allows. Given the explosion in available information resources of all types, it remains to be seen whether the majority of users will be better served by simplified access to a wider range of materials, or whether increased access will be useless without more sophisticated and discriminating retrieval capabilities.

## NOTES

1. *Guidelines for the Use of Field 856*, prepared by the Network Development and MARC Standards Office. Washington, D.C.: Library of Congress, 1995. (Available by sending email to listproc@loc.gov with the message "GET USMARC 856_GUIDELINES")

2. Nancy B. Olson, ed. *Cataloging Internet resources: A manual and practical guide*. Dublin, Ohio: OCLC, 1995. (URL: http://www.oclc.org/oclc/man/9256cat/toc.htm)

3. *CONSER Cataloging Manual: Module 31: Remote Access Computer File Serials*, prepared by Melissa Beck. Washington, D.C.: Cataloging Distribution Service, 1995.

4. Stuart Weibel, Jean Godby, Eric Miller, Ron Daniel. *OCLC/NCSA Metadata Workshop Report*. Dublin, Ohio: OCLC, 1995. (URL: http://www.oclc.org:5046/conferences/metadata/dublin_core_report.html)

5. Library of Congress, Network Development and MARC Standards Office. "Discussion Paper No. 86: Mapping the Dublin Core Metadata Elements to USMARC." Washington, D.C.: Library of Congress, 1995.

6. Library of Congress, Network Development and MARC Standards Office. "Discussion Paper No. 88: Defining a Generic Author Field in USMARC." Washington, D.C.: Library of Congress, 1995.

7. Library of Congress, Network Development and MARC Standards Office. "Discussion Paper No. 87: Addition of Subfield $l (Uniform Resource Locator) in Linking Entry Fields 76X-78X in the USMARC Bibliographic Format." Washington, D.C.: Library of Congress, 1995.

# Cataloging for Digital Libraries

Judith M. Brugger

**SUMMARY.** Using grant funding, some prominent creators of digital libraries have promised users of networked resources certain kinds of access. Some of this access finds a ready-made vehicle in USMARC, some of it in the TEI header, some of it has yet to find the most appropriate vehicle. In its quest to provide access to what users need, the cataloging community can show leadership by exploring the strength inherent in a metadata-providing system like the TEI header. *[Article copies available from The Haworth Document Delivery Service: 1-800-342-9678. E-mail address: getinfo@haworth.com]*

I am an ex-cataloger. Since I cataloged for ten years or so, there is a kind of stamp on the way that I think that cannot be eradicated, like antibodies in the blood. Cataloging is a semiotic of surrogacy and order. Catalogers want connected things to be connected and distinct things to be distinct according to an impulse called bibliographic control. So, when I think about digital libraries, I think about them from this lofty and noble place called bibliographic control. When other people think about digital libraries–and this includes a large percentage of the people who are currently creating digital libraries–"bibliographic control" (the exactitude of the phrase is important) never voluntarily crosses their minds. If it did, it might seem like something subsidiary, peripheral, almost nineteenth-century.

---

Judith M. Brugger is Information Technology Librarian, Cornell University's Central Technical Services, 107B Olin Library, Ithaca, NY 14853-5301.

[Haworth co-indexing entry note]: "Cataloging for Digital Libraries." Brugger, Judith M. Co-published simultaneously in *Cataloging & Classification Quarterly* (The Haworth Press, Inc.) Vol. 22, No. 3/4, 1996, pp. 59-73; and: *Electronic Resources: Selection and Bibliographic Control* (ed: Ling-yuh W. Pattie, and Bonnie Jean Cox) The Haworth Press, Inc., 1996, pp. 59-73. Single or multiple copies of this article are available from The Haworth Document Delivery Service [1-800-342-9678, 9:00 a.m. - 5:00 p.m. (EST). E-mail address: getinfo@haworth.com].

 

## *FEDERAL GRANTS FOR DIGITAL LIBRARIES*

In 1994, the National Science Foundation (NSF) together with the Department of Defense Advanced Research Projects Agency (ARPA), and the National Aeronautics and Space Administration (NASA) granted a total of $24.4 million to fund six Digital Library Initiative (DLI) projects.[1] The six awards went to Carnegie Mellon University, the University of California at Berkeley, the University of Michigan, the University of Illinois, the University of California at Santa Barbara, and Stanford University. The goal is for these institutions to work both independently and collaboratively to collect, store, and organize information in digital forms, and then to make this information available for searching, retrieval and processing via communication networks. Digital, spatial, video, and audio information resources show up in proposal after proposal–not just text, certainly not just bibliographic records. Each project takes a slightly different tack in its examination and manipulation of the resources it pulls into its testbed: Carnegie Mellon–technologies for natural language understanding; Berkeley–automated indexing, intelligent search and retrieval processes; Michigan–systemizing large amounts of heterogeneous information; UCSB–creating electronic catalogs of geographical data; the University of Illinois–retrieval techniques and usage patterns, and Stanford–the Information Bus.

The Stanford Integrated Digital Library Project (SDLP) has been specifically designed to test three aspects of the digital information space that its creators have deemed most crucial: "massiveness," "geographical distribution," and "heterogeneity."[2] At first, I thought this all sounded more like physics or geology than it did information science, but then I learned that in order to explore these properties, SDLP staff had defined an "Information Bus." Now in electronic terms a "bus" is "one or more conductors in a computer along which information is transmitted from any of several sources to any of several destinations."[3] To my delight, the more I got into the Information Bus the more I saw it as the digital, mobilized equivalent of bibliographic control, that meta-language of the catalog record. In fact, I eventually came to see the Information Bus as central to all of Stanford's endeavor. I wondered if I'm on track with this, or if it was just because I'm a cataloger. I mean, an ex-cataloger.

## *THE INFORMATION BUS*

I'd like to try to lay out exactly what the elements are that the Information Bus is meant to deliver. According to the proposal, the Information Bus is made up of "protocols, service definitions, and interfaces [that provide] the necessary distinctions and properties for describing a variety of basic dimensions (such as document identity and versioning, authority, ownership, access rights, summarizing of information, etc.)."[4] Some of these elements are elements in traditional bibliographic control; and some are not. But the proposal goes on. Even before users retrieve documents, it says, they might want to know something about the "the size, or authenticity of information, the cost, the completeness of the collection, and/or the access time."[5] Almost none of these things are part of traditional bibliographic control. Worse yet, "none of the existing protocols and systems," meaning "Z39.50, World Wide Web, Dialog,[and] OCLC [gives users the ability to] deal gracefully with widely varied resources. They all count on their ability to legislate conformity to a single or small number of uniform implementations."[6]

In the United States, one of these uniform implementations is the meta-language of bibliographic control which is documented in three separately maintained sources: the *Anglo-American Cataloging Rules* (2d ed., rev.),[7] the USMARC formats,[8] and the *Subject Cataloging Manual.*[9] Catalogers call these the rule book, the formats, and the *SCM*, or the "subject manual." I will be comparing some of the explicit directives within these sources to the specific access dimensions laid out in SDLP, but first I'd like to grapple with underlying principles, the idea of meta-information itself. SDLP challenges the status quo here. "Meta-information is a domain," says SDLP, "that requires new conceptual structuring."[10] SDLP sees meta-information as consisting of two parts:

> a core language that serves as a "structural glue" and an extensible collection of conceptual frames each dealing with

> one aspect of information, such as summarization, ownership, or access rights. Looking more deeply, we find a complex bundle of different notions of ownership, relevant to different kinds of actions that people take (writing, putting on line, copyrighting, selling, . . . ). We can work out a set of distinctions that keeps these appropriately separate, and is based on a clear semantics of who has done what (or can do what) with the information. These in turn can be formalized into a set of specific attributes that can be used for describing and operating on information items. This resulting structure is not a part of the core language, but forms a conceptual module of the Information Bus protocol. Each of today's network standards can be seen as taking a cut through a bundle of conceptual domains, using its own structural core to express a subset of issues from the conceptual areas that the designers deemed most salient. By partitioning the problem into separable modules we provide the basis for working on parts that are most directly relevant and useful, and to take advantage of work done by others, just as programmers today take advantage of libraries of shared modules or objects in doing their programming.[11]

The various conceptual frames correspond not only to network standards and to aspects of the information resource in question, but also to the various protocols and systems that users might invoke. The core language is the Information Bus. If we translate the components of traditional bibliographic control into this formula, we make the standard identification of the USMARC formats with the network or communications standards and AACR2 (together with the subject manual) as guidance for taking advantage of that communications standard. They are not seen as methods for enmeshing the USMARC communications standard into a partnership with other standards or responding to expanded needs (like the Information Bus). Traditional bibliographic control, then, seems to be parallel not with the core language, but with a subset of the conceptual areas that have been deemed salient. We (I mean, they, the traditional catalogers) are indeed peripheral. On the other hand, a New

Improved bibliographic control might be brought into parallel being with the Core Language/Information Bus.

And some of the access dimensions cited by the SDLP proposal do, in fact, map to tagging authorized by the formats, although there is neither a one-to-one correspondence between information and tag nor a sufficient source of guidance for effective tagging. In Table 1, I extract from the SDLP access parameters cited as potentially useful, and I assign them to potential USMARC tags.

## *SDLP ⇒ USMARC*

It is clear that the fit between USMARC and the access points described as necessary in SDLP is not very good. The concept of "content categorization," for example, maps so poorly that even in the quickest of overviews (mine), at least 6 USMARC fields might be said to carry information relevant to a query about content of the document. Use of the leader byte 06 (record type), for example, could weed out the published materials for a searcher who only wanted manuscript sources. The title is often a good clue as to content. A general material designation such as "interactive media" tells the user to expect a content that contains hyperlinks and options. Similarly, the concept of "origin" is bigger than the publication statement, because both author and publisher might fruitfully be construed to be the origin of a particular piece. Perhaps all those "sponsored by" statements catalogers stuff into 500 notes could also be usefully included in the category "origin." "Cost" is another poorly controlled data element in USMARC because catalogers have seen it as both too dynamic and as unrelated to description and access. There is a smattering of less-than-perfect places to put it: 018, 020$c, 037$c, 852$s. "Completeness," "authenticity," and "point of views," are completely out of scope for USMARC, because they require a kind of assessment grounded in the intellect rather than in transcription or "literary warrant." See Table 1 for a summary comparison of these and other access points cited in SDLP.

Despite its shortcomings, USMARC enjoys a well-deserved reputation for its ability to carry lots of information in standard, easy-to-process, clearly-designated sequences of bytes. Surely we should

TABLE 1. SDLP to USMARC

| Information to be Accessed | Possible MARC Tagging | Format |
|---|---|---|
| content categorization | Leader 06 (record type) | Bib |
| | Leader 07 (bibliographic level) | Bib |
| | 245$ h (general material designation) | Bib |
| | 505 (contents note) | Bib |
| | call number 153 | Holdings |
| | 6XX | Bib |
| origin | 245$ c (statement of responsibility) | Bib |
| | 260$ a (place of publication) | Bib |
| | 260$ b (publisher) | Bib |
| summarizations | 520 (summary note) | Bib |
| availability | 856 (electronic access) | Holdings |
| | 876-878 [MARBI Draft Proposal 92-21] | Holdings |
| relevance | [nowhere] | |
| document identity/versioning | 250, 260, 500 | Bib |
| access rights | 506 | Bib |
| size | 256, 300 | Bib |
| access time | [nowhere] | |
| cost | 018, 020$c, 037$c, 852$s, | Bib, Holdings |
| completeness | [nowhere] | |
| authenticity | [nowhere] | |
| for what purpose? | [nowhere] | |
| from what point of view | [nowhere] | |

be able to salvage something from USMARC's vision of bibliographic control and bring it to the expanded universe of the digital library. We need USMARC's precision, but we need to apply it to a universe as unlike the book universe as the Internet is different than a museum. The blame for the poor fit between USMARC and SDLP cannot be shouldered by USMARC alone. AACR2's Chapter

9, insofar as it tries to keep computer file cataloging parallel to book cataloging, is equally to blame.

## *THE TEXT ENCODING INITIATIVE*

Something new happened when cataloging issues began to be addressed by the existing digital libraries, my example of which will be the Center for Electronic Texts in the Humanities (CETH), especially in their collaboration with the Text Encoding Initiative (*TEI P3*),[12] and most especially in the bit of code called the "TEI header." CETH's document collection comprises primarily marked-up ASCII texts, appended to each of which is one of these headers. While CETH's collection is not, obviously, as heterogeneous as some of the proposed digital library collections currently under development, it is in fact a library in the computer file format. Although the existence of the TEI header cannot be construed as completely radical, because its documentation cites ISBD(G), AACR2, and ANSI Z39.29 as "influential in developing the content of the TEI file header,[13] its development is still the single most important milestone to date on the way towards accessing collections of information stored as computer files. Here's what Susan Hockey, CETH's Director, has to say about it:

> A TEI conformant text consists of a header followed by the text itself. The header consists of a set of SGML elements which provide documentation about the text and its encoding. It represents the first to provide a method of in-file documentation for electronic texts which can be processed by the same software as the text itself. It provides metadata which is needed by librarians who will catalogue the text, scholars who will use the text, and software programs which will operate on the text. The header has four major sections. The file description contains a bibliographic description of the electronic text and can be used as a chief source by catalogers. It is the only part of the header that has mandatory elements. These include the title statement which gives the title of the work and those responsible for its intellectual content, the publication statement which provides information about the publication or dis-

> tribution of the text, and the source description which records details of the source from which the electronic text was derived. The encoding description documents the editorial principles used in the transcription of the text, for example the treatment of hyphenation, quotations and spelling variation, and any sampling methods used. The profile description is most relevant for spoken texts where it documents the participants in the conversation. The revision history provides a change log indicating who made each change to the text and when. For a corpus or composite text, there is one header which includes elements common to the entire corpus and individual headers for each text within the corpus.[14]

Now let's run the same access dimensions that were cited by the SDLP proposal, and which I compared above to the USMARC formats, across the TEI header.

## *SDLP TEI*

No perfect fit here, either, but the scheme is entirely different. Whereas USMARC designates field content by means of 3-digit tags and alphabetical (occasionally numerical) subfields, the TEI uses the Standard Generalized Mark-up Language (SGML) convention of enclosing tagged data within a pair of angle-bracketed designators, such as <title> </title>, with the closing designator preceded by a slash. This gives the effect of nesting pieces within pieces, as opposed to USMARC's more linear feel. Similar to USMARC, there is often more than one place from which relevant information might be extracted. In the first example under Table 2, the "<textDesc>" (i.e., the "text description"), the "<particDesc>" (description of the participants in a linguistic interaction), the "<settingDesc>" (the setting in which a linguistic interaction takes place) and the "<catRef>" (a categorization of the text containing classification terms) are all found nested within the Profile Description, the third major element of the TEI header. The element "<title>," on the other hand, is part of the File Description, the first major element of the TEI header.

While much of the TEI header's second major area, the Encoding

TABLE 2. SDLP to TEI

| Information to be Accessed | Possible TEI Tagging | Where Nested |
|---|---|---|
| content categorization | <textDesc> | <profileDesc> . . . . . . . . . . . </profileDesc> |
| | <particDesc> | <profileDesc> . . . . . . . . . . . </profileDesc> |
| | <settingDesc> | <profileDesc> . . . . . . . . . . . </profileDesc> |
| | <catRef> | <profileDesc> . . . . . . . . . . . </profileDesc> |
| | <title> | <fileDesc><SourceDesc><bib1Struct<br>> . . . . . . . </biblStruct></SourceDesc><br>▶<br></fileDesc> |
| | <language> | <profileDesc><langUsage> . . . . .<br></langUsage></profileDesc> |
| origin | <author> <funder> <sponsor><br><principal> | <fileDesc><titleStmt><title></title>.<br>. . . . . . . . </titleStmt></fileDesc> |
| | <resp> + <name> | <fileDesc><titleStmt><title></title><br><respStmt> . . . . . . . . . . . . . </respStmt><br></titleStmt></fileDesc> |
| | <resp> + <name> | <fileDesc><editionStmt><respStmt<br>. . . . . . . . </respStmt></editionStmt><br>▶<br></fileDesc> |

TABLE 2 (continued)

| Information to be Accessed | Possible TEI Tagging | Where Nested |
|---|---|---|
| summarizations | <classCode> | <profileDesc><textClass> . . . . . </textClass> </profileDesc> |
| | <list> | <profileDesc><textClass><keywords> . . . . . . . </keywords></textClass> </profileDesc> |
| availability | <imprint> | <fileDesc><sourceDesc><biblStruct> . . . . . . . . </biblStruct></sourceDesc> </fileDesc> |
| relevance | | |
| document identity/versioning | <change><date></date><name> </name><what> . . . </what></change> | <fileDesc><sourceDesc>. . . . </sourceDesc><fileDesc> |
| access rights | | |
| size | | |
| access time | | |
| cost | | |
| completeness | <sampling> | <encodingDesc> . . . . .</encodingDesc> |
| authenticity | | |
| for what purpose? | <settingDesc> | <profileDesc> . . . . . . . . . . . </profileDesc> |
| | <creation> | <profileDesc> . . . . . . . . . . . </profileDesc> |
| from what point of view | <projectDesc> | <encodingDesc>. . . . . </encodingDesc> |

Description, tends towards document identity and authenticity, the flavor of the versioning in the TEI is different than the flavor of the versioning in SDLP. In fact, SDLP's sense of versioning more nearly approaches that of the USMARC edition statement (250), while the TEI's approaches USMARC's 567–Methodology. For example, the TEI mark-up designates the exact place a textual change has occurred, by means of the tags "<step>," "<state>," and "<milestone>."

Relevance and access time, which have no place in USMARC, are equally out of place in the TEI header as it presently exists. I would like to see information scientists devise some way of constructing a fifth TEI header area: <AccessDesc>. This would be no simple task since it would involve assessing the client's computer power, among other things, and would have to happen on the fly.

It should, however, still be easier to define new TEI-conformant mark-up tags than it would be to corral new MARC fields or subfields. One can easily run out of 3-digit numbers and single-letter subfield codes, but one can never run out of words. I'm assuming that anyone who is still reading this paper knows a fair amount about USMARC (i.e., is probably a cataloger or an ex-cataloger) but has quite a bit less knowledge about the TEI header. For that reason I think it is now appropriate to parse a TEI-conformant header right here on the page. If, after all, I am going to convince anyone that the TEI header holds more promise for the digital libraries of the future than do USMARC-based bibliographic records, we cataloging-types will need some time to develop a feel for what we'll be getting everybody else into. The example in Table 3, I will explicate is taken directly from the TEI documentation.[15]

## *READING THE TEI CODES*

Here is a rough, line-by-line translation of the preceding example.

***<!DOCTYPE ihs system teishd2.dtd>***

"What follows is a comment (!). Before we start with the actual coding, let me just state the fact that I'm going to be reporting out headers without their associated texts (ihs), and those headers are

TABLE 3. Headers

| | |
|---|---|
| <!DOCTYPE ihs system 'teishd2.dtd'> | ! = comment |
| <ihs> | ihs = independent header system |
| <teiHeader> | c.f. teishd2 = independent header system |
| <fileDesc> ... </fileDesc> | declaration |
| <encodingDesc> ... </encodingDesc> | teiwsd2 = writing system declaration |
| <profileDesc> ... </profileDesc> | teifsd2 = feature system declaration |
| <revisionDesc> ... </revisionDesc> | teitsd2 = tag set declaration |
| </teiHeader> | |
| <teiHeader> | |
| <fileDesc> ... </fileDesc> | |
| <encodingDesc> ... </encodingDesc> | |
| <profileDesc> ... </profileDesc> | 3 headers in this concatenation, the first |
| <revisionDesc> ... </revisionDesc> | two showing markers for all four major |
| </teiHeader> | components, the set of three bounded by |
| <teiHeader> ... </teiHeader> | the <ihs> </ihs> tag pair. |
| <!-- ... etc. —> | |
| </ihs> | |

going to invoke (system) the auxiliary Document Type Definition (dtd) for Independent TEI Headers (teishd2)."

***<ihs>***

"What follows is an independent header file. Look for the </ihs> element later in this file to signal the end of the file."

***<teiHeader>***

"What follows is not just any independent header, but a TEI header. Watch for the </teiHeader> element later in this file to signal the end of this particular TEI header."

***<fileDesc> . . . </fileDesc>***

"All elements that could legitimately be substituted for the elipses here form part of the file description area. Some examples might be: titles, series, source, or note statements, much like a bibliographic record in the AACR2 sense."

***<encodingDesc> . . . </encodingDesc>***

"All elements that could legitimately be substituted for the elipses here form part of the encoding description area. Some examples might be: a project description, a sampling declaration, a declaration of the piece's metrical scheme, etc."

***<profileDesc> . . . </profileDesc>***

"All elements that could legitimately be substituted for the elipses here form part of the profile description area. Some examples might be: a statement of the languages used, a standard classification number, a description of the participants in a linguistic interaction, etc."

***<revisionDesc> . . . </revisionDesc>***

"All elements that could legitimately be substituted for the elipses here form part of the revision description area. Some examples might be: a list of changes to the text and the dates or statements of responsibility associated with them."

***</teiHeader>***

"This TEI header is now finished."

***<teiHeader>***

"The next TEI header is now beginning."

And so forth, until finally we read </ihs>, which means the file is over. There are three headers in the example. "In practice," say the TEI documentation, "headers might be stored in separate operating system files, to reduce redundant storage requirements."[16] Another advantage might be the heightened opportunity to perform authority control on the data in these headers.

The signal difference between the possibilities trailing in the wake of TEI and those trailing in the wake of MARC is that TEI is something one applies to a document as well as to a document surrogate. Trailing in the wake of this distinction is the greater possibility, need, and usefulness of having data carry within itself information about its own character. Metadata (or data about data) should be the place to carry this information for, as I quoted from the SDLP proposal earlier, metadata "is a domain that requires new conceptual structuring."[17]

That's why I was so excited to see my first Internet draft of metadata sometime last March. In its "Definitions and Examples for a Core Metadata Set," however, the Dublin Group proposes a baker's dozen of terms meant to assist "Discovery" that are categorically identical to, but much less granular than, terms found in *AACR2R* and *TEI (P3)*. This dataset is unsatisfactory in that it proposes only a subset of what AACR says must be in a record, instead of examining what it is that creators of digital libraries have said they want to distribute and/or what creators of networked objects are capable of providing. Its virtue, on the other hand, is that it is truly syntax independent. The defined terms are: subject, title, author, publisher, Other Agent, Date, Identifier, ObjectType, Form, Relation, Language, Edition, and Source.[18] Terms meant to assist "Management" were not included in the Dublin Core, even though they would more closely match the metalinguistic dimension of the Information Bus. If these networked objects could carry with them the right kind of management metadata,[19] users of networked information objects would benefit from a quantum leap in the level of their empowerment.[20,21]

## *CONCLUSION*

Because it uses words instead of numbers, it seems to me that the TEI header could be flexible enough to give users of networked resources what they say they want. We can run out of 3-digit numbers and letters of the alphabet, but we cannot run out of words. It is also important for an <AccessDesc> area to be devised that contains not hard data but (perhaps) mini-programs associated with expert systems, or querying routines that comply with the Z39.50 protocol. Thirdly, authority control methodologies need to be devised for TEI-compliant strings, perhaps by writing them over into USMARC, for which those kinds of file processing applications are already available. Most important of all, however, is that we pay attention to what the creators and users of digital libraries say they want us to provide for them, and that we do not close ourselves off to a radical re-thinking of USMARC.

# REFERENCES

1. "NSF Announces Awards for Digital Libraries Research," http://http.cs.berkeley.edu/~wilensky/proj-html/nsf-press-release.html.

2. *Stanford Digital Libraries Proposal (SDLP). Part II. Project Description*, http://www-diglib.stanford.edu/diglib/pub/proposal/partII/node1.html#SECTION 00010000000000000000.

3. *McGraw Hill Dictionary of Scientific and Technical Terms*, 3rd ed.

4. *SDLP. Part II.B.1. Information Bus Infrastructure and Models*, "http://Mjosa.Stanford.EDU:80/diglib/pub/proposal/partII/node4.html#SECTION00040000000000000000

5. *SDLP. Part II.B.1.1. II.B.1.1. Definition of the problem area*, http://Mjosa.Stanford.EDU:80/diglib/pub/proposal/partII/node5.html#SECTION0004100000000000000

6. Ibid.

7. Michael Gorman, ed., *Anglo-American Cataloging Rules*, 2nd ed. rev., (Chicago: American Library Association, 1988).

8. Library of Congress. Network Development and MARC Standards Office, *USMARC Concise Formats*, (Washington, D.C.: The Library, 1991- ).

9. Library of Congress. Cataloging Distribution Service, *Subject Cataloging Manual: Subject Headings*, 4th ed., (Washington, D.C.: The Library, 1991- ).

10. *SDLP. Part II.B.1.3. Our approach to the problems*, http://Mjosa.Stanford.EDU:80/diglib/pub/proposal/partII/node7.html.

11. Ibid.

12. Michael Sperberg-McQueen and Lou Burnard, eds., *Guidelines for Electronic Text Encoding and Interchange (TEI P3)*, (Chicago, TEI, 1994).

13. Ibid., vol. 1, p. 137.

14. Susan Hockey, *Describing Electronic Texts: The Text Encoding Initiative and SGML*, http://lcweb.loc.gov/catdir/semdigdocs/hockey.html.

15. TEI P3, vol. 1, p. 678.

16. TEI P3, vol. 1, p. 678.

17. *SDLP. Part II.B.1.3. Our approach to the problems*, http://Mjosa.Stanford.EDU:80/diglib/pub/proposal/partII/node7.html.

18. Stuart Weibel [and others], *OCLC/NCSA Metadata Workshop Report*, http://www.oclc.org:5046/conferences/metadata/dublin_core_report.html.

19. Robyne M. Sumpter, *Whitepaper on Data Management*, http://www.llnl.gov/liv_comp/metadata/papers/whitepaper-draft.html.

20. Judith M. Brugger, "Cataloging the Internet," in *McJournal; The Journal of Academic Media Librarianship*, Available as "brugger mcj01006" via anonymous FTP from "ubvm.cc.buffalo.edu." (1993).

21. Ron Daniel, Jr. and Michael Mealing, *URC Scenarios and Requirements*, Available as "draft-ietf-uri-urc-req-01.txt" via anonymous FTP from "ds.internic.net", (March 24, 1995).

# Selection, Access, and Control in a Library of Electronic Texts

David M. Seaman

**SUMMARY.** The Electronic Text Center at the University of Virginia has been mounting SGML full-text databases on-line since 1992, and actively building a user community around this Internet resource. Conceiving of what we do as firmly a library operation, we have sought to integrate the electronic text databases into the training, cataloging, preservation, and collection development areas of our library. Central to our selection criteria is the desire for software- and platform-independent texts–if it's not SGML, it's ephemeral– and central to our cataloging endeavors is an SGML bibliographic record such as the Text Encoding Initiative header. *[Article copies available from The Haworth Document Delivery Service: 1-800-342-9678. E-mail address: getinfo@haworth.com]*

## *INTRODUCTION*

The Electronic Text Center at the University of Virginia is in every sense a library operation, existing in and being funded by the

---

David M. Seaman is Coordinator of the Electronic Text Center at the University of Virginia Library, where he is responsible for building and maintaining a Library-Based Electronic Text Center and on-line archive of texts. He holds a BA in English Studies from the University of East Anglia, Norwich and an MA in Medieval Studies from the University of Connecticut.

The author is grateful to the School of Information and Library Studies at Curtin University of Technology in Perth, Australia, for a Visiting Fellowship in August/September 1994 that amongst other things allowed him time to finish this article.

[Haworth co-indexing entry note]: "Selection, Access, and Control in a Library of Electronic Texts." Seaman, David M. Co-published simultaneously in *Cataloging & Classification Quarterly* (The Haworth Press, Inc.) Vol. 22, No. 3/4, 1996, pp. 75-84; and: *Electronic Resources: Selection and Bibliographic Control* (ed: Ling-yuh W. Pattie, and Bonnie Jean Cox) The Haworth Press, Inc., 1996, pp. 75-84. Single or multiple copies of this article are available from The Haworth Document Delivery Service [1-800-342-9678, 9:00 a.m. - 5:00 p.m. (EST). E-mail address: getinfo@haworth.com].

 

University Library. From our earliest planning stages in late 1991 we assumed that the electronic information in which we were investing our resources was amenable to traditional library skills. I use the word "traditional" unapologetically; indeed, coming from outside the library profession to create the Center, one of my first efforts was to coordinate with such areas as collection development and cataloging, whose involvement is central to any successful digital library. The rapid growth in both our on-line holdings and our user community has been predicated firmly on the notion that an electronic text center has to be *of* the library and not merely *in* the library. Moreover, we are beginning to see the benefits of keeping the electronic collections in the hands of the librarians who know the content, even if they have to learn the mechanics of the new media and machinery–science librarians are planning our Science Data Center, fine arts librarians run our Digital Image Center, and so on, as we develop a loose confederation of electronic centers that integrate with the other document access and control disciplines in our library system.

## *ACCESS*

The majority of our electronic texts are on-line, marked up in Standard Generalized Markup Language coding (hereafter SGML),[1] and are accessed through a single commercially available search tool.[2] It was a founding principle of the etext archive that this would be so. By purchasing SGML texts such as the *Oxford English Dictionary* or Chadwyck-Healey's *Patrologia Latina Database* as on-line data rather than as objects–by treating these titles as text on a networked server rather than on CD-ROMs or floppy disks–we can allow remote access 24-hours a day and we can have a common piece of interface software for a multitude of different titles.[3] The search program we purchased comes with X Windows, MS Windows, and VT100 interfaces to the Unix-based search tool; in addition, we can now offer forms-based World Wide Web interfaces of our own devising, which are increasingly the most popular way to access the on-line materials. There are some exceptions to our ability to move our electronic holdings on-line. Material in character sets such as Greek and Hebrew is still difficult to deliver over a network to a disparate set of users, and there will be for some time a subset of titles for which we cannot obtain on-line permissions. These items are available in the library building, but not on the Internet.[4]

HyperText Markup Language, the simple form of SGML that currently underpins the World Wide Web, is unsuitable as a primary markup language for most full-text items, but the Web is a valuable, convenient, and desirable delivery mechanism for many of our texts. Our provision of World Wide Web access does not require us to maintain a duplicate set of HTML-encoded files, in addition to our other SGML formats–that degree of duplication would be unmanageable. Instead, the texts are all held on the server in forms of SGML more sophisticated than HTML, and are converted to HTML "on the fly" using a PERL script of our own creation that is triggered each time a user browses a text or searches a database. This, then, allows us to have Web access without reducing the markup of our data to the rather impoverished level of HTML. Despite its inability to describe database structure in a text (as opposed to typographic or spacial layout), the growing popularity of HTML has done much to raise the awareness of the value of standardized markup in our publishing and library communities.

The burden of setting-up and running the Unix server and the databases stored on it falls to the Library, with the work shared between the Etext Center staff and Jeff Herrin, our Unix specialist in the Library Systems Department. As most of the major commercial databases are already coded in SGML, there is relatively little to do to these databases prior to indexing them on the server. There is a significant investment in skills and time when running these databases as on-line resources, but the on-line access provides a more sophisticated service to our library patrons, and the use of a single interface greatly simplifies the task of providing user training and support. Users access the databases from their homes or offices, or from public machines at the University, so there is also much less need for the library to buy and maintain the PCs that allow users to access the electronic texts. Moreover, the Library's early lead in providing networked information has done much locally to ensure that the information professionals in the library system take a leading role–surely to everyone's benefit–in the longer-term development, description, and archiving of the mass of Web-engendered texts that are pouring from every part of our university.

## *SELECTION AND COLLECTION DEVELOPMENT CRITERIA*

If the electronic library is to develop congruent with the larger print collections it is important that its holdings be informed by the same selection criteria that govern any other item added to the library. An electronic text is not suitable for inclusion in a library if it runs counter to the collection development policies that govern the long-term vitality of that collection. The knowledge of the collections specialists and subject bibliographers in evaluating texts is entirely appropriate to the selection of electronic product.

The new media bring new selection criteria concerned with the long-term viability of data. Chief among these new criteria is the degree to which the electronic data conforms to the media- and platform-independent SGML standards. Irrespective of its content, the electronic text that is held in a software- and medium-*dependent* format has little relevance to long-term library development, although an item may have sufficient short-term utility to make it worth purchasing. The etext conceived of as having a life only as a CD-ROM disk, and usable only with a particular piece of software included on that disk, is much less desirable for libraries and (increasingly) for publishers and consumers alike than the standards-based and networkable SGML text. There are certainly non-SGML titles that are valuable parts of our etext collection today, but it is most unlikely that those databases encoded in proprietary formats will be viable data in a decade, and even today the CD-ROM bound texts are cumbersome in comparison to networked data.

For some electronic text collections we have undertaken the work ourselves of turning a proprietary database into networkable SGML (working, of course, with the compliance of the publishers). The philosophy texts from InteLex Corp. are a good example of this. The work of adding the SGML tagging is an additional cost associated with such a product, but it is less than the cost of housing the text as a standalone object, of maintaining the machinery to use it, and of running training sessions in that particular product. The mechanics of the conversion to SGML varies with the nature of the source text, but typically the bulk of the work involves a series of "search and replace" operations, perhaps performed within a word processor such as WordPerfect, but more often using the Unix utilities SED and PERL to write short scripts that locate a proprietary or implicit way of indicating document structure or typography and replace it with explicit SGML tags.

## *CONSORTIA*

As we get used to the inclusion of networked data in our libraries, we see the possibilities of consortial purchasing arrangements emerge, especially for large and expensive databases. The University of Virginia Library brokered a deal in 1993 to purchase a group site license for Chadwyck Healey's *English Poetry Full-Text Database,* to allow five Virginia universities to access the on-line copy of the data at UVa. Building on this lead, the Virtual Library of Virginia (VIVA) has bought a 39-site group license for a range of Chadwyck-Healey databases, all housed at the University of Virginia Library, including the *English Poetry Database,* its companion *English Verse Drama Database,* and the *African-American Database,* and other states are doing similar consortial deals with publishers of electronic data.[5] These arrangements are in everyone's interest at present: the publishers get a greater volume of sales from a given state than they would by selling the items simply to individual institutions, and smaller colleges get access to massive amounts of data that they could not afford to buy as single products. This latter point is especially true for collections such as the *English Poetry Full-Text Database,* which is monumental in both scope and cost, and out of reach as a single product for the majority of college libraries.

## *CATALOGING THE ELECTRONIC TEXT*

Earlier in this article I noted the close links developing between the Electronic Text Center and our Cataloging Department. It is a natural alliance that has benefitted the electronic text endeavor considerably, and all the more so since our library has been able to add to its staff Jackie Shieh, our first Cataloguer of Electronic Resources. We are still perfecting the details of the workflow, but what follows is a description of the cataloging processes from the perspective of the Etext Center, for those texts that we encode or create ourselves.

All of the texts we encode are marked up in SGML according to the tenets of the *Text Encoding Initiative Guidelines* (hereafter TEI). Chief amongst the document control benefits of the TEI Guidelines is the provision of a sophisticated "TEI header" that begins each text.[6] The TEI header functions for us as an electronic titlepage, a record of the creation of the text, of its print source, of any corrections made to it, and it provides various date and keyword fields for our search tools. The version of the header used by us exists as a "fill in the blanks" template that is concatenated to the top of a text before we start work on it. In brief, the four major sections of our TEI header are as follows:

1. *The File Description*–<fileDesc>–contains a full bibliographical description of the computer file–title, author, creator of electronic version, publisher of electronic version, the size of completed file in KB–along with information about the printed source from which the electronic text was derived (contained within the <sourceDesc>).
2. *The Encoding Description*–<encodingDesc>–describes whether (or how) the text was normalized during transcription, how the encoder resolved ambiguities in the source, what levels of encoding or analysis were applied, and so on.
3. *The Text Profile Description*–<profileDesc>–describes non-bibliographic aspects of the text, specifically the languages used, the situation in which it was produced, the participants, and their setting.
4. *The Revision History Description*–<revisionDesc>–allows present and future encoders to provide a history of changes made during the development of the electronic text.

After we have finished tagging and parsing a text, a copy of the completed header goes to a "headers-incoming" directory where the catalogers take over [for an example of a completed TEI header from our collection, see the Appendix]. The header is the source for the MARC record that the cataloging staff create. At present, this is a manual process, but our library (like a number of others) is exploring mechanisms to create automatically a MARC record from a TEI header.

In the process of using the TEI header as a source of information, the catalogers are also proofreading it, and correcting errors or bibliographical gaucheness on our part. When we re-attach the corrected header to the text, we have a more accurate and standardized record, and due to feedback from the catalogers my staff and I are learning to be more precise bibliographers. The accuracy of the header is particularly important as the collection of etexts grows, because the header to a text is often the prime source of information for our search tool's ability to limit an operation to works by a particular author or publisher, or to works created (but not necessarily published) within a certain range of dates. The fields that identify a work as belonging to one of these subsets are often located only within the header.

While we are not doing this at present, I am beginning to think that it is in our interest to scan as a digital image the titlepage for any text we process, while we have the book in hand for other tagging and scanning purposes. This would take little extra time, and would be a useful source of reference later, in the event, for example, of a data-entry omission or error in the header.

As we found ourselves with a growing number of electronic texts that include related digital images–book illustrations, titlepages, manuscript scans from our Special Collections–it dawned on me that the TEI header was a viable attribution record (and perhaps a cataloging form) for these book-related images too. We are now going through the process of modifying our TEI header template to allow for the inclusion of more information about related image files. The use of the TEI header to record information about images addresses a pressing practical need. When these images are accessed through the Web, there is little or nothing on them to identify their source or provenance. Once we realized that we could bury the tagged text header in the image file itself–so that a single image file carries both the binary code of the digital image and also the SGML text cataloging record itself–it did much to overcome our unease at sending images out onto the Web with no indication of whence they came or to what text they belonged. This is in theory, and increasingly in practice, a regular part of our attempts to maintain bibliographical control over our on-line etext collections, especially as more and more of them are not single text files but interconnected multi-file and multi-format documents.[7]

## *CONCLUSION*

After three years of operation as a public "walk-in" Center, as a place for user-training and electronic text creation, and as a large online collection of SGML-encoded texts, we are increasingly sure that the decision to treat this new enterprise as a textual endeavor that uses computers–rather than a computer operation that gets fed electronic texts–has paid off. By embracing SGML encoding as a means to ensure the long-term viability of our texts, and by using the TEI header as a way to maintain bibliographic control over them, we are confident that our on-line electronic text holdings will continue to be useable many years from now. "If it's not SGML, it's ephemeral" is a motto we keep firmly in mind. Moreover, as our archives of digital data grow rapidly it is increasingly evident that only through the library disciplines of collection development and acquisitions, of cataloging and user training, can we continue to manage and nurture our digital collections.

## NOTES

1. More information about Standard Generalized Markup Language can be found at: http://etext.lib.virginia.edu/sgml.html
2. We chose PAT, a Unix-based indexing and search tool from OpenText: http://www.opentext.com/
3. A list of electronic texts available on-line at the University of Virginia can be found at: http://etext.lib.virginia.edu/uvaonline.html
4. A list of electronic texts available off-line at the University of Virginia can be found at: http://etext.lib.virginia.edu/offline.html
5. For more information about the Virtual Library of Virginia, see: http://www.vcu.edu/ulsweb/viva/viva.html
6. More information on the TEI header can be found in the *Text Encoding Initiative Guidelines,* available online at: http://etext.lib.virginia.edu/TEI.html

7. Our first attempts at using the TEI header as an attribution record for digital images are recorded in the following article: David M. Seaman. "Campus Publishing with TEI and SGML" in *Paying the Piper* (Washington D.C.: Association of Research Libraries, 1994), pp. 93-102. This item is available online at: http://www.lib.virginia.edu/etext/articles.html

More recent developments can be found in the *Illustrations* section of the *Electronic Text Center Introduction to TEI and Guide to Document Preparation* at: http://etext.lib.virginia.edu/teiguide.html

# APPENDIX: A Sample TEI Header

<TEI.2>
<teiHeader type=aacr2>
<fileDesc>
<titleStmt><title>The history of Lady Julia Mandeville [a machine-readable transcription]</title>
<author>Brooke, Frances, 1724?-1789 </author>
<respStmt>
<resp>Creation of machine-readable version: </resp> <name>Barbara Smith, University of Virginia English Department </name>
<resp>Creation of digital images: </resp><name>David Seaman, University of Virginia Library Electronic Text Center </name>
<resp>Conversion to TEI.2-conformant markup: </resp> <name>University of Virginia Library Electronic Text Center</name>
</respStmt></titleStmt>
<extent>ca. 390 kilobytes </extent>
<publicationStmt><publisher>University of Virginia Library</publisher>
<pubPlace>Charlottesville, Va.</pubPlace>
<idno type="ETC">Modern English, BroLady</idno>
<availability><p>URL:
http://etext.lib.virginia.edu/modeng.browse.html</p>
</availability>
<date>1992</date>
</publicationStmt>
<seriesStmt><p></p></seriesStmt>
<notesStmt><note>Illustrations have been included from the print version.</note>
<note>This text was created for use by Professor Patricia Spacks and her students. </note></notesStmt>
<sourceDesc><biblFull>
<titleStmt><title>The history of Lady Julia Mandeville</title>

<author>Frances Brooke </author>
<respStmt><resp></resp><name></name></respStmt>
</titleStmt>
<editionStmt><p>4th ed </p></editionStmt>
<extent></extent>
<publicationStmt><publisher>J. Dodsley </publisher>
<pubPlace>London </pubPlace>
<date>1765 </date></publicationStmt>
<seriesStmt><p></p></seriesStmt>
<notesStmt><note></note></notesStmt>
</biblFull></sourceDesc></fileDesc>
<encodingDesc>
<projectDesc><p>Prepared for the University of Virginia Library Electronic Text Center</p></projectDesc>
<editorialDecl><p>All quotation marks retained as data</p>
<p>All unambiguous end-of-line hyphens have been removed, and the trailing part of a word has been joined to the preceding line.</p>
<p>The images exist as archived TIFF images, one or more JPEG versions for general use, and thumbnail GIFs.</p>
<p id=ETC>Keywords in the header are a local Electronic Text Center scheme to aid in establishing analytical groupings</p>
</editorialDecl>
<refsDecl>
<p>ID elements are given for each page element and are composed of the text's unique cryptogram and the given page number, as in AusEmma1 for page one of Jane Austen's Emma.</p>
</refsDecl></encodingDesc>
<profileDesc>
<creation><date>1763 </date></creation>
<langUsage><language>English </language></langUsage>
<textClass>
<keywords><term>fiction; prose</term></keywords>
</textClass></profileDesc>
<revisionDesc>
<change><date>May 11,1994</date>
<respStmt><resp>cataloger</resp><name>Allison M. Sleeman, University of Virginia Library, Cataloging Services Dept</name></respStmt>
<item>TEI header completed</item></change>
<change><date> July 1993</date>
<respStmt><resp>corrector</resp><name>David Gants, University of Virginia Library Electronic Text Center</name></respStmt>
<item>Tagging and header updated</item></change>
</revisionDesc>
</teiHeader>

# Control of Electronic Resources in Australia

Giles Martin

**SUMMARY.** This article describes various ways that electronic resources on the Internet are being controlled in Australia, and in particular how various special networks and projects are linking users of information with documents, often using the World Wide Web. It also examines the implications for libraries and for cataloguers. *[Article copies available from The Haworth Document Delivery Service: 1-800-342- 9678. E-mail address: getinfo@haworth.com]*

## *INTRODUCTION*

This article is a snapshot of the control of electronic resources in Australia, as of the end of November 1995. The situation is so fluid that by next week something new will have happened, and this article will be out of date–but the pointers that I have provided in the article to World Wide Web (WWW) documents should lead to more current information.

I interpret "control of electronic resources" broadly. Control is not just the electronic equivalent of using card catalogues: it is all

Giles Martin is Quality Control Librarian, University of Newcastle, Australia, responsible for authority control, cataloguer training and OPAC record quality. He is a member of the Australia Committee on Cataloguing at the Dewey Decimal Classification Editorial Policy Committee.

[Haworth co-indexing entry note]: "Control of Electronic Resources in Australia." Martin, Giles. Co-published simultaneously in *Cataloging & Classification Quarterly* (The Haworth Press, Inc.) Vol. 22, No. 3/4, 1996, pp. 85-96; and: *Electronic Resources: Selection and Bibliographic Control* (ed: Ling-yuh W. Pattie, and Bonnie Jean Cox) The Haworth Press, Inc., 1996, pp. 85-96. Single or multiple copies of this article are available from The Haworth Document Delivery Service [1-800-342-9678, 9:00 a.m. - 5:00 p.m. (EST). E-mail address: getinfo@haworth.com].

 

the links between users of information and the documents that contain information. This includes government policies, networks to link people to information, projects to investigate and set up links between users and documents, and a variety of service organisations (many of which do not look like traditional libraries, but which do offer much the same kinds of services as libraries).

This means that we are seeing catalogues of electronic resources, which don't call themselves "catalogues," and which are being created by people who would not call themselves "cataloguers," alongside of "catalogues" of electronic resources being created by "cataloguers" in "libraries."

It no longer makes sense to think of control of electronic resources solely in a library context. The Internet and the WWW are no respecters of boundaries–either national or institutional. Once the users of information have access to the Internet and the WWW, they are not limited to the services provided by libraries.

I am also including some projects that control documents generally–not just electronic resources–since they use networked electronic media to provide control.

Some general comments that can be made about Australian control of electronic documents are:

- WWW is the preferred mode of access to networked documents and information now–replacing Gopher, Archie, FTP, etc. The Web is currently seeing explosive growth, as libraries, government departments, and commercial organisations rush to set up their home pages on the Web, and as every newspaper and magazine gives advice to their readers on how to access the Web.
- Libraries are among the main players in controlling electronic materials–particularly the National Library of Australia, most of the state libraries, and many of the academic libraries. But there are other organisations involved, which are not traditionally seen as providing access to information–both government departments, and commercial organisations.
- There is a lot of experimentation, and a lot of possible duplication of effort, which may be both confusing to the user and wasteful of resources. I have listed a variety of Australian WWW services in the Appendix–and it is clear from that list that there is a lot of

duplication, e.g., the half dozen or so indexes to Australian WWW sites.

## *GOVERNMENT POLICY*

Several recent Government reports have emphasised the importance of access to information for all Australians.

### *The Broadband Expert Services Group Report*

"The ability to communicate and the right to have access to information are fundamental to a democratic society. Access to digital information and the ability to communicate electronically may become just as fundamental in the future."[1]

### *Creative Nation*

"Access to information for all Australians is an important element of Commonwealth cultural policy."

"Information is a key resource for all Australians–for full participation in our society, and for our quality of life. The Government will continue to work with the States to ensure that existing information resources and the new networking technologies are widely available."

"The Government will work with the States to enable the resources in libraries throughout the nation to become available to all."[2]

As a result of these policies, the Australian Government has supported both networks to provide access for all, and projects to help people find and retrieve documents and information.

## *ACCESS NETWORKS*

Several networks are already running, or are in the process of being set up in Australia, to provide access to electronic resources. Four such networks, set up by governments, and targeted either to educational institutions or to disadvantaged groups, are:

***The Community Information Network (CIN)***
*<http://www.cin.gov.au/>*

"CIN will provide free access to government and community information, communication facilities and services, initially through 100 Local Access Points (LAPs) situated in DSS offices, libraries and community organisations."[3] This network was launched by the Minister for Social Security, Peter Baldwin, in July 1995.

***EdNA (Education Network Australia)***
*<http://www.deet.gov.au/edna/ednahome.htm>*

"EdNA will link all schools, TAFE colleges, Universities and other education and training providers across Australia." Announced by the Minister for Employment, Education and Training, Simon Crean, on 9 June 1995.[4]

***Open Net***
*<http://www.opennet.net.au/>*

Open Net is a network service for open learning students in schools, TAFE (Technical and Further Education) and universities. It was launched by the Minister of Employment, Education and Training, Simon Crean, on 19 May 1995, and is run by Open Net Pty. Ltd.[5]

***VICNET: Victoria's Network***
*<http://www.vicnet.net.au/vicnet/vicnet.html>*

"VICNET is a joint project of the State Library of Victoria and RMIT, and is being established thanks to funding from the Victorian State Government's Community Support Fund."[6]

## *PROJECTS*

Two major projects are currently under way in Australia to provide access to electronic resources. The first (IDA) involves providing access with tools developed by others, and the second (WORLD 1) is developing new systems to provide access to electronic resources as part of a larger project.

***The IDA Project (Integrated Document Access Project)***
*<http://www.ida.unisa.edu.au/ida.html>*

This project is being conducted by the University of South Australia on behalf of the Council of Australian University Librarians (CAUL). Funding for the project has been provided by the Department of Employment, Education and Training (DEET) under the Evaluations and Investigations Program (EIP).

The IDA project falls into two main parts. The first part of the project is to identify and describe:

- finding tools/indexes used for research and teaching information with an emphasis on electronic publications
- projects that aim to integrate tools/indexes for print and electronic publications
- projects for the document delivery of print and electronic publications

The second part of the IDA project is to analyse the tools and projects identified as above and make recommendations in relation to their testing as models for integrated delivery of information to Australian research institutions.[7]

***WORLD 1 and The National Document & Information Service (NDIS) Project***
*<http://www.nla.gov.au/2/NDIS/>*

"WORLD 1 is a new online information service being developed by the National Library of Australia. It will provide all Australians with access to recorded knowledge held in libraries and databases in Australia and overseas, through one easy to use service.

WORLD 1 was announced, on 18 July 1995, as the Australian brand name for the service being developed by the National Document and Information Service (NDIS) Project."[8]

WORLD 1 will do a lot more than provide access to electronic resources, but because it is being developed at this time, electronic resources will be important to it–both provision of access and delivery to the user.

## *SOME AUSTRALIAN ACCESS SERVICES ON THE WWW*

As well as the two major projects, there are a number of smaller Australian services on the WWW that provide access to electronic resources. These have been set up by a variety of organisations: libraries, government departments, and commercial firms.

The National Library of Australia has taken a lead in providing control over electronic resources, seeing this as a natural extension of its role in controlling conventional resources.[9,10] Thus, several of the services listed below are run by the NLA.

### *INDEXES TO AUSTRALIAN WWW SERVERS AND HOME PAGES*

The Aussie index <http://www.aussie.com.au/>
A database of Australian businesses and their Web pages.

Australian Announce Archive (AAA). <http://www.com.au/aaa/index2.html>
Run by Big Country Radio AM/FM.

Australian Internet Directories <http://www.sofcom.com.au/WWW.AU/index.html>
Includes "WWW.AU–The Australian Web Directory" and "EMAIL.AU–The Australian Email Directory." Operated by Sofcom Distributors Pty Ltd.

Australian WWW servers <http://www.csu.edu.au/links/ozweb.html>
"This service provides various means of locating Web services in Australia. . . . This project was partially funded from the National Priority (Reserve) Fund allocation for improved Library infrastructure administered by the AVCC Standing Committee on Information Resources."

Operated by Charles Sturt University.
Definitive Guide to (over 5,000) Australian webs. <http://gwb.com.au/gwb/guide.html>
Run by Global Web Builders.

Little Aussie Web Wombat Search Engine <http://www.intercom.com.au/wombat/>
"The little Aussie Web Wombat is a web crawling robot. The Wombat wanders the net day and night searching for pages that might be of interest to you."
Run by Internet Communications.

The Registry of Australian Web Servers. <http://www.csu.edu.au/Harvest/brokers/OzRegistry/>
"Broker Query Interface to Home pages of Registered Servers. This Broker was built using the Harvest system."

## *INDEXES TO OTHER AUSTRALIAN ELECTRONIC SERVICES*

Australian Libraries <http://info.anu.edu.au/ozlib/>
An index to Australian library catalogues, operated by Mark Nearhos, The Library, The Australian National University.

Index of Australian Indexes. <http://www.moreinfo.com.au/ausindex/>
An index of indexes to Australian WWW resources. Run by MoreInfo Internet Publishing

OZLISTS : a List of Australian electronic mailing lists
<http://www.gu.edu.au/gint/ozlists/ozlists_home.html>
"A compilation of those electronic mailing lists or discussion groups that are based in Australia."
Operated by Griffith University.

## *INDEXES TO AUSTRALIAN DOCUMENTS*

The Australia Index. <http://sin.csu.edu.au/australia/>
"This project was partially funded from the National Priority

(Reserve) Fund allocation for improved Library infrastructure administered by the AVCC Standing Committee on Information Resources."

"The Australia Index is a collaborative project that aims to develop a comprehensive on-line index of Australian information, and information about Australia and to make it available on the Internet. The Index will include comprehensive, searchable databases as well as structured guides and interpreted views ("virtual libraries") of the information aimed at particular needs, especially education, tourism, research, government and commerce."

Australian Electronic Journals <http://www.nla.gov.au/oz/ausejour.html>

"This is a current list of Australian electronic journals and magazines with a presence on the WWW–including overseas works with Australian content or an Australian emphasis."
Run by the National Library of Australia.

"This service is one of the closest to traditional library cataloguing done by traditional catalogers–but even this service has had to adjust to the different reality of electronic resources."[11]

Australian Governments' Entry Point <http://www.nla.gov.au/oz/gov/>

Run by the National Library of Australia. This provides access to federal, state and local government information services."

Guide to Australia <http://www.csu.edu.au/education/australia.html>

"This GUIDE TO AUSTRALIA project aims to compile links to all available on-line information resources about Australia for distribution via World Wide Web. Our aim is that ultimately it will grow into an on-line, hypertext encyclopaedia." Editors, David Green and Jim Croft. Publishers, Charles Sturt University and the Australian National Botanic Gardens.

Internet Directory Australia <http://www.ida.com.au/>

"Internet Directory Australia is a commercial World Wide Web Publishing Service. Our largest client base is in the tourism, travel and hospitality industries."

This is Australia. <http://www.telstra.com.au/meta/australia.html>

"This page represents links to all sorts of information about this great country of ours–Australia."
Run by Telstra.

## *INDEXES TO THE WORLD (CREATED BY AUSTRALIAN LIBRARIES)*

ELISA, the Electronic Library and Information Service at ANU <http://info.anu.edu.au/elisa.html>

Run by Tony Barry at the Australian National University.

The State Library of Tasmania home page <http://www.tased.edu.au/library/library>

University of Adelaide Subject Guide to Selected Internet Services <http://library.adelaide.edu.au/net/topics/index.html>

World Wide Government Information <http://www.nla.gov.au/gov/govinfo.html>

"Information about and from the governments of: Australia, New Zealand, Pacific Islands, Asia, Canada, United Kingdom, United States of America, Europe, Africa, The Middle East." Run by the National Library of Australia.

## *IMPLICATIONS FOR LIBRARIES*

Libraries do not have any choice about whether to provide access to Internet resources–an increasing part of the information needed by their users is only available from the Internet. The choice is about how to do it:

- Integrate access into the normal OPAC?
- Put access on a WWW page created by the library?
- Cooperate with other libraries–either through bibliographic utilities like WORLD 1, or through a project like IDA–to provide access?
- Leave it up to commercial services not traditionally associated with libraries?

Few Australian libraries have attempted to include Internet resources. The only one that I am aware of is the University of Adelaide Library.[12] In this case, there has been a deliberate decision only to include resources "academically relevant" to the University.[13]

More Australian libraries have provided access through WWW pages, as indicated in the list above: the NLA, some state libraries, and some academic libraries. The disadvantages of this approach are that you must help your users to find and use the WWW, and that this separates access to Internet resources from the access to resources within your own library. The advantage is that you can, with a small effort, provide a seamless link to information resources created by others on the WWW.

The invention of the MARC record meant that it no longer made sense to catalogue for one library alone. Similarly, the WWW means that an electronic information resource needs to be maintained only once to be available anywhere in the world. Most libraries need only maintain a simple home page on the WWW in order to provide links to WWW pages maintained by others. However, there will need to be some coordination, through projects such as IDA and WORLD 1, to ensure that work is only done once, but that the whole information universe is adequately covered.

Within this information universe, there is room for commercial providers. No one would want to duplicate Telstra's "White Pages" and "Yellow Pages," for example. However, most commercial WWW services will either concentrate on selling a product, or use automated WWW search programs to generate indexes to the WWW at a minimal cost. What libraries are likely to be best at is the application of human intelligence to help link users with the most appropriate Internet resources.

## NOTES

1. Broadband Services Expert Group. "Final report, Chapter 4: Providing Access." <http://www.dca.gov.au/chapt4.htm>
2. Australian Government. "Creative Nation, Information for all Australians." <http://www.dca.gov.au/creative_nation/info.htm>
3. Baldwin, Peter. "The Community Information Network Bridging [sic] the Information Gap." <http://www.nla.gov.au/oz/gov/press/baldwin4195.html>
4. Crean, Simon. "Australia's Schools and the Information Highway," 9 June 1995 <http://www.deet.gov.au/edna/itec.htm>
5. Open Net Pty Ltd. "Information on Open Net Pty Ltd" <http://www.opennet.net.au/OPENNET/company_info.html>
6. "VICNET: Victoria's Network" <http://www.vicnet.net.au/vicnet/vicnet.html>

7. "What is the IDA project?" <http://www.ida.unisa.edu.au/whatisida.html>
8. "WORLD 1 and The National Document & Information Service (NDIS) Project." <http://www.nla.gov.au/2/NDIS>
9. Bezear, Lesley. "Defining the National Library of Australia's Role in the Acquisition, Control and Preservation of Australian Electronic Publications." <http://www.nla.gov.au/nla/staffpaper/catpaper.html>
10. Henty, Margaret. "Networked Information Resources: Collection Development, Cataloguing and Preservation in the National Library of Australia." <http://www.nla.gov.au/nla/staffpaper/npomh.html>
11. Henty, Margaret. "Electronic Journals and the National Library of Australia." <http://www.nla.gov.au/oz/ausejour/henty.htm>
12. University of Adelaide Library. Telnet to library.adelaide.edu.au, and login as "library." An example of a record is that for "Current Cites."
13. Thomas, Steve. Personal communication.

## APPENDIX: Acronyms and Other Jargon

ABN. Australian Bibliographic Network. A utility run by NLA to provide cataloguing and inter-library loan services to Australian libraries. <http://www.nla.gov.au/2/abn/abnhome.html>

ALIA. Australian Library and Information Association. The Australian professional society for librarians. <http://www.alia.org.au/>

ANB. Australian National Bibliography.

AVCC. Australian Vice Chancellors' Committee. <http://www.avcc.edu.au/avcc/>

CAUL. Council of Australian University Librarians. <http://www.anu.edu.au/caul/>

CJK Project. The National Chinese Japanese Korean Project. A project to provide access to CJK material using CJK script, run by the NLA. <http://www.nla.gov.au/1/asian/ncjk/cjkproj.html>

DEET. The Australian Department of Employment, Education and Training. <http://www.deet.gov.au/>

DNC. The Distributed National Collection. The concept of the totality of the library collections in Australia as one collection. Coordinated by the Distributed National Collection Office in the NLA. <http://www.nla.gov.au/dnc/dnchome.html>

IDA Project (Integrated Document Access Project) <http://www.ida.unisa.edu.au/ida.html>

III. Improved Information Infrastructure–Network Information Support. A project of the AVCC <http://www.gu.edu.au/alib/iii/iii-home.htm>

JEDDS. Joint Electronic Document Delivery Software Project <http://www.gu.edu.au/alib/iii/docdel/jointdev.htm>

Kiwinet. A collection of bibliographic and other databases run by NLNZ.

NDIS Project. National Document and Information Service Project. The working name of the project being run by NLA and NLNZ to replace ABN, Ozline, NZBN and Kiwinet. <http://www.nla.gov.au/2/NDIS/>

NLA. National Library of Australia. <http://www.nla.gov.au/>

NLNZ. National Library of New Zealand. <.http://planet.natlib.govt.nz/>

NZBN. New Zealand Bibliographic Network. The counterpart in New Zealand of ABN, run by NLNZ.

Ozline. "Australian Information Online"–a collection of bibliographic and other databases run by NLA. <http://www.nla.gov.au/2/ozline/ozlinehome.html>

Telstra. Formerly Telecom Australia. The main supplier of telephone and telecommunication services in Australia. <http://www.telstra.com.au/>

WORLD 1. The brand name of the Australian half of the NDIS Project. <http://www.nla.gov.au/2/NDIS/>

# "Parallel Universes" or Meaningful Relationships: Envisioning a Future for the OPAC and the Net

Diane I. Hillmann

**SUMMARY.** Over the past year, innumerable discussions on the relationship between traditional library OPACs and the newly burgeoning World WideWeb have occurred in many libraries and in virtually every library related discussion list. Rumors and speculation abound, some insisting that SGML will replace USMARC "soon," others maintaining that OPACs that haven't migrated to the Web will go the way of the dinosaurs. *[Article copies available from The Haworth Document Delivery Service: 1-800-342-9678. E-mail address: getinfo@haworth.com]*

## *THE OPAC AND THE NET– IS A RELATIONSHIP POSSIBLE?*

Underneath all these discussions lies a basic concern that the rapidly expanding Internet, particularly the WWW, has undermined forever the ideal of universal bibliographic control, or at least muddied the waters sufficiently to make formerly widely accepted goals and standards no longer unquestioned. No one has seriously pro-

---

Diane I. Hillmann is Head, Technical Services Support Unit, Cornell University Library, 107 Olin Library, Ithaca, NY 14853. E-mail: dih1@cornell.edu.

[Haworth co-indexing entry note]: " 'Parallel Universes' or Meaningful Relationships: Envisioning a Future for the OPAC and the Net." Hillmann, Diane I. Co-published simultaneously in *Cataloging & Classification Quarterly* (The Haworth Press, Inc.) Vol. 22, No. 3/4, 1996, pp. 97-103; and: *Electronic Resources: Selection and Bibliographic Control* (ed: Ling-yuh W. Pattie, and Bonnie Jean Cox) The Haworth Press, Inc., 1996, pp. 97-103. Single or multiple copies of this article are available from The Haworth Document Delivery Service [1-800-342-9678, 9:00 a.m. - 5:00 p.m. (EST). E-mail address: getinfo@haworth.com].

 

posed that libraries can "catalog the net" completely (at least, not lately), but there are still very real questions concerning the usefulness and validity of library standard cataloging when applied to networked resources.

But what is the alternative? In the early days of both books and the Internet, the cosmos was small enough that no special tools were needed to navigate the known world. It has not been possible for many lifetimes for libraries to operate without detailed catalogs. In the compressed time of the Internet, those lifetimes have also passed. The navigational tools devised by the network denizens maneuver only within the limits of the net itself–they have no capability to search the record of the human past. Are librarians to enforce those same limitations and describe only non-electronic resources in our catalogs? Will our users benefit by having to search two parallel universes to find what they need?

## *DO WE STILL NEED TO SELECT?*

The traditional library model of selection/cataloging/maintenance is often cited as one that will allow libraries to pull into their catalogs the best and most useful resources available on the Net. Central to this idea is the belief that networked resources are "just another format," not unlike the once-new videotapes, music CD's and microfiche. Just as these formerly outlaw formats have been mainstreamed into our general selection processes, using the same or similar criteria formerly applied to conventional printed materials, so will materials in computer file formats of all kinds, from diskettes to data "out there" on the Internet take their place in the enlarged realm of the catalog.

Using selection criteria, the networked "universe" that needs to be considered becomes much smaller and more manageable. These criteria remove from consideration the multitudes of library homepages that distribute the electronic version of desk handouts (describing hours, circulation policies, etc.). Also most libraries will no longer consider the hundreds (probably already thousands) of promotional sites, sites distributing software and ephemera, and the increasing numbers of personal homepages springing up on the Net.

Left after that initial screening are several categories of potentially useful databases, substantive Web sites (and the documents available on them), resources available by subscription through dial-up or telnet, ftp sites, and others. What still stymies much of the selection portion of the process are questions about who will select, whether pointers will be used or materials archived locally, and how selection decisions will be conveyed to catalogers, since the physical object that formerly served that purpose can no longer carry the message.

## *RESOURCE VOLATILITY AS A FACTOR IN "CONTROLLING" DOCUMENTS– IS IT THAT MUCH DIFFERENT THAN "BOOKS SPROUTING LEGS?"*

Early discussions of cataloging Internet resources invariably included concerns about the volatility of these resources. Didn't the addresses used for access change often? How could users be protected from dead ends? Realists pointed out that books had a long history of "sprouting legs," and that we hadn't talked about doing regular inventories of shelves because users sometimes couldn't find what they needed where we said it should be. For many resources, this question seemed only valid for the short term, since clearly if automatic connection from the OPAC to remote resources ever became a reality, it would be a short jump from there to regular, automatic inventorying of remote resources using the same mechanism.

But volatility can still be an issue at some levels. Efforts some years ago to catalog the individual databases in the WESTLAW and Lexis systems came to grief partly because the vendor regularly reorganized the structure of the databases to reflect the constantly growing nature of the full-text data in those systems. Catalogers' attempts to nail down the location of these databases within that structure could not keep up with the changes. Since these databases are firmly proprietary in nature and not available freely through the Internet, it seems unlikely that solutions designed for Web-based resources will solve the inherent problems of describing individual databases within Lexis/Nexis or the like.

## *COLLECTIONS vs. SINGLE DOCUMENTS–WHICH MAKES SENSE?*

What the push to "catalog the Net" has done, however, is to bring into sharper focus the choices we have made in the past about levels of cataloging. When a group of related resources is gathered together under one homepage or as part of a large database offered as a whole, should they be cataloged as a collection or as separates? This is not a dissimilar question from those the archival community has been dealing with forever, nor from the question of analytics for microform sets, but the hypertextual nature of the Web has complicated the issue somewhat.

The archival community has traditionally been more comfortable with making collection level decisions for their materials than general library selectors and catalogers have been with theirs. The proliferation of microform sets over the past few decades has forced a certain uneasy tolerance between macro- and micro-level treatment, but until now we've been able to leave the more extreme "collections"–the actual databases themselves–and the extreme "analytics"–journal articles–out of the mix. In the world we see developing in our near future, we will need to accommodate more varying levels in the traditional catalog, particularly if we want to retain the OPAC as the central point of contact between our users and the information we purchase and make available on their behalf.

## *STANDARDS OLD AND NEW–ARE THEY THE TOOLS FOR THE JOB?*

An important focus of AACR2 has been to attempt to proscribe sources of information strictly. The idea was to ensure uniform results–an essential point for isolated catalogers working independently on similar materials in various sites. Remotely accessed resources that exist in one place, which are not replicated in each library but instead are pointed to from various catalogs have an important quality in common with traditional archival collections–they are often one of a kind. In this context will it really matter if the title or other descriptive elements harken to a looser standard? Particularly if we can link directly to the item itself?

The problem of versioning for electronic documents is one we've just begun to grapple with, and to some extent we know from our experience with other formats that this is likely to challenge us mightily. Clearly the problem is not with dynamic databases, which change continually (as do their print analogs, the infamous loose-leaf services), but with individual documents, where an updated document could conceivably be linked to an outdated catalog record with no one being the wiser. This is an area where the record of libraries in setting standards and finding solutions has been less than stellar (whisper "multiple versions" to any cataloger and you'll see what I mean). And it may be useful to look for some technological solution that does not rely on the frayed nerves of catalogers to implement.

The recently approved 856 field in the USMARC Holdings Format has just begun to be used widely as a locator for remote resources, and some libraries have implemented automatic linking from the catalog to the resource itself using URLs. There's still some uneasiness about relying on easily changed URLs, but there is as yet not enough experience with the capability to make any generalizations about how users will react when they fail to make connections. It is sincerely to be hoped that their reaction is to complain, so at least we'll be able to follow through.

## *POINTS OF CONTACT–CONNECTING THE OPAC AND THE NET*

Although library catalogs are sometimes termed dinosaurs by the proponents of the Web, perhaps the movie *Jurassic Park* has taken much of the sting from that epithet. Dinosaurs may be linked to our past, but they are powerful and impossible to ignore. The difficulty becomes defining the relationship between these two important technologies, each in a different stage of life, without denying the power or usefulness of either.

Traditional cataloging rules and procedures have essentially been based on the handling of separate items, primarily individual printed paper packages with covers and title pages. Extending the rules, the formats and our minds around things like serials, looseleaf services, microfilm compilations, curriculum kits, videotapes of speeches, and the other diverse kinds of materials we catalog today has not always been comfortable, but for the most part, it has worked to bring these diverse media into the mainstream of the catalog and the users' attention.

The approach taken by the Text Encoding Initiative in their use of a mandatory TEI header in their standard SGML application is the first since CIP to explore attaching bibliographic information to the item itself. All TEI conformant documents are required to contain a header, and the standard headers are designed to be easily translatable into USMARC. These developments presage the era of the self-cataloging document in ways that the initiators of CIP could never have imagined!

There is growing support in some quarters for the idea of attaching "metadata" (usually defined as "data-about-data–in an earlier life we called this "bibliographic data") to resources themselves, so they can carry some of the identification information that users and information systems need to make use of them. This is roughly analogous to the CIP data on the verso of books. A major difference is that some of this metadata will of necessity be provided by the creator of the information, instead of a cataloger, just as publishers now supply CIP data sheets. Presumably, if a cataloger has the opportunity to update the metadata that arrives with a resource, perhaps by adding standard thesaurus terms or additional access, that updated information could also be attached to the resource.

This model envisions a future with the most important resources eventually coming with cataloging attached, thereby searchable either within a traditional catalog (perhaps with some judicious tweaking and the addition of some modest authority control) and, in addition, as an identified point in the ever expanding Internet. The model recognizes that the structure of information that has formed the basis for traditional catalogs can, with some additions particular to the format of electronic objects, serve the purposes of those who "surf the nets" as well as users who approach information through the more traditional catalog.

As is probably obvious from the foregoing discussion, I believe that catalogers and cataloging skills, selectors and acquisitions librarians will be as essential in the newly evolving world as they have been in the past. But to take their important place as the organizational gurus of cyberspace, catalogers will need to become as comfortable with their Internet browsers as they are with AACR2, as proficient in cyberspeak as they are in talking MARC tags.

They'll need to convince their administrators and systems people that when the revolution comes, catalogers will not be the first to go, but rather the ones who, when the breadcrumbs get eaten by the birds, know how to find the way.

# Electronic Theses and Dissertations: Merging Perspectives

Gail McMillan

**SUMMARY.** Theses and dissertations as electronic files transferred from the student author to the Graduate School to the Library may well be the first major source of electronic texts that many libraries encounter. To prepare for this potential influx of electronic texts, an ad hoc task force considered work flow and cataloging guidelines. The author suggests expanding current theses cataloging and taking advantage of online information prepared by authors so that the bibliographic records provide OPACS with much more valuable information than does traditional theses cataloging. This should not require a lot of extra work. *[Article copies available from The Haworth Document Delivery Service: 1-800-342-9678. E-mail address: getinfo@haworth.com]*

An experienced cataloger moving on to process electronic texts steps back from those years of training and practice and takes the opportunity to examine *all* the available MARC tags. She does not just look for the new fields that are available to describe the attributes particular to computer files. She systematically works through the tags and imagines an electronic text (e-text) that could be defined and described by each one.

In the spring of 1994 there were three primary sources of this

---

Gail McMillan is Associate Professor and Director, Scholarly Communications Project, and Head, Special Collections Department, University Libraries, Virginia Polytechnic Institute and State University.

[Haworth co-indexing entry note]: "Electronic Theses and Dissertations: Merging Perspectives." McMillan, Gail. Co-published simultaneously in *Cataloging & Classification Quarterly* (The Haworth Press, Inc.) Vol. 22, No. 3/4, 1996, pp. 105-125; and: *Electronic Resources: Selection and Bibliographic Control* (ed: Ling-yuh W. Pattie and Bonnie Jean Cox) The Haworth Press, Inc., 1996, pp. 105-125. Single or multiple copies of this article are available from The Haworth Document Delivery Service [1-800-342-9678, 9:00 a.m. - 5:00 p.m. (EST). E-mail address: getinfo@haworth.com].

 

information: the Bibliographic Standards,[1] the CETH (Center for Electronic Texts in the Humanities) guidelines,[2] and the University of Virginia's online cataloging manual.[3] These were joined by the OCLC Internet cataloging manual.[4] The cataloger acquired each of these tools in a unique way. The Bibliographic standards are part of her cataloging department's reference collection. CETH guidelines availability were announced as accessible by FTP (file transfer protocol) on a listserv (probably on several). UVa's guidelines were discovered by browsing library World Wide Web sites while looking for examples of cataloging department home pages. For an experienced cataloger, it is not necessary to reexamine *AACR2R*,[5] but it is reassuring to have the rules cited with the MARC tags in the CETH guidelines. The cataloging rules for computer files are sketchy and it quickly becomes a matter of applying logic to what the user might want to learn from the bibliographic record and what information a computerized access and retrieval system might need. Later, in the endless search for answers, TEI (Text Encoding Initiative) header guidelines[6] were added to the electronic catalogers' expanding tool kit. Many of these tools quickly became the much-thumbed source of the cataloger's queries and provided reassurance that not every initiate to cataloging electronic texts (hereafter referred to as e-cataloger) is starting from ground zero when she's faced with her first electronic text (e-text).

What would these e-texts actually be? At Virginia Tech and other university libraries, electronic theses and dissertations may become the first significant body of electronic materials regularly requiring cataloging. Staff at the Virginia Tech library became aware that electronic theses[7] were in the offing in the spring of 1993 when the Associate Dean of the Graduate School (ADGS) contacted the library's theses liaison to discuss a partnership for providing access.

## *WHY E-THESES?*

The ADGS presented several reasons for providing students with the opportunity to prepare electronic dissertations and over time several more reasons became clear:

- Greater freedom for authors to demonstrate creatively the result of their independent research

- More flexibility in theses presentation
- Ability to include active links to other electronic research and resources
- Ability to include illustrations with sound, and/or motion, etc.; computer simulations
- Alternative ways to share drafts among authors and committee members
- More channels for timely feedback
- Continued communication with committee members who may be away from the university
- Development of both the faculty member and the student as electronic scholars
- Ease of preparation of PDF (portable document format) files
- Reduced costs to produce the final product
- Improved access to the information in graduate research because it becomes immediately available to a vast audience through the Internet

There are also advantages to e-theses from the library's point of view.

- Better stocked digital library
- More timely public access to current research
- All day, every day availabiliy
- Never checked out, never overdue
- Serve more users with reduced library staff
- Fewer physical copies to handle, so staff not needed to circulate and (re)shelve
- No expense to ship for microfilming
- No shelf space required to store them
- Reduced processing costs

- Cataloging record derived largely (programmatically) from existing e-text
  No need to bind

The director of the Scholarly Communications Project (SCP) (and also a cataloger) met with the ADGS and library theses liaison because this unit of Virginia Tech's University Libraries is largely responsible for experimenting with electronic scholarly publishing.

The SCP director agreed to coordinate staff from all the pertinent areas of the library to discuss possible scenarios for processing e-theses. This ad hoc task force included the head of cataloging, the theses liaison (also a cataloger), the university archivist, and the SCP programmer.
Two goals initially evolved:

1. Determine a process for handling e-theses so that access would be at least as good as it is for hard copy
2. Find a way to derive cataloging information from the electronic text and avoid rekeying as much as possible.

The ad hoc task force drafted the steps to get the document into the library for cataloging and public access (see Figure 1).

Initially the task force planned for processing ASCII (i.e., text only) files and providing Gopher access. However, the Graduate School adopted the PDF (Adobe Acrobat's Portable Document Format) file as its standard. PDF has several advantages over ASCII because, not only can it be viewed identically from Macs and PCs without any additional work, it very faithfully retains the look and feel of the original document, whether it was created with Word, WordPerfect, LaTeX, Excel, PowerPoint, PhotoShop, or other applications. Control of how the document looks online is left entirely up to the author.

The Scholarly Communications Project established its World

FIGURE 1. Electronic theses: From author to public access

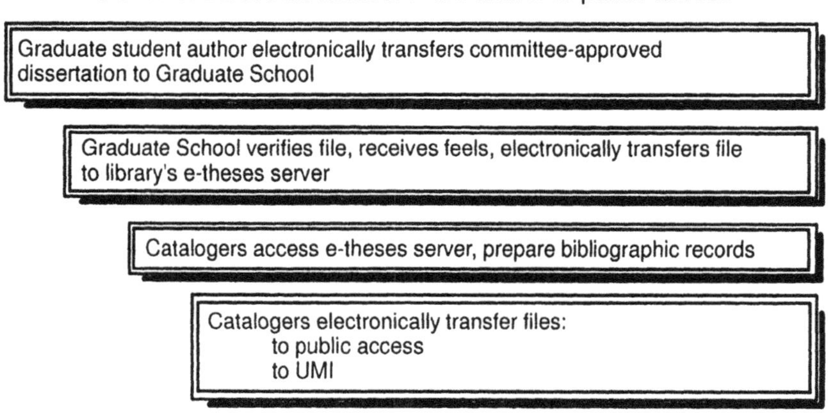

Wide Web presence in the winter of 1993 and the Adobe Acrobat Reader, a viewer for PDF files, became available at no direct cost to the user shortly thereafter. The SCP also adopted PDF as its standard file format as it developed the Libraries' electronic reserve system. One result–some adjustments were made in the original workflow design for e-theses that reduced the number of steps required to process e-theses.

Additional considerations in the processing of e-theses evolved from a regional initiative called the Monticello Electronic Library (MEL) Project (sponsored by SURA, 13 universities forming the Southeastern University Research Association and SOLINET, SOutheastern LIbrary NETwork). A group focusing on electronic dissertations, theses, and technical reports was created at the first general meeting held in July 1993 in Atlanta. Further discussions took place when this group met a year later at Virginia Tech. Largely due to the leadership role of the Virginia Tech Graduate School and its work with the University Libraries, the MEL Working Group on Electronic Theses, Dissertations, and Technical Reports charged the SCP director with coalescing work that was being done by SURA participants to create bibliographic (or bibliographic-like) descriptions for a variety of databases and catalogs. This involved learning about how TEI (Text Encoding Initiative)[6] headers (derived from SGML, Standard Generalized Markup Language) were being used at the University of Virginia to create MARC bibliographic records for publications issued by its Electronic Text Center, and learning about the codes used to create descriptors for WATERS (Wide Area Technical Report Server),[8] a WAIS-based distributed technical report repository.

## *MARC BIBLIOGRAPHIC RECORDS*

Evaluating the potential value of an e-thesis bibliographic record provided the ad hoc task force with the opportunity to propose a substantially enhanced record of real and continuing value to OPAC users. Before looking at new descriptors for computer file cataloging, the Virginia Tech catalogers focused on what fields were currently included in the MARC bibliographic record for theses and whether these would be the same or different for e-theses. Currently, even the full MARC record for a dissertation is not very robust and often has a local twist, presenting valuable information in a unique format that can be seen only at the originating institution because it is masked to users of OCLC or other centralized cataloging repository. The ad hoc task force also studied the fields that could be supplied from the electronic documents using the copy/paste features of word processors. It would have been optimal to work with programmers in library automation so that author, title, abstract, or other information could have been programmatically adapted to the appropriate MARC fields. Their priorities, understandably, were not the same as the task force's. The extent of *AACR2R* compliance was another complicating factor. For example, would programming change upper-case letters to lower case?

While the ad hoc task force was looking at how to do things differently, we also chose this opportunity to press the Graduate School to require authors of theses (in all formats) to provide keywords for use in the bibliographic record. Cataloging had been impressed for years with how labor-intensive was the task of assigning LC subject headings, so having the authors assign (even uncontrolled) subject headings was an appropriate alternative. Since the Graduate School would be rewriting its handbook for student authors, we successfully lobbied for this change to be included in the Graduate School's first *Electronic Dissertation Manual*.[9] The principal cataloger determined that MARC tag 653 would be appropriate for theses author-assigned terms and pointed out to us that without Library of Congress subject headings, our records would be considered "minimal level," rather than full level, cataloging. This seemed particularly unjust to us since e-theses cataloging would be more robust than previous theses cataloging because we planned to include additional information.

The catalogers on the ad hoc task force suggested including tables of contents (MARC tag 505) and abstracts (MARC tag 520) since the standard copy-and-paste features of today's word processors would make this a relatively easy process. The table of contents for theses, however, proved to be quite generic, usually containing only the standard dissertation topics (e.g., literature review, methodology, findings, etc.) and, therefore, not an enhancement to the information available about the work from the OPAC. The abstract, however, contains valuable information and provides a real enhancement to the information about the work available from the OPAC record. The 520 tag is also an indexed field in our online catalog and, therefore, a word-searchable field for OPAC users. Adding the abstract (250-350 words) can, however, add tremendously to the length of the MARC record (see Figures 2 and 3).

While including abstracts and tables of contents is not necessarily a unique feature of e-text cataloging, cataloging conventions have not generally included the name of the thesis' author's department as a standard feature of the bibliographic record. Therefore, another consideration was the opportunity to modify our local practice of creating a pseudo-series statement in order to have the name of the department in a searchable MARC field. Since about 1987 VPI theses catalogers had been creating local notes with the name of the student's department. These 590 notes for OCLC were retagged as 440, with indicators 90 once the record was imported into our local system, VTLS.

440 90 VPI & SU. Mechanical Engineering. Ph. D. 1955

Taking advantage of the opportunity to incorporate changes in theses cataloging, we discussed using MARC tag 502, the dissertation note field, to include the degree, institution, and year the degree was granted and expanding institution to include the name of the department. The new note would follow this example:

502 Thesis (Ph. D. in Mechanical Engineering)–Virginia Polytechnic Institute and State University, 1955.

Evaluating the potential value of an e-thesis bibliographic record provided us with the opportunity to propose a substantially enhanced record of real and continuing value to OPAC users. And, conformance to the accepted interpretation of *AACR2R* was a repeated consideration. In reviewing her *Cataloging Internet Resources: A Manual and Practical Guide*, Nancy Olson states that when cataloging Internet-accessible documents, consider them to be published documents. The ad hoc task force agreed that publisher information belongs in field 260 of an e-thesis record and a 710 field could be added for that corporate body tracing also. Additional

FIGURE 2. Possible MARC bibliographic record for an electronic thesis

| | | | | | |
|---|---|---|---|---|---|
| Local lvl: 1 | Analyzed: 0 | Operator: 00 | | Edit: | |
| CNTL: | Rec stat: n | Entrd: 950321 | | Used: 950417 | |
| Type: m | Bib lvl: m | Govt pub: | Lang: eng | Source: d | Frequn: |
| File: d | Enc lvl: | Machine: 0 | Ctry: vau | Dat tp: s | Regulr: |
| Desc: a | Mod rec: | Audience: | Dates: 1994, | | |

[003-049 system assigned fields and information]

090 LD5655.V856 \b 1995.TEST

100 1 Seevers, Gary L., Jr.

245 12 Identification of Criteria for Delivery of Theological Education Through Distance Education \h [computer file]: \b An International Delphi Study / \c by Gary L. Seevers, Jr.

256 Computer data (1 file: ca. 1353 kilobytes)

260 [Blacksburg, VA: \b Scholarly Communications Project], \c 1994.

500 Title from title page (initial screen display).

500 Vita.

502 Thesis (Ph. D. in Educational Research and Evaluation)–Virginia Polytechnic Institute and State University, 1994.

504 Bibliography: leaves 92-102.

520 Distance education is one means of delivering theological education which is being used increasingly. This delivery method is particularly helpful to non-traditional students who desire higher education but who cannot leave family and work commitments for residential study. For some in both developing and developed countries, distance education is the only route open to higher theological education. Criteria for assessing effective delivery of distance education have not been established in the literature. The purpose of this study was to identify such criteria.

Data were collected with a three-round Delphi from an international panel of seventy-four members comprised of denominational and non-denominational educational administrators and distance educators, denominational district representatives, accreditation representatives, and adult education representatives. Two pilot studies were conducted to test the questions used for round one. Criteria statements were retained if they were deemed "important" or "very important" by at least 80 percent of the respondents on rounds two and three. The panel's responses were found to be independent of respondent location–national or international–and the category of the respondent's group membership.

The findings of the study led to the identification of a set of thirty-one criteria in eight categories which may be useful for evaluating existing distance education programs or guiding the development of new programs. The eight categories were ethical concerns, commitment, curriculum, evaluation, support, technology, feedback, and faculty. There was a 100 percent consensus in rating these thirty-one criteria as "important" or "very important" by the panel members.

538 System requirements: World Wide Web browser and Acrobat Reader.

590 Workstations are available in Newman Library MEDIA CENTER.

653 Higher theological education; mediated instruction; learning; teaching

710 20 Virginia Polytechnic Institute and State University. \b University Libraries. \b Scholarly Communications Project.

856 3 \u http://scholar.lib.vt.edu/theses/seeversgl/DISSERTA.pdf

949 GMc 4/18/95

FIGURE 3. Public display for an electronic thesis from the Virginia Tech VTLS opac

| | |
|---|---|
| CALL NUMBER: | LD5655 V856 1995 TEST |
| AUTHOR: | Seevers, Gary L., Jr. |
| TITLE: | Identification of criteria for delivery of theological education through distance education [computer file] : an international Delphi study / by Gary L. Seevers, Jr. |
| FILE TYPE: | Computer data (1 file : ca. 1353 kilobytes) |
| IMPRINT: | Blacksburg, VA : Scholarly Communications Project, 1994. |
| NOTE: | System requirements: World Wide Web browser and Acrobat Reader. |
| REMOTE ACC.: | http://scholar.lib.vt.edu/theses/seeversgl/DISSERTA.pdf |
| NOTE: | Public access terminals are available in Newman Library Media Center. |
| NOTE: | Title from title page (initial screen display). |
| NOTE: | Vita. |
| NOTE: | Thesis (Ph. D. in Educational Research and Evaluation)–Virginia Polytechnic Institute and State University, 1994. |
| NOTE: | Bibliography: leaves 92-102. |
| SUMMARY: | Distance education is one means of delivering theological education which is being used increasingly. This delivery method is particularly helpful to nontraditional students who desire higher education but who cannot leave family and work commitments for residential study. For some in both developing and developed countries, distance education is the only route open to higher theological education. Criteria for assessing effective delivery of distance education have not been established in the literature. The purpose of this study was to identify such criteria.<br>Data were collected with a three-round Delphi from an international panel of seventy-four members comprised of denominational and non-denominational educational administrators and distance educators, denominational district representatives, accreditation representatives, and adult education representatives. Two pilot studies were conducted to test the questions used for round one. Criteria statements were retained if they were deemed "important" or "very important" by at least 80 percent of the respondents on rounds two and three. The panel's responses were found to be independent of respondent location–national or international–and the category of the respondent's group membership.<br>The findings of the study led to the identification of a set of thirty-one criteria in eight categories which may be useful for evaluating existing distance education programs or guiding the development of new programs. The eight categories were ethical concerns, commitment, curriculum, evaluation, support, technology, feedback, and faculty. There was a 100 percent consensus in rating these thirty-one criteria as "important" or "very important" by the panel members. |
| KEY WORDS: | –Higher theological education;–mediated instruction;–learning;–teaching. |
| ADDED ENTRY: | Virginia Polytechnic Institute and State University. University Libraries. Scholarly Communications Project. |

fields required for cataloging computer files include tag 256 for computer file characteristics, tag 538 for notes of system details, and tag 856 for formatted electronic location and access information. These and other additional fields (505, 260, 710, for example), however, also increase the length of the record and, therefore, had to be carefully considered for the usefulness of the information provided in meeting the combined needs of OPAC users and computerized access and retrieval systems.

Following by more than eight months the work of the ad hoc e-theses committee, the Libraries' Task Force on Cataloging Electronic Texts (TFCET) began reviewing the broader topic of bibliographic control of electronic publications. Richard Sapon-White chaired this task force that included representatives from cataloging, reference, archives, and new media, and scholarly communications.

The TFCET focused on adding to current cataloging practices those fields that would enhance the opac users' access and conform to *AACR2R*. So many of the fields describing computer files appear to be redundant, 245 \h, 256, 516, 538, for example, which tell the OPAC user over and over that the item is a computer file. To stay within the stringent restrictions of full-level cataloging, the task force members saw no way to avoid requiring catalogers to use all the available fields. However, the TFCET concentrated on the MARC tags that would provide information about access. The principal fields we addressed included: 256 (computer file characteristics), 506 (restrictions on access note), 516 (type of computer file or data note), 530 (other formats available), 538 (system details note), 556 (accompanying documentation), and 856 (electronic location and access).

Current OPACS, in addition to the limitations of hardware and workstations, however, still prevent most OPAC users from accessing electronic texts or images directly and smoothly from one menu or even from one workstation. However, workstations are gradually becoming available that permit OPAC users to copy the URL from the bibliographic record and paste it into a World Wide Web browser for accessing an e-text from a single workstation. Knowing this is possible made the TFCET's discussion about including the MARC tag 856 a brief one.

Prolonging the discussion, however, was the need to better understand the possible consequences of using subfield u or splitting the URL into the multiple subfields. We went for simplicity and decided to format the 856 subfield u so that it could be copied and pasted more easily into a World Wide Web browser. Again, we were not willing to wait for the programming that would be necessary to combine the separate subfields into a clickable URL and directly linked to the e-thesis.

Determining the fields appropriate to the MARC bibliographic record was only a part of the charge from the Monticello Electronic Library Project e-theses subgroup. The matrix (Figure 4) shows how the MARC tags correlate with the fields being assigned to describe technical reports available in the WATERS (Wide Area Technical Report Service) searchable database (developed by the computer science departments at Old Dominion University, Virginia Tech, University of Virginia, and SUNY Buffalo).

Cataloging has greatly benefitted from advances in library automation and the cataloging of e-texts is ripe for further automation. It is now possible to derive MARC cataloging from text mark-up languages, subsets of SGML, such as TEI headers, and possibly even HTML (hypertext markup language) tags. Therefore, to the matrix of WATERS and MARC fields, were added the TEI headers (Figure 5).

As one way of getting from the e-text to the MARC record, the TFCET discussed the possibility of having authors assign TEI headers so that a basic record could be created that would include author, title, publisher, file size, file type, abstract, formatted contents notes, and the like. However, it will be more timely to use an e-thesis submission form, begun by the author, added to by the Graduate School, and then the library, as the basis for the cataloging record. The first draft of this form asks the author to supply the following information, to which are added the MARC tags (see Figure 6).

## *ELECTRONIC THESIS PROCESSING*

In addition to considering the MARC record and the cataloging department work flow, the staff of the Scholarly Communications

FIGURE 4. Variable fields for describing electronic theses

| **WATERS** *symbols* | **MARC** *variable field tags* | **TEI Header** *tags* | **Labels/Comments** *MARC variable field information should be in subfield a (#a), unless otherwise noted; indicator codes have not generally been listed.* |
|---|---|---|---|
| A | 100 | <titlStmt>... <author> </author></titlStmt> | WATERS allows multiple authors in one field; MARC uses multiple 700 fields for added authors. WATERS puts names in direct order; MARC uses last name first, etc. (indicators describe the type of name for order or display). After #a, MARC's principle subfield is #d for date of author's birth. |
| T | 245 | <titlStmt> <title> </title>...</titlStmt> | MARC #b = subtitle; #c = statement of response-ability; #h = medium. Initial articles: WATERS includes them; MARC has "indicator" codes that describe the number of characters to ignore |
| dsize | 256 | <extent></extent> | WATERS: document size; MARC: computer file characteristics (i.e., no. of files and no. of bytes) |
| D | 260 | <pubStmt><date> </data></pubStmt> | MARC #c: provide year only; WATERS is often date-specific |
| K | 653 | <txtClass><keywords scheme = ></txtClass> | Keywords, uncontrolled index terms |
| R | | | Report number |
| | 090 | <clasCode scheme = LC> | Locally assigned Library of Congress call number |

| | | | | |
|---|---|---|---|---|
| U | 856 #u | * | | URL = Uniform Resource Locator |
| host | 856 #a | * | | e-location host name |
| | 856 #b | * | | e-location IP address |
| port | 856 #p | * | | e-location port number |
| | 500-590 | | <noteStmt><note> </note></noteStmt> | Notes |
| I | | | | WATERS: Institution–includes department name |
| | 502 | | | MARC: Dissertation Note–includes degree, institution name, year |
| | 500 | | | General Note [VPI: Vita]; Title from |
| | 504 | | | Bibliographic, etc. note |
| | 505 | * | | Formatted Contents Note |
| | 520 | * | | Summary, etc. note [i.e., abstract] |
| | 538 | * | | System Details Note [e.g., System requirements: Adobe Acrobat Reader] |
| | 7xx | | | Added authors |
| doc | | | | Document name |
| dtype | | | | Document type |
| | 035 | | | System assigned unique control number |
| | 040 | | | Source of cataloging [VPI #c VPI] |
| | 049 | | | OCLC local holdings symbol [VPII] |
| | | * | | *Fields not currently included in theses cataloging* |

FIGURE 5. MARC fixed fields for electronic theses cataloging

| TEI header tags | MARC fixed fields | Labels/Comments for MARC |
|---|---|---|
| | 001 | OCLC record number [VTLS label = CNTL] |
| | ldr/06 | Type: m = materials being described are computer files |
| <biblFull> or <header type=aacr2> | ldr/07 | Biblvl: m = computer files that are monographs (or that are not serials or multi-part) |
| | 008/35-37 | Lang: eng = text is English; Lang: NA = text is not completely textual |
| | 008/39 | Source: d = non-Library of Congress cataloging |
| | 008/18-21 | Illus: a = there are illustrations, b = maps, g = music, o = photographs, [blank] = no illustrations |
| <encDesc></encDesc> | ldr/17 | Enc lvl describes how complete is the bib description enc lvl: [blank] = full cataloging Enc lvl: k = less than full cataloging |
| | 008/15-17 | Ctry: xx = theses are not considered "published" so there is no country of publications, per AACR2r |
| | 008/06 | Dat tp: s = a single date of publication (i.e., not serial) |
| | 008/07-10 | Dates: [year of publication] |
| <fileDesc></fileDesc> | 008/26 | File: [type of computer file: d = text, m = combination c = image; others |
| <srcDesc></srcDesc> | ldr/18 | Desc: a = cataloged according to AACR2r; i = preAACR2r |
| OR <headertype = AACR2> | | |

FIGURE 6. Theses submission form *First Phase* scholarly communications project, university libraries, Virginia Tech

Instructions: Please fill out form completely. Be sure to provide filenames for each item submitted. Submit only electronic files in Acrobat PDF format. Do not forget to place file in Drop folder or FTP it to our server. Incomplete forms and restricted works will be rejected.

Name

[MARC tag 100]

Title

MARC tag 245]

Document Type (check one):

| | | |
|---|---|---|
| Thesis | Dissertation | |
| Special Project | Major Paper | Technical Report |

Abstract:

[MARC tag 520]

Keywords: [MARC tag 653]

1.

2.

3.

4.

5.

Department:

[MARC tag 502]

Degree

[MARC tag 502]

| Filename(s) | File size(s): |
|---|---|
| 1. / | [MARC tag 256] |
| 2. / | |

Files delivered via: Appleshare FTP
Appleshare server is currently: macintoy in LIBRARY zone; FTP server is vatech.lib.vt.edu.

Date submitted to Graduate School:

[MARC 008/07-10]

SEND

Project considered a procedure for getting the files from the Graduate School, the mechanics of making an e-thesis available to a cataloger (from the secure and private environment of the server) and for moving an e-thesis into public access (see Figure 7). We suggested that the cataloger forward a copy as each one is processed to a server at UMI. If UMI prefers batch processing, files could be accumulated (i.e., stored in a directory on the e-theses server) for batched file transfer, or perhaps a UMI-access point could be established on the e-theses server from which UMI staff could retrieve them. This decision has not been reached (see "UMI's Concerns").

With input from the University Archivist and to address a concern from the Graduate School, long term preservation and access of e-theses was also factored into the procedures. The current plan includes periodically writing e-theses to CD-ROMs for security back-ups and possibly longer term preservation. While this may not be the final answer, an alternative has not been brought forward; how frequently this would be done has also not been determined.

Draft documentation from the Scholarly Communications Project about e-theses processing is available through the Internet. It includes converting a dissertation to a PDF file, submitting an approved e-thesis to the Graduate School, how the files would be transmitted to the University Libraries, and how readers could access, read, print, and download e-theses. This information along with some background on the e-theses project at Virginia Tech is available at http://scholar.lib.vt.edu/theses/theses.html.

## *FACULTY AND STUDENT CONCERNS*

At the early October 1995 meeting of the Commission on Graduate Studies and Policies (CGSP), the ADGS announced that e-theses would replace traditional theses beginning with fall 1996 masters and doctoral candidates. Exemptions, he said, may be requested by the committee chairs, but he anticipates that they will be granted only for special circumstances such as when architectural drawings (or the like) cannot be digitally (re)produced with good online results. Later that month at the annual retreat of the Graduate School with deans and department heads from throughout the university, they previewed the sequence an e-thesis might complete,

FIGURE 7. Processing electronic theses: A possible scenario

1. **Graduate School**

Electronically Transfers approved file to library theses server

E-mails Theses Transmission Form to library theses coordinator

2. **Library/Cataloger**

Downloads e-thesis from closed server to cataloger's workstation

Prepares cataloging (see figure 4 above)

Adds e-page for call number and property "stamp"
("memos" feature of Acrobat–later reconsidered)

Moves file to server for public access

Electronically transfers file to UMI or moves to UMI holding area

3. **Library Theses Server Administrator**

Indexes text for word searchability

Integrates new index with existing index

Maintains server, including back-ups stored on- and off-site

Removes files from closed server following processing to public access

Makes CD-ROMs

4. **Special Collections Department/University Archive**

Retains e-theses CD-ROMs

Works with Theses Server Administrator to ensure archival files will be accessible (including refreshing data as necessary) moving through screen displays of submission to the Graduate School to public access from the library OPAC and World Wide Web access.

At this meeting faculty asked about specific points that they wanted clarified, some of which have no answers. For example, "How long does it take to download and/or print an electronic thesis?" This is dependent upon the RAM available on the computer, the size of the document, the type of telecommunications lines being used, and even the time of day that an electronic document would be accessed. Faculty also had personal concerns, such as the current portability and readability of a paper document versus being limited to terminals and/or workstations to access works in progress. E-theses will require changes in working habits, on a different scale, perhaps, but similar to the way e-mail has changed–where and how mail is sent, received, opened, and read.

Clearly, education about PDF and e-thesis preparation is needed and will be an important factor in faculty and student acceptance of this new research and publishing process.

"Exchange" software is needed to prepare a PDF file from existing online document. Acrobat's Distiller will convert LaTeX, for example, to PDF. It can be purchased today from the campus bookstore for less than $30. It is also available at this time for public use in at least two computer labs on campus and more sites will be available as the demand increases. Faculty may have Exchange installed on their office computers without charge through campus license agreements with Adobe. Another option that the programmer/analyst at the Scholarly Communications Project recently successfully experimented with is creating a PDF file by using Distiller on a remote server.

Faculty and students may also not be aware that in several campus computer labs there are quality scanners available for use to convert pictures to digital images. Equipment and software are available without charge but there is a cost-recovery fee for printing.

Students who were part of the CGSP asked what will become a common question: What kind of software should one use to prepare an e-thesis so it will be easily exchanged for a PDF file? The Graduate School and the Libraries have experience with many of the popular word processors, spreadsheet packages, and presentation display formats, so we know that Word, WordPerfect, LaTeX, Excel, PowerPoint, and others 'exchange' to PDF files without any problems. The more unusual and less frequently used software will have to be tested or Adobe should be consulted.

In addition, many do not know that one of the benefits of PDF files is that entire documents do not have to be sent back and forth. As long as sender and receiver (author and reviewer, student and faculty/committee member) are working from the same version of the electronic document, only the "margin notes" need to be shared because they are tied to the place in the document from which they came. This is another example of how e-theses will require changes in working habits.

Copyright is another issue. E-theses authors will be asked to give permission to the university for the library to provide electronic access because e-theses are considered published documents once they become available on the Internet. The university does not intend to do as most publishers do and require that all copyrights be assigned to it, only that nonexclusive electronic rights be shared with it for the purpose of the library providing electronic access.

## *UMI's CONCERNS*

In September 1995, UMI was not prepared to participate in the strictly Internet access to e-theses that Virginia Tech is proposing. The UMI representatives preferred to receive each e-thesis on a separate diskette containing commonly used word processor files(s). They also wanted several paper documents to accompany each thesis on diskette: the abstract, the title page, and a signed publishing agreement. Since the library is attempting to speed and streamline processing, and since it will be receiving e-theses through the campus network, the author may have to assume the added burden of preparing the diskette and the paper documents for UMI.

As of this writing, UMI was planning to print out these dissertations and then microfilm them. In the near term this may work but when students take advantage of the added creativity an e-theses allow them to demonstrate, microfilming and printing a work that was never intended for paper will, in some cases at least, be impossible.

## *CONCLUSIONS*

Theses and dissertations as electronic files transferred from the Graduate School to the Library may well be the first major source of electronic texts that many libraries and their catalogers will regularly encounter. Catalogers can enhance the OPAC users search results by expanding current theses cataloging and taking advantage of online information prepared by authors. Catalogers can use the information available in a variety of online sources including the document itself or from the online submission form to provide the basic descriptive MARC fields. Whether programmatic changes can be made or standard copy-and-paste features of word processors are incorporated, enhancing the e-theses bibliographic record need not require a lot of extra work.

Some library administrators and others believe that publications available on the Internet should not be cataloged because they can be found through existing and continually-improving search mechanisms. Cataloging resources, especially personnel, are being reduced for this and other reasons. However, rarely do researchers of any kind (whether sophisticated or novice or someone in between) seek information in only one format. Rather they are often looking for all, or perhaps the most current information available, and they expect this from libraries' catalogs. Even with diminishing resources, catalogers can continue to create quality and quantity information for this unparalleled source of information.

MARC bibliographic records are increasingly easy to prepare for electronic publications–now through copy/paste features at all but the stand-alone systems (a.k.a. dumb terminals) and sooner rather than later, from computer programs that will assign fields to existing electronic publications. With e-theses authors assigning key words, catalogers can concentrate on providing intellectual access to the uncontrolled electronic texts also being produced in increasing numbers.

Clearly, education is a key component for everyone in the chain of information, including faculty, students, catalogers, and other librarians at VPI as well as UMI personnel. When student authors and faculty committee members learn about the ease of "exchanging" traditional theses for e-theses, all will reap benefits. Similarly, librarians will need training to use the technology to improve fully processing time and access through the OPAC and Internet to the information currently locked away in traditional theses.

## REFERENCES

1. *USMARC Format for Bibliographic Data.* (Washington: Library of Congress Cataloging, 1994).

2. Annelies Hoogcarspel, *Guidelines for Cataloging Monographic Electronic Texts at the Center for Electronic Texts in the Humanities.* Technical Report No. 1. ([New Brunswick, NJ: CETH], 1994).

3. *Cataloging Procedures Manual.* Chapter 12: Computer Files Cataloging, Part B: Electronic Texts. [Charlottesville, VA]: Cataloging Services Department University of Virginia Library, [1994]. [Accessed at http://www.lib.virginia.edu/cataloging/manual/chapxiib.html]

4. *Cataloging Internet Resources: A Manual and Practical Guide.* Nancy B. Olson, ed. (OCLC, 1995). [Accessed at http://www.oclc.org/oclc/man/9256cat/toc.htm]

5. *Anglo-American Cataloguing Rules,* 2nd ed., 1988 rev. Chicago: American Library Association, 1988. *Anglo-American Cataloguing Rules,* 2nd ed., 1988 rev., 1993 amendments. (Chicago: American Library Association, 1993).

6. C. M. Sperberg-McQueen and Lou Burnard, *TEI Guidelines for Electronic Text Encoding and Interchange (P3),* [Charlottesville, Va.: Electronic Text Center, University of Virginia, http://etext.virginia.edu/TEI.html, (last checked 9/8/95)]

7. The term "e-theses" is used in the generic sense and includes both electronic theses and electronic dissertations.

8. WATERS is at http://www.cs.odu.edu/WATERS/WATERS-GS.html. It will be replaced by NCSTRAL (Networked Computer Science Technical Report Library) at http://www.ncstrl.org

9. The Virginia Tech Graduate School's *Electronic Dissertation Manual* is available at http://gserver.grads.vt.edu/edman.html

# CATRIONA: A Distributed, Locally-Oriented, Z39.50 OPAC-Based Approach to Cataloguing the Internet

Dennis Nicholson
Mary Steele

**SUMMARY.** The aims of CATRIONA were: (1) to investigate the requirements for developing procedures and applications for cataloguing and retrieval of networked resources, and (2) to explore the feasibility of a collaborative project to develop such applications and procedures and integrate them with existing library systems. The project established that a distributed catalogue of networked resources integrated with standard Z39.50 library system OPAC interfaces with information on hard-copy resources is already a practical proposition at a basic level. At least one Z39.50 OPAC client can search remote Z39.50 OPACs, retrieve USMARC records with URLs in 856$u, load a viewer like Netscape, and use it to retrieve and display the remotely held electronic resource on the local workstation. A follow-up project on related issues is being finalised. *[Article copies available from The Haworth Document Delivery Service: 1-800-342-9678. E-mail address: getinfo@haworth.com]*

---

Dennis Nicholson is Head of Library Systems at Strathclyde University in Glasgow, Scotland. Mary Steele was the Research Assistant for Phase I of the CATRIONA Project and has jointly authored several papers relating to the CATRIONA Project.

[Haworth co-indexing entry note]: "CATRIONA: A Distributed, Locally-Oriented, Z39.50 OPAC-Based Approach to Cataloguing the Internet." Nicholson, Dennis and Mary Steele. Co-published simultaneously in *Cataloging & Classification Quarterly* (The Haworth Press, Inc.) Vol. 22, No. 3/4, 1996, pp. 127-141; and: *Electronic Resources: Selection and Bibliographic Control* (ed: Ling-yuh W. Pattie and Bonnie Jean Cox) The Haworth Press, Inc., 1996, pp. 127-141. Single or multiple copies of this article are available from The Haworth Document Delivery Service [1-800-342-9678, 9:00 a.m. - 5:00 p.m. (EST). E-mail address: getinfo@haworth.com].

 

## *INTRODUCTION*

This article is not written from the perspective of the cataloguer. One of the authors is a library systems manager and both are involved in the management and operation of a nationally funded Internet information service which aims to establish a measure of control over world wide electronic resources, currently through a subject tree approach. The article looks at the CATRIONA feasibility study[1] and its roots in the BUBL Subject Tree service, discusses possible future developments, including a proposed UK Electronic Libraries Programme project,[2] and seeks to show why the authors believe that the CATRIONA (CATaloguing and Retrieval of Information Over Networks Applications) approach–one centered upon distributed MARC based Z39.50 OPACS and resource delivery via OPAC clients–is likely to prove at least a significant part of any future solution to the problems of finding and retrieving electronic resources across local, national and international networks.

## *BEGINNINGS: THE BUBL SUBJECT TREE*

The BUBL Information Service *<URL:http://www.bubl.bath.ac.uk/BUBL/home.html>* is a UK-based Internet information service based at Bath University in England, but run over the Internet from Strathclyde University in Glasgow, Scotland. It is funded by the Joint Information Services Committee (JISC) of the UK Higher Education Funding Councils to provide a range of services to both the UK academic and research community and the UK Library and Information Science community. Included amongst these are: (1) coordination and support for co-operative and worksharing ventures within the UK LIS community; (2) weekly email based Internet resources current awareness services; and (3) a combined gopher and WWW subject tree, *<URL:http://www.bubl.bath.ac.uk/BUBL/TreeAlphabet.html>*, with 8,000 to 9,000 links to resources and services covering all major subject areas and incorporating both alphabetical and UDC-classified approaches.

The CATRIONA Phase I proposal arose partly out of a desire to offer an improved service in the third of these three areas. Whilst the BUBL Subject Tree is a popular and useful part of the service, its limitations are recognised. We would not attempt to offer access to the collections in a single medium-sized library via a hierarchical tree-menu structure, so attempting to do so for the world-wide resources of the Internet is ultimately ludicrous. In compiling the CATRIONA Phase I Proposal, however, one positive feature of the Subject Tree initiative was recognised–that of utilizing geographically distributed co-operative efforts to help solve what was potentially a huge problem (that of cataloguing Internet resources). This was identified as a useful, even vital, aspect of the developing CATRIONA model. Another aspect of the Subject Tree initiative was also influential in this respect, albeit in a negative sense: the drawbacks of relying on volunteer effort for the distributed aspects of the Subject Tree project were readily apparent. Obviously, any solution to the problem of cataloguing the Internet could not be based on volunteer effort, it had to assume qualified (and paid!) staff in real cataloguing departments taking on this task as a standard part of their everyday duties.

## *CATRIONA PHASE I: OTHER ASPECTS OF THE PROBLEM*

The main impetus behind the CATRIONA proposal put to the British Library Research and Development Department in mid 1994 was the desire to tackle library-service-related aspects of the international problem of designing and developing an adequate mechanism for finding and retrieving Internet resources distributed across the developed world. It was recognised, however, that the question had other elements and that this introduced local and regional dimensions, so that the final CATRIONA proposal sought to tackle, from a library service perspective, four related elements of what is essentially the same problem:

1. The need to offer library users a reliable and user-friendly means of finding, retrieving and using the growing range of 'Electronic Information Objects' (EIOs)–electronic texts and journals, images, sounds, interactive services, multimedia documents, programs, video, human expertise, and so on–

available over the Internet. This should be one which employs library-standard finding tools and library-standard descriptions and which preferably also encompasses access to information on traditional (i.e., non-electronic) resources.

2. A requirement recognised by systems and reference librarians to offer library and campus network users seamless library OPAC mediated access to a range of electronic information resources held, or subscribed-to, locally from a single workstation (variously, a PC, Mac or X Windows workstation).
3. Ensuring that the e-resources available at an institution are exploited fully both across campus at the institution itself and, where so desired for income-related or promotional reasons, beyond the local institution via network access–the idea being that cataloguing these resources in the network-accessible library OPAC may be the best way of doing this.
4. The need to find a practical mechanism for finding, retrieving and 'viewing' or utilizing EIOs in a 'virtual library,' which, like the Internet itself, can ultimately only function if it has at its heart a system and associated infrastructure able to support a sustainable, distributed and scalable approach to the resource discovery, description, retrieval, and presentation over networks.

In assessing the CATRIONA approach it is important to recognize that it seeks to address the problems of finding and retrieving electronic resources over networks from each of the four perspectives identified above.

## *CATRIONA PHASE I: THE CATRIONA MODEL*

The aim of the CATRIONA Feasibility Study, a 6-month project running from August 1994 to January 1995 and funded by the British Library Research and Development Department, was "to investigate the technical, organisational and financial requirements for the development of applications programs and procedures to enable the cataloguing, classification, and retrieval of documents and other resources over networks, and to explore the feasibility of a library system supplier led collaborative project to develop such applications and procedures and integrate them with one or more existing library housekeeping systems and associated OPAC interfaces." The original application (available at URL http://www.bubl.bath.ac.uk/BUBL/catriona.html) included an outline of the approach proposed as a solution to the problem described above–a model for a distributed catalogue of the Internet based on MARC, Z39.50, resource delivery via catalogue records containing URLs, and enhanced Z39.50 OPAC clients. During the feasibility study, this model was developed and improved. Further developments and improvements were expected to arise out of the Phase II demonstrator proposed in the feasibility study report.[3] However, since the Phase II demonstrator project has not yet taken place (for a full report on the current situation with this see below), the current version of the model is identical to that arrived at during the feasibility study. In summary, it contains the following main features.

## *CENTRAL ELEMENTS: Z39.50 SERVERS AND CLIENTS*

At the heart of the model are two essential elements:

1. A distributed catalogue of Internet EIOs based on regional and other building blocks and comprising a series of Z39.50 OPACs sited globally. These OPACs would be of two kinds:

   Catalogues of electronic resources created by institutions, companies, services and organisations. These would describe electronic resources which are either held locally (items created/authored locally, purchases, or free items downloaded from other Internet sites) or subscribed-to/used at the local site (e.g., BIDS, a UK data service which provides network access to a range of bibliographic databases, other Z39.50 OPACs describing electronic resources).

   'Union' catalogues of such resources (e.g., OCLC, RLG) created through co-operative cataloguing and covering a wider range of electronic resources than the average local OPAC. Again, descriptions of hard copy resources might usually be included in the same catalogue.

In both cases, items catalogued would include various types of resources including electronic text, images, multimedia documents, programs, videos, sounds, interactive services and other OPACs. In both cases, the records describing the resources would utilise the MARC standard enhanced as recommended by MARBI.[4,5,6] (Note: These were developed initially for USMARC. Implementation in other MARC formats is limited as yet.) This means, amongst other things, that they hold in 856 ≠ u a URL or URLs for each electronic resource catalogued, information that can be utilised by clients such as Mosaic or Netscape to locate, retrieve and display or 'play' the resource on a local workstation.

2. A number of enhanced Z39.50 clients capable of:

- Conducting parallel distributed searches of all of the Z39.50 OPACs which make up the core of the distributed catalogue of the Internet resources.
- Retrieving enhanced MARC records containing URLs in 856 ≠ u.
- Responding to these URLs by offering the user the option of loading an appropriate NIDR (Network Information Discovery and Retrieval) client such as WWW, Gopher, WAIS clients–and of retrieving and displaying or playing the electronic resource locally.

Since the 'playing' of such things as images, sounds, video and programs requires facilities only available on a microcomputer or workstation as opposed to a terminal, a client-server model is assumed, with at least the presentation or display level under the full control of a GUI client on a microcomputer or workstation.

## *LOCAL CONTROL OF URL CHANGES AND URL UPDATES*

The problem of changed or 'broken' URLs is dealt with by ensuring that all resources catalogued are essentially under the local control of the site doing the cataloguing. In the CATRIONA model, the updating of changed URLs in catalogue records would be managed as follows:

If URLs for major services like BIDS change, this will be widely known and local cataloguers would update the appropriate records as a result.

Local catalogues will only contain records for major BIDS type services and for locally held electronic resources. Changes of URLs would therefore either be widely known or under local control, allowing rapid and reliable updating of records.

These tasks would be backed up by automated processes for identifying and reporting on 'broken' URLs in the local system such as those employed in current HTML checking programs.

## *CATALOGUING OPACs*

The assumption behind the CATRIONA approach is that the Internet will be catalogued in a distributed fashion. In order to carry out a search of this whole distributed catalogue, therefore, it is necessary for the OPAC client being utilized to be able, in some sense, to locate and search all of the individual OPACs that make up the distributed catalogue. In existing clients this information is programmed into the client itself by the system administrator. However, the assumption in the CATRIONA model is that this information would initially be located on the local OPAC which would contain catalogue records for other OPACs selected by the library and uploaded to the client as required. It is further assumed that any given OPAC would normally only contain a small subset of all of the available OPACs and that much of the information about the rest of the distributed catalogue of the Internet will come from other OPACs and, in particular, the 'Union' catalogues. It is likely that Internet OPACs would be categorised according to their subject strengths and that users will be able to search their own local catalogues for records of other OPACs strong on a particular subject category. The user would then be able to conduct a distributed search of a selection of these OPACs as required. It is recognised that this assumption will have to be critically examined in the context of a demonstrator project and in the light of experience.

## *ACCESS TO OTHER INTERNET RESOURCES*

The model assumes that for some considerable time to come, and perhaps indefinitely, there will be many sources of information about the existence, location, and type of important Internet resources that are not part of the core of the CATRIONA model. These will include things such as catalogues (possibly Z39.50, but probably not) utilizing record formats other than MARC (IAFA templates, TEI headers and others); and cross-Internet indexing tools like Veronica, Archie, WebCrawler.

The model therefore includes the possibility that a CATRIONA client will also be able to offer the user the option in appropriate circumstances of utilising such non-standard tools to search for, retrieve and display Internet resources. In the absence of Z39.50, such searches would have to be done on a service by service basis (that is, not via a parallel/distributed search) and would entail the CATRIONA client invoking an appropriate NIDR client (WWW or Gopher or WAIS or whatever) and allowing the user to utilise this client to conduct the search as required.

## *ACCESS CONTROL*

Access control is regarded as an essential element of the model. It is assumed that libraries will wish to offer users access to most Internet and local network resources but they will wish to control access for a number of reasons:

- to encourage efficient use of the network by directing to geographically close sites first
- to direct attention to commercial resources with special discounts before more expensive alternative commercial resources
- to direct attention to local institutional sites with special inter-institutional agreements in place before sites further afield without such agreements
- to save user time through expert guidance and knowledge of local requirements to monitor use so as to obtain management

information on what users are accessing and under what circumstances

It is assumed that access control can be managed via a combination of user permissions on the local library housekeeping system and selective cataloguing and judicious classification/subject indexing of other Internet catalogues and other Internet indexing services. More work is required in the practical context of a demonstrator project to clarify exact requirements and identify feasible solutions. It is possible that there will be a requirement to develop functionality based on some aspects of Z39.50 Version 2 not yet addressed by library systems suppliers (Access Control and Resource Control).

## *CATRIONA PHASE I: RESULTS OF THE FEASIBILITY STUDY*

The conclusion reached at the end of the feasibility study was that a finding and retrieval system for network accessible electronic resources based on the CATRIONA model as developed and extended during the study was a practical proposition. The next step should be a demonstrator project aimed at clarifying some of the issues and development requirements and at establishing the kernel of a working system based on a number of co-operating institutions in Scotland. These conclusions were based partly on analysis and discussion of the CATRIONA model as it developed, but mainly upon the following information, uncovered as a result of the study:

1. Of possible schemes such as MARC, IAFA (Internet Anonymous FTP Archive), TEI, URC (Uniform Resource Characteristics), MARC offered several advantages. It is compatible with existing infrastructure and practice; MARC records are transportable via Z39.50, and, following the enhancement to the MARC record, in particular the 856 field, MARC has the capacity not only to describe but also to enable delivery of a wide range of electronic resources.
2. At least two other library systems suppliers (Geac and Dynix) had available early versions of Z39.50 OPAC clients capable

of responding to the existence of a URL in a catalogue record by loading an appropriate client or viewer, passing the URL to it, and, by this means, enabling delivery of the described electronic resource to the desktop.

3. The development of a working user-friendly system for integrated searching of a distributed catalogue of Internet resources already existing, albeit in piecemeal fashion, in the applications software of a number of library systems companies.
4. That, despite the above, significant software development was required in order to establish a working system which would handle the implications of finding and retrieving resources via a distributed catalogue in an efficient manner and that the exact nature of much of this development could only be specified clearly in the context of a demonstrator project.

Although much of this information is now widely known, the project team had not previously been aware of it and had expected to find that a much greater level of development was required to implement the model–if, indeed, it was possible at all. From this point of view alone, therefore, the study was regarded as a useful exercise. Moreover, as indicated above, it was also of help in extending and enhancing the original model.

## *CATRIONA PHASE II: IN SEARCH OF A DEMONSTRATOR PROJECT*

At the time of this writing (August, 1995), funding for a Phase II demonstrator project had not yet been secured. The UK Electronic Libraries Programme (ELib) had declined to fund a demonstrator as such but indicated a willingness to fund a CATRIONA Project follow-up along the following lines:

> An investigation of the existence of quality, locally-created, electronic resources on individual campuses, of their value beyond the local institution, of mechanisms for efficient and speedy discovery/retrievability, delivery/usability, and for the sustainable, reliable and economic maintenance and archiving

of such material for institutional and extra-institutional purposes, and of associated questions relating to institutional policy, strategy, and organizational infrastructure, with particular reference to the potential role of the library.

Although the exact details of this are still being worked out it does contain some aspects of relevance to the further development of the CATRIONA proposals. These include elements relating to the availability of locally produced electronic resources and their delivery to the desktop, questions relating to the role of the library in electronic resource discovery, delivery and maintenance, and also the possibility of a small scale non-developmental demonstrator.

Once the details of this follow-up project have been finalised, consideration will be given to finding funds for other aspects of the proposed demonstrator project. A second bid to the BLRDD is a possibility and European sources of funding may also be investigated. In addition, Strathclyde University Library has recently purchased a new library system with CATRIONA-style capabilities (Dynix Horizon) and hopes to be in a position both to co-operate with other Dynix Horizon libraries with similar capabilities and to coordinate with the company itself regarding development requirements (this is still under discussion). Moreover, BUBL is looking at the introduction of server software incorporating Z39.50 capabilities and electronic resource cataloguing facilities as an eventual upgrade path to replace the subject tree, and this, too, could have a part to play in the future of the project.

There is, therefore, every possibility that some form of demonstrator project, funded or not, will emerge in due course. Exactly how this will happen and how long it will take to establish, however, is currently uncertain.

## *CATRIONA: A FUTURE ROLE?*

Despite the uncertainty surrounding the current position, the CATRIONA Project team remain convinced that the CATRIONA approach is likely to prove at least a significant part of any future solution to the problem of finding and retrieving electronic resources on local, national, and international networks. Its strengths in this respect are most evident in the library arena, although there is also a case for its adoption in the wider world.

Libraries should find it an attractive approach for a number of reasons:

1. It offers a solution to all four aspects of the problem outlined above, potentially offering a workable approach to electronic access within the individual library environment, across campus, within a regional 'virtual library', or across the whole Internet. It also integrates access with the standard library finding tool, the OPAC, and, hence, with retrieval of information on holdings and locations of non-electronic resources.
2. Its basis is already available in the form of both Z39.50 servers and Z39.50 clients capable of responding to URLs and delivering resources to the desktop by loading an appropriate viewer. Moreover, it is an 'open' system in the sense that any library whose system supplier has Z39.50 compliant products and who uses USMARC can become part of the system. (Libraries will continue to adhere to MARC for some time to come, whatever its perceived drawbacks.)
3. Libraries will consider that cataloguing and indexing by professional cataloguers on a world-wide basis is essential in order to accurately place a resource within the universe of knowledge in a retrievable way. Natural language will not be considered adequate. Authors, it will be argued, are not familiar enough with the wider perspective and publishers will tend to be concerned with commercial considerations rather than with *appropriate* retrieval. Automated searches on attributes of the primary electronic resource, such as file and directory names and author supplied abstracts and titles, will become increasingly inefficient as the number of such resources grows. Secondary resources such as catalogue records will become essential to ensure accurate and timely searching and retrieval.
4. Local cataloguing and indexing of locally held resources is likely to be considered essential on the grounds that locally based academics, researchers and students will require locally-held electronic resources to be classified and subject-indexed in a way that is both appropriate to local expectations,

local research interests and local courses, and is integrated with the classification and indexing of hard copy resources.

5. The approach potentially entails access control via user registration on the local library system. Libraries will offer users access to most Internet and local network resources but they may nevertheless wish to control this access for the various reasons detailed above.
6. It also has the general advantages as a solution listed below.

The case for the adoption of the CATRIONA approach to the world beyond libraries may be summarized as follows:

1. A distributed approach to cataloguing the Internet is inevitable. There are too many interested parties with reasons to set up their own catalogues for a single catalogue of the whole Internet to be generally acceptable, even if it were practical. The fact that a distributed catalogue based on the CATRIONA approach is already possible, albeit at a basic level, only increases the inevitability; it is also the only practical approach to cataloguing world-wide electronic resources in the longer term. The volume of these resources may currently be small but it will ultimately be so large that only a distributed cataloguing system will be able to cope, and the only currently available solution to the problem of ensuring that changes in the URL of a resource are always reflected in the catalogue. If the site responsible for the resource or a particular copy of it is also responsible for the catalogue record and any Union catalogue copy of it then theoretically at least, the URL should always be kept up to date given that appropriate monitoring, reporting and operational procedures are in place in the cataloguing department concerned.
2. An approach based on Z39.50 clients able to load appropriate viewers in response to particular URLs is adaptable to *any* resource format, even to formats which do not yet exist.
3. Since a distributed approach is both inevitable and the only practical solution then:

   a. some means of ensuring an integrated approach to searching is essential and Z39.50 offers this possibility;

b. MARC is important because it can be handled by Z39.50 and can handle URLs, and
c. the system must be 'open' so that any interested party can join it at any time. Again, Z39.50 offers this possibility, since it allows different (but compliant) suppliers to inter-work.

4. Libraries (and their users) will have a large part to play in any Internet-wide system. They will be significant contributors to the catalogue set, significant users of the electronic resources available and significant purchasers of commercial resources. It is important, therefore, that the approach adopted by the wider world be integrated with the library approach to this problem.

## AUTHOR NOTE

Dennis Nicholson has written a number of papers on a range of library automation issues and in 1988 was recipent of the Dawson Award for Academic Innovation. He is largely responsible for the existence of the BUBL Information Service, an Internet service aimed at the UK Higher Education community and funded nationally by the Joint Information Services Committee. BUBL was the 1995 recipient of the Institute of Information Scientists Jason Farradane Award. He has managed a number of research projects, including Project CATRIONA.

Prior to this Mary Steele had completed a doctorate in linguistics, followed by an MSc in Information and Library Studies at the University of Strathclyde. Her interests are in information retrieval and the digital/electronic library area and her dissertation title was *Progress Towards the Electronic Library*. She is currently working for the BUBL Information Service.

## NOTE

Details of how to obtain the Catriona Feasibility Study Report in electronic form or hard copy are available at <URLhttp://www.bubl.bath.ac.uk/BUBL/catreport.html>

## REFERENCES

1. Dennis Nicholson et al., *Cataloguing the Internet: CATRIONA feasibility study,* Library and Information Research Report 105, London: British Library Research & Development Department, 1995.

2. ELib: UK Electronic Libraries Programme, 1995 <URL:http://ukoln.bath.ac.uk/elib/intro.html>

3. Dennis Nicholson et al., *Cataloguing the Internet: CATRIONA feasibility study,* pp. 23-26.

4. MARBI, *Proposal no. 93-4: Changes to the USMARC bibliographic format (computer files) to accommodate online information resources.* Library of Congress and OCLC Internet Resources Project. November 20, 1992. Revised March 29, 1993. <URL:gopher://marvel.loc.gov:701/00/.listarch/usmarc/93-4.doc>

5. MARBI, *Proposal no. 94-3: Addition of subfield $u (Uniform Resource Locator) to field 856 in the USMARC Bibliographic/Holdings Formats.* Library of Congress. December 6, 1993. <URL:gopher://marvel.loc.gov:701/00/.listarch/usmarc/94-3.doc>

6. MARBI, *Proposal no. 94-9: Changes to the USMARC Bibliographic Format to Accommodate Online Systems and Services.* Library of Congress and OCLC Internet Resources Project. May 6, 1994. Revised July 20, 1994. <URL:gopher://marvel.loc.gov:701/00/.listarch/usmarc/94-9.do>

# Possible Solutions for Incorporating Digital Information Mediums into Traditional Library Cataloging Services

Eric Lease Morgan

**SUMMARY.** This article first compares and contrasts the essential, fundamental differences between traditional and digital information mediums. It then reexamines the role of the online public access catalog (OPAC), refines the definition of a library's catalog, and advocates the addition of Internet resources within the OPAC. Next, the article describes the building of the Alex Catalog, a catalog of Internet resources in the form of MARC records. Finally, this article outlines a process of integrating the further inclusion of other Internet resources into OPACs as well as some of the obstacles such a process manifests.[1] *[Article copies available from The Haworth Document Delivery Service: 1-800-342-9678. E-mail address: getinfo@haworth.com]*

## *TRADITIONAL RESOURCES ARE PHYSICAL AND IMMUTABLE*

Traditionally, items listed in a library's catalog have been print resources like monographs, serials, or sheet music. Other, less com-

Eric Lease Morgan is affiliated with NCSU Libraries, Box 7111, Room 2316-b Raleigh, NC 27695-7111. E-mail: eric_morgan@ncsu.edu or http://www.lib.ncsu.edu/staff/morgan/

[Haworth co-indexing entry note]: "Possible Solutions for Incorporating Digital Information Mediums into Traditional Library Cataloging Services." Morgan, Eric Lease. Co-published simultaneously in *Cataloging & Classification Quarterly* (The Haworth Press, Inc.) Vol. 22, No. 3/4, 1996, pp. 143-170; and: *Electronic Resources: Selection and Bibliographic Control* (ed: Ling-yuh W. Pattie, and Bonnie Jean Cox) The Haworth Press, Inc., 1996, pp. 143-170. Single or multiple copies of this article are available from The Haworth Document Delivery Service [1-800-342-9678, 9:00 a.m. - 5:00 p.m. (EST). E-mail address: getinfo@haworth.com].

 

mon items included maps, globes, microfiche, phonograph records, audio cassettes, video cassettes, video laser disks, and even realia. The defining characteristic of these materials is their physical, tangible nature. Since these resources are physical manifestations of information, they can not, by definition, occupy more than one space in any single instant of time. Consequently, the cataloging process could assign codes (call numbers) to these items and place the items in designated locations. The cataloging process, for the most part, did not have to concern itself with the movement of those items from one location to another. Once items had been assigned location codes, it was rare that the location codes (and thus the actual locations) of the items would change. In short, because these materials are physical in nature, traditional resources could be physically collected and assigned specific location codes. Thus, libraries have had direct control over the locations of items in their collections.

Another characteristic of these traditional resources is their relative immutability. The contents of books or journals are not changed over time, except by the occasional patron who writes in the margins. Even more so, items like microfiche, phonograph records, or video laser disks must be completely remastered before their contents can be altered. This immutable quality of traditional information resources made it possible for libraries to create authoritative collections of materials, since the collected items were considered exact duplicates of their originals. Thus, librarians could feel relatively certain about their collection's authenticity.

## *DIGITAL RESOURCES ARE ETHEREAL AND ALTERABLE*

The advent of computers brought about a new medium for information, a digital medium. This digital information, by definition, is electronic and "general-purpose" in nature.[2] Initially used to compute tables of functions for the United States military, digital information was later found useful for the creation and storage of textual information as well as numeric information. To complicate matters, this "general-purpose" medium was designed to be interpreted by some sort of "special-purpose machine" (a computer) and manifested through various output devices (like sound speakers, video monitors, or printers) before it could be made intelligible by people.[3]

Because of its electronic nature, digital information is necessarily ethereal and non-material. This presents special problems for us librarians since we have traditionally wanted to assign location codes to the items in our catalog. Considering digital information's ethereal nature, this is a difficult task. What should we do? Should we assign location codes to a disk containing the information? Should the information be printed and then cataloged? If the item is a bibliographic index on a CD-ROM and made available to our constituents through a public access computer, then should we catalog the CD and state the location of the computer? The situation gets even worse when the same bibliographic index is mounted through our online public access catalog (OPAC) software and available from a number of locations within the library and across campus.

A corollary stemming from this new medium's electronic nature is its alterability and malleability. Once a person (or even a computer) has possession of digital information it is very easy to change and manipulate it to fit particular, individual needs. The medium was designed with these purposes in mind. Furthermore, this information can then be put back into circulation and disseminated as if the altered information were identical to the original. Consequently, it is more difficult to assess the authenticity of digital information when compared to a library's traditional mediums.

At this point in the discussion, it should be kept in mind that this digital medium can be used to communicate the same sorts of information as our traditional mediums. Digital information can be used to represent monographs such as the items in Project Gutenberg or scholarly journals like the ones listed in the *Directory of Electronic Journals, Newsletters, and Academic Discussion Lists*.[4,5] As alluded to earlier, digital information can also take the form of bibliographic indexes such as the ERIC database.[6] Works of art such as paintings and movies can also be stored in a digital medium.[7,8]

At the same time, the digital medium, especially combined with the Internet, has generated a number of new information formats as well. The best example is software, the set of codes instructing computers what to do. Along with software is the data used or created by the software, as well as the numbers and text being manipulated by the software itself. With the advent of computer networking, electronic mail (e-mail), the electronic written communications between people, becomes a new candidate for possible cataloging and classification. After computer networking, e-mail evolved into Usenet newsgroups, mailing lists, and discussion groups on local and national bulletin board systems. Unlike a lot of traditional e-mail communications, Usenet newsgroups, mailing lists, and discussion groups are sometimes archived and searchable, thus presenting libraries with opportunities for preservation, organization, and further dissemination.

As the Internet evolved from simple computer networking so did the forms of digital media. For example, FTP sites and Telnet services were one of the first "things" to make themselves available through the Internet. FTP sites presented themselves as collections of digital artifacts (software, texts, images, and others). Telnet services allowed people to take advantage of a remote computer's facilities without having to be there physically. One of the most popular types of services Telnet has provided has been our own OPACs.

As the Internet continues to mature, the services it provides are maturing as well. The gopher and HTTP (hypertext transfer protocol or more commonly called the World Wide Web or WWW) are excellent examples. These services not only provide a means for storing and accessing digital mediums, but they also provide methods for better organization and indexing of the items they contain, especially when compared to simple Telnet and FTP services.

Additionally, as the functionality of computers has increased so have the types of information, specifically multimedia. Multimedia, (like typical movies) usually includes pictures and sound. It might also include narratives and texts as well as other written materials. Distinguishing itself from these traditional mediums, multimedia is often more interactive than movies or sound recordings and consequently, the presentation of the information within the medium is a dynamic thing usually different every time it is used.

In summary, digital mediums for information have manifested themselves as traditional information resources, but they have also manifested themselves as completely new and different types of information, information that is both ethereal, dynamic, and malleable. These qualities provide libraries with new challenges when it comes to cataloging and classification issues.

## *HISTORICAL PERSPECTIVES OF CATALOGING*

This is a good place to discuss the role and possible definition refinement of the library catalog. Hanson and Daily, in the *Encyclopedia of Library and Information Science* define the library catalog as "one of the many forms of bibliography. It is generally defined as a list of books contained within a single library and is comprehensive rather than selective."[9] This simplified definition of a library catalog, where the defining characteristic is one of inventory, has been echoed in a number of other dictionaries of library science, as well as histories of librarianship.[10,11,12] It also seems to be the public's main conception of a library's catalog.

These "traditional" views have sometimes given way to enhancements of the definition and purpose of a catalog. More specifically, these enhancements make the catalog a "finding aid" or index to the library as a whole. An often quoted manifestation of this idea was put forth by Cutter.

In addition, in Rules for a Dictionary Catalog, Cutter contended that the purpose or objects of the catalog were as follows:

1. To enable a person to find a book of which either is known: author, title, or subject.
2. To show what the library has by a given author, subject, or in a given kind of literature.
3. To assist in the choice of a book: as to its edition (bibliographically) or as to its character (literary or topical).[13,14]

These ideas were echoed by the International Federation of Library Associations in 1963:

Functions of the catalog. The catalog should be an efficient instrument for ascertaining:

2.1 whether the library contains a particular book specified by:

a. its author and title, or
b. if the author is not named in the book, its title alone, or
c. if author and title are inappropriate or insufficient for identification, a suitable substitute for the title; and

2.2

a. which works by a particular author and
b. which editions of a particular work are in a library.[15,16]

Not only is this concept of a catalog defined by individuals and organizations of note, but if it has historical warrant as well.

The fifteenth principle of librarianship is: Since libraries are storehouses of knowledge, they should also be arranged according to subject. . . . All modern schemes of library classification–Dewey, Universal Decimal Classification, Library of Congress, Bliss–are designed for arrangement by subject. Prior to modern times, arrangement by subject was the rule, though in less sophisticated form. The library rooms in Ashurbanipal's palace were each devoted to a particular subject group: one room for tablets relating to history and government, another to those concerning legends and mythology, and so on.[17]

In many ways, the philosophical and pragmatic issues surrounding the cataloging and classification of digital media echo the issues raised with the introduction of audio-visual materials into our collections. At that time, just as in our own, the new media were viewed with both skepticism and jubilation.

## *A CATALOG'S DEFINITION REFINED*

The definitions of traditional and enhanced catalogs always assumed the materials (objects) of the catalog were physical in nature. Since the objects were only physical in nature, perhaps it seemed fruitless to list items beyond the library's control. Catalogs are big and difficult to maintain if they only contain the items any one library owns. The problem would be compounded if the catalog included items outside the library's collection.

With the advent of electronic items, and the desire to make the catalog a finding aid, information resources found their way into library catalogs, even though these resources were not owned by the library. Thus, the catalog has become a tool more like a bibliography than a simple list. In keeping with this idea, records have appeared in library catalogs pointing to electronic-only bibliographic indexes available only through online database vendors such as DIALOG.[18]

These electronic items, unlike physical items, are more "readily-available"; these items, assuming well maintained Internet sites and reliable connections, can be just as accessible, if not more so, than physical materials. Furthermore, these items have as much information value as many other objects in library catalogs. Therefore, since modern catalogs can be seen as finding aids to information on given subjects, and since Internet resources have as much value as traditional mediums, Internet resources should be included in library catalogs. This is seen as necessarily true when the definition of library catalogs is refined to read:

> A library catalog is an organized list of information resources arranged in all or any number of schemes (author, title, subject, accession, size, type, or others) and these resources are readily available to the intended clientele of the organized list.

## *THE ALCUIN PROJECT*

In an effort to put some of these ideals into practice, the NCSU Libraries is in the process of developing methods for effectively and efficiently introducing digital mediums (Internet resources) into our OPAC. The rest of this article describes this process, affectionately called the Alcuin Project.[19]

## *ALEX AND HUNTER MONROE*

The Alcuin Project has its roots in the Alex database and Hunter Monroe.[20] Monroe, an economist by profession and a person who has done some computer work for the cataloging department at the Bodleian Library of Oxford University, had been maintaining a list of electronic documents. His goal was to create an OPAC-type database of Internet resources. He was going to accomplish this task by using a simple dBase IV database. Gopher link files, describing Internet-based electronic documents, were intended to be created on a regular basis and then copied to a gopher server for distribution.

The NCSU Libraries was lucky enough to foster a relationship with Monroe, and consequently, the NCSU Libraries has hosted his data on its gopher server.[21] Monroe named his database Alex. David Price of Radcliffe Science Library, Oxford University hosted the first version of Alex at Oxford.[22]

Because every information system has to be browsable as well as searchable, the NCSU Libraries indexed the Alex database using the Jughead technology. Later, since the hypertext transfer protocol (WWW) was becoming popular, the NCSU Libraries experimented with methods of providing access to the Alex database using WWW browsers. While WWW browsers can interpret the gopher protocol, the WWW browsers were not being used to their fullest extent. Consequently, Monroe was asked to create a specialized report that would be easily indexable using the WAIS technology. Monroe obliged and a WWW interface to Alex was created.[23]

## *TIM KAMBITSCH AND WWW/DRA GATEWAY SCRIPTS*

At the same time the NCSU Libraries had been working with Tim Kambitsch on scripts to search our DRA-based OPAC with WWW browsers.[24] These scripts allow the searcher to specify Boolean queries to be applied to selected databases on our OPAC (book and journal catalogs, catalogs of government documents, and potentially bibliographic indexes such as *Academic Index,* or *Business Index*). After installing these scripts on our own computers, we were able to search our OPAC using WWW browsers.[25] Furthermore, by including URLs in the 856 fields of MARC records, we were able to make hot links from our OPAC to Internet resources.

As an experiment, two records were imported into our OPAC (OCLC record numbers 26226155 and 20987125). These records describe *ALAWON* and *Public Access Computer Systems Review* (*PACSR*), respectively, and the records were edited to include 856 fields. These 856 fields contain URLs linked to the NCSU Libraries local collection of *ALAWON* and *PACSR* (see Figures 1 and 2). By adding URLs to our MARC records, and by searching our OPAC for these records through Kambitsch's scripts, searchers have the opportunity to navigate directly to the electronic resources after locating items of interest.[26]

## *ALEX + GATEWAY SCRIPTS = ALCUIN*

By combining the data from the Alex database with the WWW/DRA gateway scripts, the NCSU Libraries was able to create the first iteration of the Alcuin database. The Alcuin database is a MARC-record based database of Internet resources.

This is how it was created. Monroe was contacted again and asked to create a new report from his dBase IV database. This time, instead of producing gopher link files or data that can be easily indexed by WAIS, his output was a list of rudimentary tagged MARC records (see Figure 3).

Monroe's output was then processed with a locally developed utility called Alcuin's Little Helper. Alcuin's Little Helper, written in Visual Basic and running under Microsoft Windows, is based on: The OS/2 Visual REXX program used to create LC MARC records [Which] is the result of a joint effort by Dick Thaxter and David Williamson to provide a more graphical and user-friendly interface between catalogers, electronic texts, and the systems used to create MARC records at LC.[27]

In short, Alcuin's Little Helper is a very simple MARC record editor. It can be used to create MARC records by hand or convert Monroe's tagged output to MARC records (see Figure 4).

Using Alcuin's Little Helper, Monroe's tagged output was imported and converted into true, rather simplified MARC records (see Figure 5). These records were then imported into a newly created DRA database and made available through Kambitsch's gateway scripts (see Figure 6).

FIGURE 1

The MARC record below describes an electronic newsletter called *ALAWON*. This record was imported into our OPAC and edited to include an 856 field.

```
AFW-1740    Entered: 06/16/1994   Last Modified: 02/21/1995        NCSU_CATALOG

Type: a Bib l: s Enc l:   Desc: a Ctry: dcu Lang: eng Mod:   Srce: d Freq:
 Reg: x ISDS: 1 Ser t:   Orig f:   Form:   Entire C:   Cont:     Gvt:
 Cnf: 0 Alpha: a S/L: 0 Pub s: c Dates: 1992 9999

003;    ;  a OCoLC $
005;    ;  a 19940616115148.0 $
010;    ;  a sn 93004037  $ o 26226155 $
040;    ;  a VPI $ c VPI $ d NSD $
012;    ;  1 a $
022; 0  ;  a 1069-7799 $
042;    ;  a nsdp $ a lcd $
```

```
082; 10;  a 025 $ 2 12 $
090;    ;  a Z673.A5 $ b A42 $
049;    ;  a NRCC $
210; 0 ;  a ALA Wash. Office newsline $
212; 1 ;  a American Library Association Washington Office newsline $
222;  0;  a ALA Washington Office newsline $
245; 00;  a ALA Washington Office newsline $ h [computer file] : $ b ALAWON :
         an electronic publication of the American Library Association
         Washington Office. $
246; 10;  a ALAWON $
260;    ;  a Washington, DC : $ b The Office, $ c [1992- $
265;    ;  a American Library Association Washington Office, 110 Maryland Ave.,
         NE, Washington, DC 20002-5675 $
310;    ;  a Irregular $
```

FIGURE 1 (continued)

```
362; 0 ;  a Vol. 1, no. 1 (July 9, 1992)- $
500;   ;  a Mode of access: Electronic mail on BITNET; listserv@uicvm;
         SUBSCRIBE ALA-WO First Name Last Name $
500;   ;  a Title from title screen. $
650;  0;  a Libraries $ z United States $ x Periodicals. $
650;  0;  a Information services $ z United States $ x Periodicals. $
610; 20;  a American Library Association. $ b Washington Office $ x Periodicals.
          $
710; 20;  a American Library Association. $ b Washington Office. $
936;   ;  a Vol. 2, no. 18 (May 10, 1993) LIC $
856; 00;  u http://www.lib.ncsu.edu/stacks/alawon-index.html $
```

FIGURE 2

The MARC record below describes an electronic journal, *The Public Access Computer Systems Review*. This record was imported into our OPAC and edited to include an 856 field.

```
AFW-1741   Entered: 06/16/1994   Last Modified: 06/17/1994        NCSU_CATALOG

Type: a Bib l: s Enc l: 7 Desc: a Ctry: txu Lang: eng Mod:   Srce: d Freq: t
 Reg: r ISDS: 1 Ser t: p Orig f:   Form:   Entire C:   Cont:     Gvt:
 Cnf: 0 Alpha: a S/L: 0 Pub s: c Dates: 1990 9999

003;    ;  a OCoLC $
005;    ;  a 19940616115330.0 $
010;    ;  a sn 90000811  $ o 20987125 $
040;    ;  a NSD $ c NSD $ d CAS $ d NSD $
012;    ;  j 1 $ l a $
022; 0  ;  a 1048-6542 $
030;    ;  a PACRES $
```

FIGURE 2 (continued)

```
042;   ;  a nsdp $ a lcd $
082; 10;  a 025 $ 2 11 $
049;   ;  a NRCC $
210; 0 ;  a Public-access comput. syst. rev. $ b (Electron. ed.) $
222;  4;  a The Public-access computer systems review $ b (Electronic ed.) $
245; 04;  a The Public-access computer systems review $ h [computer file]. $
246; 10;  a Public access computer systems review $
246; 13;  a PACS review $
250;   ;  a [Electronic ed.]. $
260;   ;  a Houston, TX : $ b University Libraries, University of Houston, $ c
         1990- $
265;   ;  a PACS Review, c/o University Libraries, University of Houston,
         Houston, TX 77204-2091 $
310;   ;  a Three times a year $
```

```
362; 0 ;  a Vol. 1, no. 1- $
500;   ;  a Mode of access: Electronic mail on BITNET and Internet; Send an
          e-mail message to: (BITNET) LISTSERV@UHUPVM1 or (Internet)
          LISTSERV@UHUPVM1.UH.EDU that says: Subscribe PACS-P First Name Last
          Name; also available through a subscription to the Public-access
          Computer Systems Forum, PACS-L@UHUPVM1.BITNET $
500;   ;  a Description based on printout of online display; title from title
          screen. $
580;   ;  a Also available in an annual print ed. under the same title. $
710; 20;  a University of Houston. $ b Libraries. $
775; 1 ;  t Public-access computer systems review (Print ed.) $ x 1063-164X $ w
          (DLC)sn 92004809 $ w (OCoLC)25907292 $
856;   ;  u http://dewey.lib.ncsu.edu/stacks/pacsr-index.html $
```

FIGURE 3

This is a sampling of an output file from Hunter Monroe. The file represents extremely simplified tagged MARC records from his Alex database. Each caret-underbar symbol (^_) represents ASCII character 31, end of subfield. Each field is delimited by a new line. Each record is delimited by a blank link. Thus, this figure lists only four records from the almost 2000 records in the Alex database. This file can be retrieved from ftp://ftp.lib.ncsu.edu/pub/stacks/alex/alex-950224-tagged.txt.

```
041;0 ;^_aeng
100;1 ;^_aDoctress Neutopia
245;00;^_aCold war still burns
856;  ;^_s3k ^_ugopher://english-server.hss.cmu.edu:70/00ftp%3aEnglish%20Ser
ver%3aPoetry:Cold%20War%20Still%20Burns
959;  ;^_aPoetry

041;0 ;^_aeng
245;00;^_aMagna carta
```

```
856;  ;^_ugopher://gopher.vt.edu:10010/11/119

959;  ;^_aHistory


041;0 ;^_aeng

245;00;^_aHard driving

856;  ;^_slk ^_ugopher://english-server.hss.cmu.edu:70/00ftp%3aEnglish%20Ser
ver%3aPoetry:Hard%20Driving

959;  ;^_aPoetry


041;0 ;^_aeng

100;1 ;^_aShakespeare, William^_d1564-1616

245;00;^_aComplete Shakespeare

856;  ;^_ugopher://cs.uwp.edu:70/11/pub/etext/shakespeare

959;  ;^_aDrama
```

FIGURE 4

This is screen shot of Alucin's Little Helper, a very simple MARC record editor. By selecting the buttons and pasting text, the cataloger can create valid MARC records for their OPAC database. Alternatively, the cataloger can import the output shown in Figure 3 to create MARC records as well. The process takes about 15 minutes to process all of the data in the Alex output file. This program and its source code are available at ftp://ftp.lib.ncsu.edu/pub/software/dos/alhelper.zip.

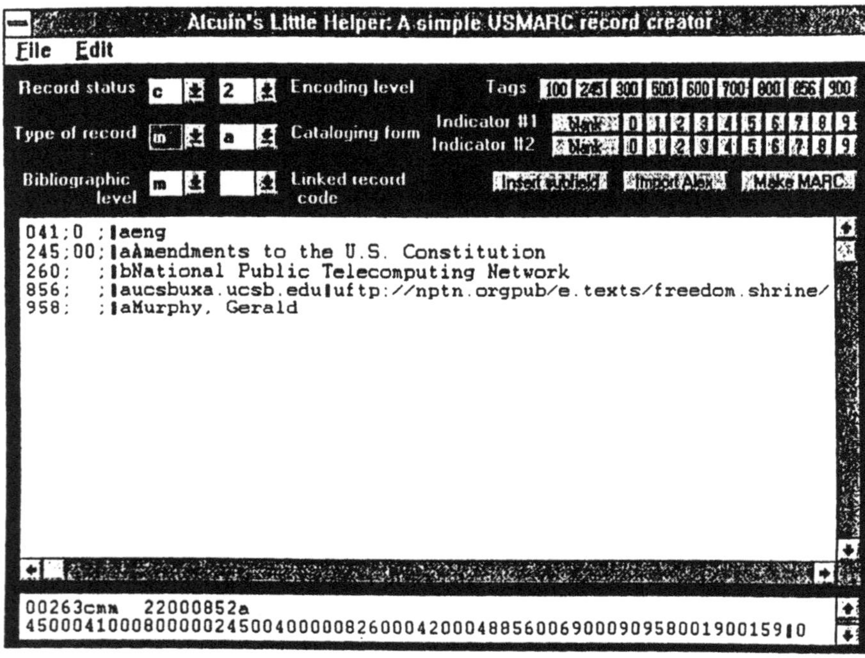


## *FORMALIZING THE PROCESS*

So far the philosophic rationale for including Internet resources into OPAC has been established. Additionally, the technical aspects of including Internet resources into our OPAC have been demonstrated. What remains is to formalize the collections/acquisitions/cataloging processes needed to make it all come together.

## *THE COLLECTION AND ACQUISITIONS PROCESS*

Before an item can be put into the Alcuin database, it must be selected and possibly acquired. This aspect of the process may be

FIGURE 5

These are three MARC records are examples of tagged manifestations of the MARC records created by Aluin's Little Helper. These records were created from the file listed in Figure 3. The sum of these records, in true MARC communications format, is available at ftp://ftp.lib.ncsu.edu/pub/stacks/alex/alex-950224-marc.txt and should be completely compatible with any OPAC database software.

```
DBCN: PAA-0647              Entered: 03/13/1995        Modified: 03/13/1995

Type: m Bib l: m Enc l: 2 Desc: a

041; 1 ;a angeng $
100; 1 ;a Plato $
245; 00;a Collected works $
700; 1 ;a Jowett, Benjamin $d 1817-1893 $
856;   ;u gopher://gopher.vt.edu:10010/01/131 $
959;   ;a Philosophy $
```

FIGURE 5 (continued)

```
DBCN: PAA-0481              Entered: 03/13/1995        Modified: 03/13/1995

Type: m Bib l: m Enc l: 2 Desc: a

041; 1 ;a angeng $
100; 1 ;a Aristotle $
245; 04;a The Athenian constitution $
260;   ;c BC $
700; 1 ;a Kenyon, Frederic G. (Frederic George), Sir $d 1863-1952 $
856;   ;u gopher://gopher.vt.edu:10010/02/39/3 $
959;   ;a History $
```

```
DBCN: PAA-0386              Entered: 03/13/1995        Modified: 03/13/1995

Type: m Bib l: m Enc l: 2 Desc: a

041; 0 ;a eng $
100; 1 ;a Twain, Mark $d 1835-1910 $
245; 04;a The adventures of Huckleberry Finn $
260;    ;a New York $b Harper & Brothers $c 1912 $
773;    ;a Writings of Mark Twain Volume XIII $
856;    ;s 390k  $u gopher://wiretap.spies.com:70/00/Library/Classic/huckfinn
          mt $
956;    ;b 1912 $
957;    ;a PG  76 WT $b pg/etext93/sawyr10.txt $
958;    ;a Dell, Thomas $b dell@wiretap.spies.com $
959;    ;a Fiction $
```

FIGURE 6

This is a screen shot of the Alcuin database as it appears in a WWW browser's window. The database itself is available itself at http://library.ncsu.edu/drabin/alcuin/. Using this interface you should be able to search the contents of the Alex database. The database consists of MARC records containing URLs in the 856 fields. The interface this service works through is based on Tim Kambitsch's DRA/WWW gateway scripts and translates the contents of subfield u of 856 fields into "hot links."

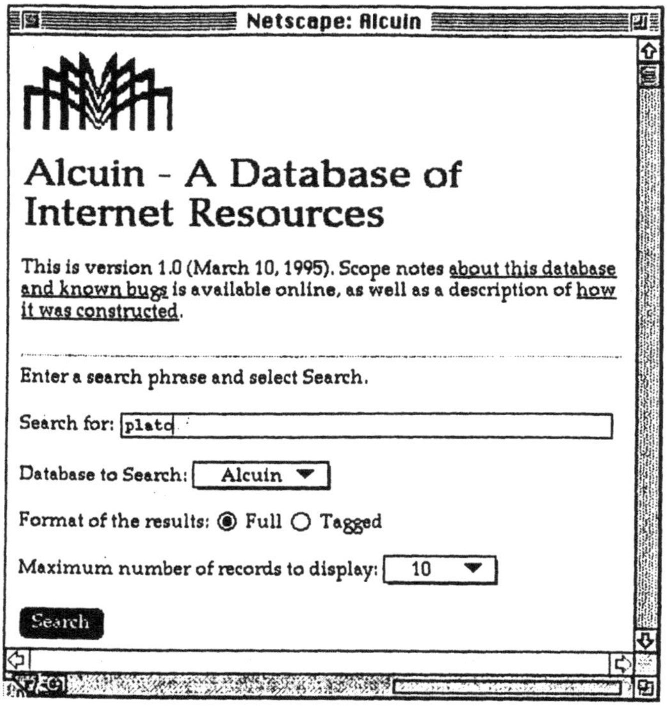


handled by the collection management and acquisitions departments, respectively. First, our collection management department "listens" to the Internet. Based on their knowledge of the needs of the library's clientele, collection managers select Internet resources to be added to the database. If the Internet resource is an item the library actually wants to own, then a URL pointing to the resource is passed on to the acquisitions department. At that time, the acquisitions department retrieves the item and puts it in an "electronic inbox" for the cataloging department. If the Internet resource is not something the library wants to own, then the URL pointing to the resource is passed directly to the cataloging department bypassing the acquisitions department.

## *CREATING AND ADDING ITEMS TO ALCUIN*

Once a cataloger becomes aware of a new item to added to the database, the cataloger uses his/her professional skills to analyze the resource and create a MARC record describing the resource based on his or her analysis. To ease the creation of these original records, Alcuin's Little Helper, which allows a cataloger to cut, copy, and paste data from various Internet client applications, is used. The records generated by Alcuin's Little Helper are then added to the Alcuin database.

## *PROVIDING ACCESS TO ALCUIN*

Providing effective access to any information system requires varying degrees of browsablility and searchability. To facilitate our clientele's ability to browse Alcuin an HTTP server has been put into place. The data contained on this server is generated on a regular basis from the contents of the Alcuin database. This data is essentially a large set of hypertext markup language documents.

The ability to browse an information system has its advantages and disadvantages. For example, the advantages of a browsable system include:

- Readers see entire system at a glance
- Knowledge of a vocabulary is not necessary
- Like items are grouped together
- Easy to navigate
- Fosters serendipity
- Stimulates thinking

On the other hand, they are not perfect and can hinder information discovery a number of ways:

- Easy to get "lost"
- Classification system may be foreign to reader

- Classification breaks down as quantity of information increases
- Classification changes over time

By providing a method for searching an information system some of those disadvantages can be overcome. More specifically, the DRA/WWW gateway scripts will provide the search features for the database.

## *CONCLUSION*

This essay has described a philosophy of cataloging advocating the addition of Internet resources into our OPAC databases. This was validated through the following definition of a library catalog:

> A library catalog is an organized list of information resources arranged in all or any number of schemes (author, title, subject, accession, size, type, etc.) and these resources are readily-available to the intended clientele of the organized list.

Defining an OPAC as a simple catalog or list of materials owned by a library would have made our lives as librarians much easier and less complex. On the other hand, if we limit our OPACs to only items we own, then we are doing our user populations a great disservice. This is because many valid information resources exist beyond our immediate control but still prove very useful to our clientele. If we exclude Internet resources from our OPACs, then we do not evolve with the times and provide the sorts of services our user populations have come to expect and desire. Furthermore, if libraries do not provide these sorts of services, then commercial services will. Consequently, libraries would be lackadaisical in fulfilling their mission of equal access to information, especially considering that many Internet resources are freely available.

This essay also described a method the NCSU Libraries is exploring for including Internet resources into its OPAC database (catalog). This method works much like our present-day method of collection where:

1. A collection manager selects a resource
2. Acquisitions people retrieve the resource
3. Catalogers analyze the resource in terms of its identifying characteristics (author, title, subjects, medium, etc.)
4. The resource is made available through a database program like our OPAC

This process includes the creation of MARC records with URLs in the 856 fields of these records. It also includes, in the case of the NCSU Libraries, the use of a DRA/WWW gateway script allowing searchers to locate records in the database and render the contents of the 856 fields as "hot links."

There are a number of obstacles impeding a library's ability to effectively add bibliographic records of Internet-based serials to its OPAC. The first is the dynamic nature of the Internet, and therefore, the potentially dynamic nature of the things our OPAC contains. If a library were to rely on the addition of uniform resource locators (URL) in the 856 fields of MARC records, then librarians may spend much of their time tracking down "broken" URLs. Hopefully, the concept of the uniform resource identifier (URI) will come to fruition and reduce (if not eliminate) the numerous reasons why the "file not found" error occurred in the first place.[28]

Until the concept of a URI becomes a reality, I can imagine a number of short-term solutions to this problem. The least likely solution is the addition of a new feature to OPAC software by vendors. This feature would examine all the records in the database(s) containing 856 field(s) and check for the validity of the URL(s) found there. Invalid URLs would then be added to a list and regularly sent to a database maintenance team. A more likely solution is to do this ourselves using the report generation services already included in our OPAC software. Another solution, and quite possibly the most implementable, is the creation of a separate, locally maintained database of Internet resources. This database is not necessarily MARC-based, but it would contain the fields essential to create a complete MARC record. More importantly, it would be able to extract the URL of a record and check for its validity. Then, on a regular basis, when all the URLs had been verified, this database would create a report in the form of MARC records, and these records would be imported into the OPAC overwriting any duplicates found there. Realistically, none of these solutions is ideal, but they may be necessary for the short-term.

The inclusion of Internet resources into our OPACs presents fundamental challenges to our conceptions of a library catalog. It also presents technical difficulties. It necessitates a lot of librarian re-education and retraining, but none of these obstacles are unsurmountable. The solutions require persistence, ingenuity, and a respect for change. In short, they require a propensity for professionalism and a commitment to excellence in service.

## AUTHOR NOTE

Eric Lease Morgan has been a Systems Librarian at the North Carolina State University Libraries since 1991. Before that he was a medical librarian at the Catawba-Wateree AHEC library in Lancaster, SC. He has a bachelors degree in philosophy from Bethany College, Bethany, WV and an MIS from Drexel University in Philadelphia, PA. Eric considers himself a librarian first and a computer user second. His professional goal is to discover new ways to use computers to improve library service. To that end he has been the architect of the NCSU Libraries WAIS, FTP, List Processor, gopher, and WWW servers. One of the projects in which he takes particular pride is his Mr. Serials Process, a project of systematically and automatically collecting electronic serials.

## NOTES

1. This text can also be found at http://www.lib.ncsu.edu/staff/morgan/cataloging-digital-mediums.html
2. Arthur W. Burks, Herman H. Goldstine, and John von Neuman, "Preliminary Discussion of the Logical Design of an Electronic Computing Instrument Part I, Vol. I." Report prepared for U.S. Army Ord. Dept. under contract W-36-034-ORD-7481 in A. H. Taub, ed. *John von Neuman Collected Works Vol. V: Design of Computers, Theory of Automata and Numerical Analysis*. (New York: Pergamon, 1963), p. 35.
3. Ibid.
4. http://jg.cso.uiuc.edu/pg/lists/list.html
5. gopher://arl.cni.org:70/11/scomm/edir
6. telnet://eric@sklib.usask.ca/
7. http://pmwww.cs.vu.nl/archive/images/arts/.html/

8. http://www.msstate.edu/Movies/

9. Eugene R. Hanson and Jay E. Daily "Catalogs and Cataloging" in Allen Kent and Harold Lancour, ed. *Encyclopedia of Library and Information Science* (New York: Marcel Dekker, 1970), v. 4 p. 242.

10. Thomas Landau, ed. *Encylopedia of Librarianship*, 3rd ed. (London: Bowes & Bowes, 1966) p. 90.

11. Elizabeth H. Thompson. *ALA Glossary of Library Terms with a Selection of Terms in Related Fields*. (ALA: Chicago, 1943), p. 24.

12. James Thompson, *A History of the Principles of Librarianship*. Hamden, CN: Linnet, 1977

13. Thomas Landau, ed. *Encylopedia of Librarianship*, 3rd ed. (London: Bowes & Bowes, 1966), p. 245.

14. Martha, M. Yee, "What Is a Work? Part 1: The User and the Objects of the Catalog," *Cataloging & Classification Quarterly* 19(1994): 12.

15. Ibid.

16. Yee cites an earlier version of this statement in Martha, M. Yee, "What Is a Work? Part 1: The User and the Objects of the Catalog," *Cataloging & Classification Quarterly* 19 (1994):15.

17. James Thompson, *A History of the Principles of Librarianship*. (Linnet: Hamden, CN, 1977), 223.

18. Sanford Berman, ed. "Appendix A," *Cataloging Special Materials: Critiques and Innovations*. (Phoenix, AR: Oryx Press, 1986), pp. 161-169.

19. Alcuin of York (b. circa 735-d. May 19, 804) was a Medieval librarian and advisor to Charlemagne. A respected scholar of the time, Alcuin was a driving force behind the Carolingian Renaissance. Alcuin is being honored here because he exemplifies the ideals of librarianship. He took the learning of his time, organized it, and provided a means for disseminating it for the benefit of society.

20. http://www.lib.ncsu.edu/stacks/alex-index.html

21. gopher://vega.lib.ncsu.edu:70/11/library/stacks/Alex

22. gopher://rsl.ox.ac.uk:70/11/lib-corn/hunter

23. http://www.lib.ncsu.edu/stacks/alex-index.html

24. http://dmcpl.dayton.lib.oh.us/~kambitsch/niso/www2dra_forms_NL.html

25. http://ncsulib4.lib.ncsu.edu/drabin/niso_forms

26. You can give this a try by pointing your WWW browser to http://library.ncsu.edu/drabin/niso_forms and then searching for "alawon" or "public and access and computer and systems and review."

27. http://lcweb.loc.gov/catdir/ecip/ecip.html

28. As you may or may not know, URIs are to URLs as the Internet names of computers are to Internet protocol (IP) numbers. All computers on the Internet are uniquely identified by IP numbers. For example, the IP number of the computer on my desk is 152.1.24.177. This computer has a name as well, emorgan.lib.ncsu.edu. If I were to get a new computer it would be assigned a new IP number, but the domain name service (DNS) of our campus could make sure the new number would be associated with the old name. Thus, I could always tell

people to connect to my computer (emorgan.lib.ncsu.edu) and they would find it available. URIs will work the same way. There will be a database of URIs. Each one will be associated with one or more URLs. As URLs change, the database is updated. To use the Internet, people would use URIs instead of URLs and consequently, URIs would never be broken as long as the database were kept up-to-date.

# Cataloging at the Library of Congress in the Digital Age

Beth Davis-Brown
David Williamson

**SUMMARY.** The Library of Congress is participating in a number of initiatives to explore issues surrounding description and cataloging of digital materials. Additionally, programs have been written by LC staff which enable electronic enhancements in cataloging activities, such as the receipt of online information from publishers in the Electronic CIP Program. This paper is both an overview of the status of cataloging-related digital projects at LC and a description of software which facilitates productivity through the provision of advanced search capabilities and the elimination of repetitive keying. *[Article copies available from The Haworth Document Delivery Service: 1-800-342-9678. E-mail address: getinfo@haworth.com]*

Like many libraries considering the impact of the highly touted "information superhighway" on their services, the Library of Congress (LC) has moved to embrace the digital age. The National Digital Library Program (NDLP) has received financial support from the U.S. Congress, and the private sector has supported the program with over $20 million in gifts through 1995. The goal of the NDLP is to make available on the Internet five million digitized

---

Beth Davis-Brown is Senior Digital Conversion Specialist with the Library of Congress National Digital Library Program. David Williamson is affiliated with the Library of Congress.

The authors would like to thank John Byrum, Regina Reynolds, and Sarah Thomas for their review and comments on earlier drafts of this article.

[Haworth co-indexing entry note]: "Cataloging at the Library of Congress in the Digital Age." Davis-Brown, Beth, and David Williamson. Co-published simultaneously in *Cataloging & Classification Quarterly* (The Haworth Press, Inc.) Vol. 22, No. 3/4, 1996, pp. 171-196; and: *Electronic Resources: Selection and Bibliographic Control* (ed: Ling-yuh W. Pattie, and Bonnie Jean Cox) The Haworth Press, Inc., 1996, pp. 171-196. Single or multiple copies of this article are available from The Haworth Document Delivery Service [1-800-342-9678, 9:00 a.m. - 5:00 p.m. (EST). E-mail address: getinfo@haworth.com].

images and texts from the Library's unique collections by the year 2000. In addition to the NDLP, initiatives such as digitizing text and images from Library exhibits, THOMAS (legislative information updated daily on the World Wide Web), and the establishment of World Wide Web home pages and GOPHER services by Library reading rooms make LC one of the largest content providers on the Internet.

But the Library of Congress is "becoming digital" through more than just the NDLP and associated Internet offerings. In the first portion of this article, an overview of what is currently happening at LC in terms of cataloging digital materials will be presented. This is by no means a policy statement, but rather a look at the process of determining practices and investigating the important issues in dealing with digital materials. In the second portion of this article, David Williamson describes the Electronic CIP program at the Library of Congress. "E-CIP" enables the Cataloging Directorate to accomplish its traditional purpose of providing Cataloging-in-Publication information for printed monographs, but newly devised electronic means are used to accelerate delivery, processing, and return of the data to the publisher. About a week in mailing time is saved on both ends of the process through the electronic delivery of information to and from the participating publishers.

One of the first times that the flourishing digital information environment and its impact on cataloging was systematically addressed at LC was on October 12-14, 1994, when Director for Cataloging Dr. Sarah E. Thomas sponsored the Seminar on Cataloging Digital Documents. The meeting allowed over 75 North American catalogers, library and information science faculty, computer scientists, and systems administrators to come together for three days in Washington. Presentations on the Text Encoding Initiative and Standard Generalized Markup Language, the LC American Memory Program and its approach to bibliographic representation, and a presentation by OCLC on its approach to the Internet Cataloging project were but a few of the talks which stimulated discussion of how cataloging departments would deal with digital materials. The questions that came out of the Seminar were along the following lines: with shrinking staffs and reducing budgets the norm at many institutions, how would libraries handle a potentially exponential growth in their workloads brought on by the advent of readily available yet volatile digital materials? Should Uniform Resource Locators (URLs) be the means of accessing the materials, or would an alternate means of providing links to materials be more stable? Or, should digital materials even be cataloged in the traditional sense, given the multitude of World Wide Web browsers and meta-indexes that categorize Internet resources already? These and other questions encouraged participants to begin thinking about policies for handling digital materials at their home institutions as well as how national cooperation might take place in representing CD-ROM and Internet resources.

The proceedings from the Seminar, including notes from the last day's discussions and formation of an action plan, are available on the World Wide Web at the following address: http://www.loc.gov/catdir/semdigdocs/seminar.html. The proceedings are also accessible from the LC homepage under the "LC Services and Publications" choice on the main menu. The address for the homepage is http://www.loc.gov.

About a year after the Seminar on Cataloging Digital Documents was held, Barbara Tillett, chief, Cataloging Policy and Support Office (CPSO), initiated a three-day meeting to lay the foundation for developing consistent cataloging policies and guidelines for digital materials. Participants included Tom Delsey, Director-General, Corporate Policy and Planning, National Library of Canada, as well as several staff members from throughout Collections Services. The meetings were held September 20-22, 1995, at the Library of Congress.

The starting point for discussion was the conceptual model of bibliographic information developed by the IFLA Study Group on the Functional Requirements of Bibliographic Records, for which Tillett and Delsey have served as consultants. The IFLA model incorporates the salient features of a general bibliographic data model developed for an information engineering project at LC in 1991. The model was used to focus discussion on how digital materials fit into the traditional bibliographic universe. The conceptual model as presented identified three basic categories (entities) of bibliographic data: intellectual or artistic content (the entities WORK and EXPRESSION); generalizable physical description (the entity MANIFESTATION); and individual instances or copies (the entity ITEM). The participants endorsed the basic categories, and agreed that they held true in the digital world. They also agreed on the need for more precision in the vocabulary used to discuss 'digital' materials, and recommended maintaining a distinction between online resources and digital works that are published and maintained as physical materials. The results of the meeting were incorporated into a report made available by CPSO in the first quarter of 1996. It can be obtained through LC MARVEL, accessible either through the LC World Wide Web homepage or at gopher://marvel.loc.gov.

In addition to sponsoring seminars and working groups to discuss issues in cataloging digital materials, LC has been active in national cooperative projects which impact the development of standards for library materials on the World Wide Web. Four LC staff members–Sarah Thomas and Beth Davis-Brown, National Digital Library Program; Janice Ruth, Manuscripts Division, and Helena Zinkham, Prints and Photographs Division–attended the Berkeley Finding Aid Conference in April, 1995. This meeting was important in that it brought together many institutions who wish to cooperate in the use of a Standard Generalized Markup Language (SGML) Document Type Definition (DTD) for online archival finding aids. Through the development of this standard, researchers will ultimately be able to utilize full text search capabilities for archival materials across collections and across institutions, a functionality which is presently not possible.

After the conference, LC staff tested the Berkeley Finding Aid SGML DTD using different SGML software packages. The NDLP sponsored a consultant with expertise in SGML and DTD development to analyze the Berkeley proposed standard and critique it. This critique and other LC suggestions were carried by Janice Ruth and Helena Zinkham to the Bentley Fellowship-sponsored group which met to make refinements to the DTD in Ann Arbor, Michigan in July. On November 1-3, 1995, the National Digital Library Program sponsored a meeting to follow-up on the work begun by the Bentley group by again hiring Deborah Lapeyre as SGML consultant to meet with the original Bentley group to discuss the latest revisions to the Berkeley Finding Aid DTD, now known as the Encoded

Archival Description standard (EAD). Working with Daniel Pitti of UC-Berkeley, other members of the Bentley team, and six other LC staff as additional resources, Lapeyre prepared the Alpha release of the EAD in early 1996. LC is one of the "early implementors" of the EAD and has used the EAD to place online registers of LC archival collections on the World Wide Web using SGML. The SGML DTD for the Encoded Archival Description is available via FTP from the Library of Congress. Please contact the authors via e-mail to request instructions on how to obtain it.

Along with supporting the EAD standard for SGML finding aids, a committee has been established to organize LC efforts to create an SGML DTD for the MARC record. This would provide a mapping of MARC to SGML according to the appropriate international standards that govern both types of data structure. A number of other organizations and agencies have asked the Network Development/MARC Standards Office (Net Dev/MSO) for guidance in undertaking such mapping. The committee's charge is to make choices among options for the characteristics of a draft DTD for the MARC record and to attempt to insure that such a draft would reflect any particular concerns of the Library. Sally McCallum, chief of Net Dev/MSO, is chair of the committee, and Randall Barry of Net Dev/MSO is also participating in the examination and discussion of several approaches to such a DTD. The MARC-SGML DTD should be available in mid-1996. To obtain a copy of it, please contact Net Dev/MSO at the Library of Congress, which is the international maintenance agency for the standard. The e-mail address is ndmso@loc.gov.

As can be seen from the cases above, the Library of Congress is grasping the issues in cataloging a variety of digital materials. A collection policy statement exists at LC for the selection of digital materials, but the addition of Internet resources to the collection has not yet become a routine practice. Even though the acquisitions step is somewhat different when "acquiring" online digital materials, the step of cataloging is still crucial to let library users know of the existence of digital materials through records in the library catalog. When cataloging digitized materials, LC makes a distinction between documents which are digital in nature, such as a software program, and items which have been digitally reformatted, such as texts, moving and still images, and sound recordings converted into electronic form. Digital items (digital originals) are generally cataloged by entering separate bibliographic records for each item in LC's main catalog. For digitized reproductions of items, there is usually already a record for the source item, and the existence of the digitized form is recorded on that record. In the event that the source item has not yet been cataloged, a computer file record is created. Currently, LC assigns subject headings and classification numbers to computer file records for original digital materials.

For digitally reformatted items, LC generally uses its existing record for the original format, adding appropriate information to indicate that the item is now also available in digitized form. This is done primarily by processing staff in the Geography and Map, Prints and Photographs, and Motion Picture, Broadcasting, and Recorded Sound Divisions. LC is currently unable to utilize copy cataloging procedures for records for computer files from bibliographic utilities due to limitations in the local automated system. It is hoped that this capacity will be attained in the near future. The Cataloging Directorate at the Library of Congress is a participant in the OCLC Intercat project. The Computer Files/Microforms team in the Special Materials Cataloging Division has cataloged LC resources on the Internet, such as THOMAS and the "Recovered Walt Whitman Notebooks" exhibit. The team is also cataloging software and CD-ROM materials that come to the Special Materials Cataloging Division.

Catalogers in the National Serials Data Program (NSDP) have been working with online electronic serials since as early as 1988. Regina Reynolds, head of NSDP, estimates that 250-300 International Standard Serial Numbers (ISSN's) have been assigned to electronic serials since the first "electronic newsletter" was submitted in 1988. NSDP is also participating in the OCLC Intercat Project. Since NSDP records are created primarily to serve as ISSN identification records, it should be noted that they are not full LC bibliographic records. The materials they represent have not been through the LC acquisitions and selection process, and the records themselves lack full CONSER authentication. In other NSDP activities, Regina Reynolds gave a workshop entitled "Cataloging Electronic Serials (Remote Access)" at the ALCTS Serials Cataloging Institute on "Serials Cataloging in the Age of Format Integration." NSDP and CONSER also gave input into a revision of the International Standard for Bibliographic Description for Computer Files (ISBDCF).

CONSER, a cooperative serials program that is coordinated by LC staff, has been active nationally in issues concerning the cataloging of electronic serials. In developing module 31 of the *CONSER Cataloging Manual*, which deals with remote access serials, CONSER had to make interim decisions on how to describe electronic materials. LC staff contributed to a November 1995 CONSER taskforce report, recommending to the CONSER policy committee and with which the committee agreed, that it was not in CONSER's scope to archive online serials cooperatively, but that it should devote resources toward further refining cataloging practices. An issue that is currently unresolved by the CONSER taskforce is whether the definition of a serial should be modified to accommodate online resources that do not meet the current serial designation, such as WWW homepages. A homepage is currently considered to be like a loose-leaf service, and it is cataloged as a monograph.

Another question with which CONSER grapples is this: what constitutes a reproduction as opposed to an edition? Should a record for the print version be adapted with an 856 field added, or should a new record be created? Also, should the policy be different for a cooperatively created database of bibliographic records rather than a locally used and maintained database? It is hard to determine at LC, since the institution is basically doing both. Also, the issue of verification of the URL is difficult, in that what the publisher states as the URL might not be correct. The issue of how specific the URL should be and how actively the catalogers should research it comes up frequently.

Finally, CONSER has drafted a proposal to the National Information Standards Organization (NISO) that a committee on standards for title presentation for electronic serials be established. The committee would recommend to creators of electronic serials principles for imparting traditional masthead information such as publisher, frequency, and numbering of issues. Additionally, electronic publishers would be steered to presenting in a standardized way the technical and header information libraries must have to store and access these materials.

A final notable project with electronic serials at LC is the Electronic Journals Project. The Electronic Journals Project includes full LC cataloging in the serials format for each title included in the project. About 20 serial titles have been "gopherized" and made available online on LC MARVEL. Currently at LC, the policy for cataloging online electronic serials is that one record is created for all file formats. Serials cataloging staff made a separate record for each computer file serial in the Electronic Journals Project, but they did not make a separate record for ASCII, hypertext and PDF versions of the serial. (The *Journal of Postmodern Culture* is a good example of how a title with printed and electronic versions was treated by LC for the project.)

As can be seen from the diverse activities and initiatives at the Library of Congress, LC is still developing an approach to cataloging digital materials and has not yet established firm policies. The following description of the Electronic CIP Program and the software and hardware it uses shows the other side of the coin of how advances in electronic communication are enhancing traditional cataloging operations at the Library of Congress.

The 1990s have seen an explosion in desktop publishing, personal computers, Internet use, and information exchange. The publishing community has been a part of that explosion, venturing into new forms of information publishing with electronic books, compact discs, and World Wide Web pages. With the emergence of this electronic market, publishers are now interested in conducting associated business electronically and, in their relationships with the Library of Congress, this means registering for copyright protection or applying for cataloging-in-publication (CIP) data.

The Cataloging-in-Publication Division at the Library of Congress began receiving questions about electronic applications for CIP data in the early 1990s. In April 1993, this division formed a study group to examine the feasibility of creating an electronic version of the CIP process. The group was responsible for examining technological aspects, workflow, and electronic file requirements. Publishers were contacted by phone to solicit interested participants for an experiment. In November 1993, the University of New Mexico Press submitted the first electronic application and manuscript for processing.

The manuscript file contained the complete text of the manuscript as it existed when transmitted. It was an ASCII text file and was sent to the Library of Congress over the Internet by file transfer protocol (FTP). After receiving the manuscript file, cataloging staff began to develop methods for extracting bibliographic information from the file. Initially, simple cut-and-paste methods were used to copy information from the file into the bibliographic record for the publication represented by the manuscript file. The cut-and-paste operation evolved quickly into a set of complex macros attached to a text editor. These macros relied on ISBD punctuation to scan highlighted information and to convert that information into MARC fields automatically.

Catalogers at the Library of Congress are now using a desktop computer to perform their work. This computer, called the bibliographic workstation (BWS), is an off-the-shelf PC functioning under the OS/2 operating system. It uses customized 3270 terminal emulation software to communicate with the LC mainframe over a TCP/IP network. The OS/2 enhanced system editor, EPM.EXE, is capable of reading REXX computer language macros and performing the instructions contained in them. These macros formed the basis for the program now in use for cataloging electronic CIP manuscripts.

The program, *On the MARC*, is an OS/2 application written in Visual REXX that can take text from any source (electronic file, Internet screen capture, keyboard input) and convert that text into MARC fields. The operator supplies appropriate ISBD punctuation to the text, highlights the text to be converted, and then tells the program which field to create based on the highlighted text. Figure 1 shows the screen that is displayed when the operator starts the program (filling the entire screen).

The upper box is the text area where the electronic data are displayed or to which the operator would paste information clipped from the source. The bottom box is where the MARC record is displayed as it is being created. There are slider bars on the right side of each box so the operator can scroll through each display.

Along the left side of the program window are the program operation buttons. They perform the following functions:

| | |
|---|---|
| File | Opens an electronic file (further details below) and displays it in the upper box |
| Paste | Pastes text from the OS/2 clipboard (e.g., Internet OPAC screens) into the upper box |
| 100 | Creates the main entry field (see also the section on database searching) |
| 245 | Creates the title field |
| 250 | Creates the edition field |
| 260ab | Creates the imprint field when the data are presented as place : publisher, date |
| 260ba | Creates the imprint field when the data are presented as publisher : place, date |
| 300 | Creates the collation field usually from an Internet OPAC record |
| 440 | Creates the series field (see also the section on database searching) |
| 500Quote | Gives selected data as a quoted note. |
| 504 | Creates the bibliographical references note usually from an Internet OPAC record |
| 505/TOC | Constructs a contents note from the selected elements of the table of contents (see also the section on constructing a 505 field for further details) |
| 520/Abs | Creates the summary note from text provided as an abstract or other summary |
| 020 | Creates the ISBN field |
| 700 | Creates an added entry field (see also the section on database searching) |
| 700, ill. | Creates the illustrator added entry field for children's literature titles, adding subfield e ", ill." |
| 856 | Creates the 856 Universal Resource Locator (URL) field [experimental] |
| C[up]C[down] | Clears the boxes. C[up] clears the upper box and C[down] clears the lower box |
| NAR | Creates a skeletal name authority record (NAR) |

| | |
|---|---|
| | based on the data in the lower box (see also the section on creating NARs) |
| APIF | Sends the MARC record being created into the LC database. |

## *OPENING AN ELECTRONIC FILE*

To open an electronic file for processing, the operator uses a mouse to point to the File button and then clicks on this button with the left mouse button (mouse button 1) to cause a dialog box to appear as seen in Figure 2.

The "Open File" dialog box is a standard Common User Access (CUA) compliant dialog box, such as is used in OS/2 or Windows programs. The operator adjusts the various boxes, if needed, to find the manuscript file. Clicking on the name and then on the "OK" button will bring the file up in the upper window of the program. The operator may click on "Cancel" to stop the file opening process. The file is read and displayed in the upper window of the cataloging program.

## *CATALOGING FROM THE FILE*

Once the file is loaded, the operator needs to insert ISBD punctuation in the various subfields. In Figure 3, notice the punctuation added–colon after the title, slash after the subtitle, and a comma after the first author's name. After inserting the ISBD punctuation, the data are highlighted as shown. The operator then clicks on the button on the left side of the screen to tell the program what field to create. For the 245 field title information highlighted in Figure 3, the results are shown in the lower window.

FIGURE 1

On the MARC version 1.4
File
Paste
100
245
250
260ab
260ba
300
440
500 Quote
504
505/TOC
520/Abs.
020
700
700, ill.
856
C↑
C↓
NAR
APIF

FIGURE 2

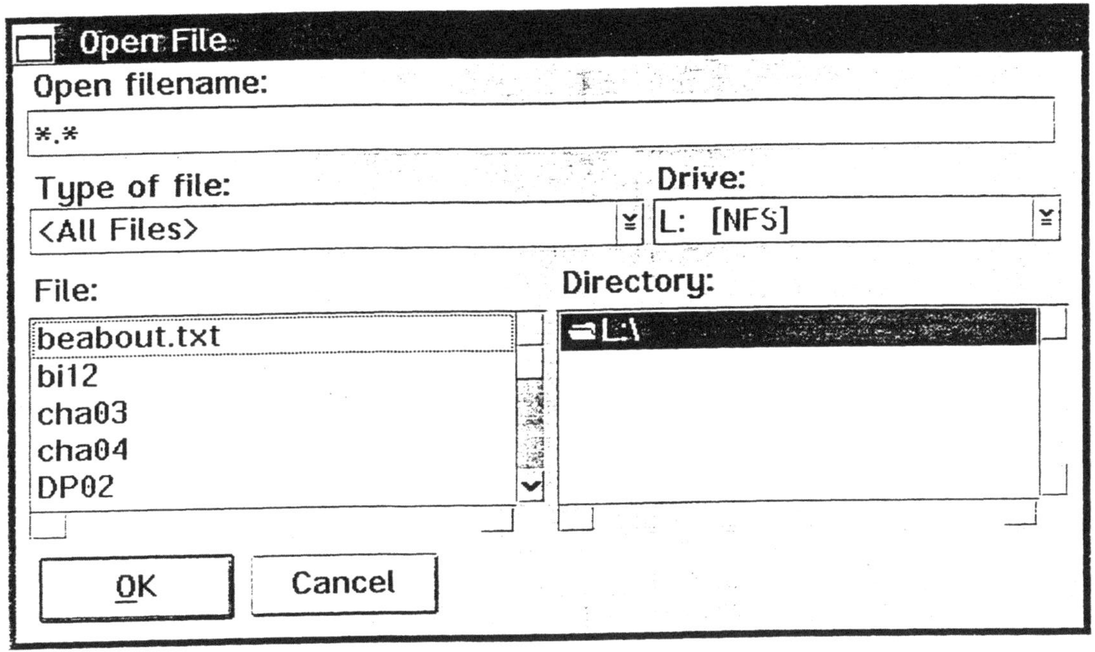
Open File
Open filename:
*.*
Type of file:
<All Files>
Drive:
L: [NFS]
File:
beabout.txt
bi12
cha03
cha04
DP02
Directory:
L:\
OK
Cancel

FIGURE 3

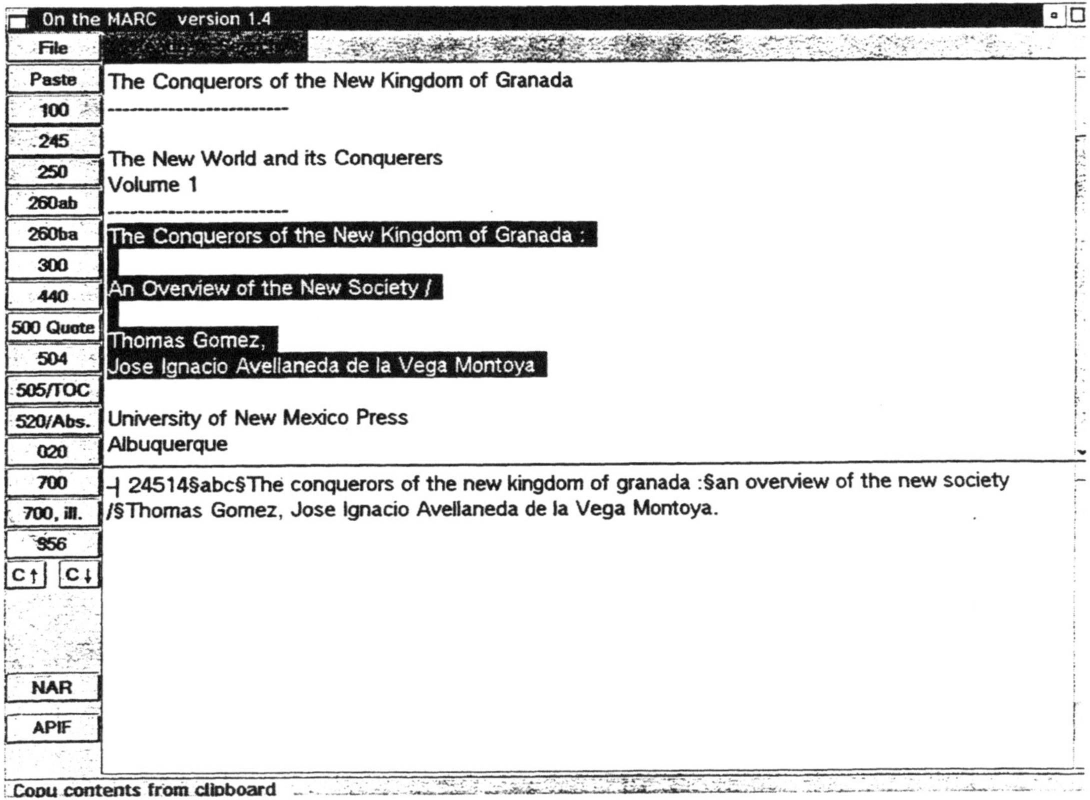
On the MARC version 1.4
File
Paste
100
245
250
260ab
260ba
300
440
500 Quote
504
505/TOC
520/Abs.
020
700
700, ill.
856
C↑
C↓
NAR
APIF
The Conquerors of the New Kingdom of Granada
The New World and its Conquerers
Volume 1
The Conquerors of the New Kingdom of Granada :
An Overview of the New Society /
Thomas Gomez,
Jose Ignacio Avellaneda de la Vega Montoya
University of New Mexico Press
Albuquerque
┤24514§abc§The conquerors of the new kingdom of granada :§an overview of the new society
/§Thomas Gomez, Jose Ignacio Avellaneda de la Vega Montoya.
Copy contents from clipboard

Notice the following in the lower window (all coding is in LC MARC):

1. The indicators '14' are provided. The '1' is a default value. The '4' is computed by the program. The program is aware of the three English articles–*the*, *an*, and *a*, and will properly code the second indicator so that any initial article in the title can be ignored in automated searching.
2. The first word of the title is uppercased and the rest of the title and subtitle are lowercased. It is easier to uppercase the proper nouns than to lowercase all other words in the title and subtitle. To uppercase proper nouns, the operator simply double-clicks on the word that needs changing. The authors' names are given without changing capitalization.
3. The program inserted the correct number of subfield codes and delimiters in the appropriate places.

## *AUTOMATIC DATABASE SEARCHING*

*On the MARC* is a multi-threaded program–one in which processes can be programmed to run as if they were separate programs. This has advantages over single-threaded programs. The operator goes through the manuscript file, highlighting data and telling the program to process the data as appropriate. Whenever the operator creates a 100, 440, or 700 field, the program spawns a new thread which initiates a search against the LC database. The advantage in using a separate thread for searching is that the cataloging thread of the program is not affected by a problem with the LC database search (e.g., a system crash), and the operator can continue cataloging.

In the example being cataloged, the operator would highlight 'Thomas Gomez' and then click on the 100 button. The 100 field would be created with the author's name inverted and properly coded for forename, single, or multiple surname. When the search is formulated, it is sent to a BWS search session. The search screen is brought automatically to the foreground and the operator can see the search and any results immediately as shown in Figure 4.

The LC search for this name would be the search command 'ppnk,' the author's name, inverted, and the file qualifier ';f=na' to tell the LC system to limit its search to the name authority file. The results allow the operator to see immediately which authors' names are close to the heading sought and to compare the heading created

FIGURE 4

```
PAGE Gomez, Thomas;f=na
NUMBER OF HITS=2      [PPNK]  [MUMS]     SEQUENTIAL RECORDS          1 TO 2
¶
1  Gomez, Thomas. [authority heading]
                                                                   n85-48557
2  Gomez, Thomas, 1905-1971 [authority heading]
                                                                   no90-11055
```

by the program to the heading in the LC name authority file. If there are differences in the forms retrieved, the operator can either do further searching to find the desired heading or use cut-and-paste techniques to adjust the form in the record being created. Future enhancements will allow the name authority form to be automatically returned to the program.

## *CONSTRUCTING A 505 FIELD FROM THE TABLE OF CONTENTS*

One of the advantages of receiving electronic files for cataloging is that the table of contents (TOC) data may be included in the manuscript file. Because the techniques used to create basic cataloging data from electronic text can also be applied to TOC data, the data can be processed very quickly and accurately. The operator may need to do some manual editing to delete some data given in the TOC. This is because the program cannot predict or consider all possible combinations of data, formatting, and layout that the text might contain. The program is able to handle two common situations. If there are chapter numbers given, the program will ignore these and not include them in the 505 field. If the table of contents is from a scanned source and there are dot leaders followed by page numbers, the program will also ignore these. Any other intervening words (such as part titles or blank lines between chapter titles), SGML coding, or complicated spacing used in the layout will have to be deleted manually by the operator. At LC, if the TOC requires extensive editing or excessive time to modify the data to enable the program to process the information, the cataloger is instructed not to include it in the record. In this example, the TOC data are presented simply and in a format the program can manipulate with no additional editing. The operator highlights the data as shown.

Only the chapter titles are included as they provide further understanding as to the nature of the work or additional key word access for searching. Once the data are processed, the data appear in the lower window of the cataloging program as shown in Figure 5.

Notice that for each element in the 505 field, the chapter numbering is stripped out, the first word of the chapter title is uppercased, and the other words are lowercased. The program also inserted ISBD punctuation between the elements. In this example, the TOC information was processed in seconds rather than the minutes required for manually typing the same information and avoids the need to proofread for typos. With this program, as long as the data are given correctly in the manuscript file, the 505 field will be accurate. The Library of Congress is adding contents notes to bibliographic records for electronic CIPs on a regular basis, even though such notes are not normally given for hard copy materials due to the time required to key the data. This experiment has demonstrated how quickly and easily the table of contents can be formatted for a contents note. Therefore, in spite of the guidelines for manual monograph cataloging, electronic TOC data will appear in bibliographic records where possible.

One area of future potential record enhancement is the inclusion of information that summarizes or abstracts the title being cataloged. Since a summary note is just running text, no machine manipulation of the actual text would be necessary except to put the 520 field tag and subfield information in front of the text. If affordable sources of objective abstracts can be found, the abstract could be easily added to a cataloging record just as with the TOC information.

## *SENDING THE RECORD*

When the operator has created all necessary descriptive fields from the manuscript, the operator clicks on the APIF (automated process information file–the LC in-process file) button which causes the window shown in Figure 6 to appear.

The operator enters selected control information as well as information used by the CIP Division and then clicks on the OK button to send the record into the LC file. The program then brings the cataloging input session to the foreground and creates the CIP

FIGURE 5

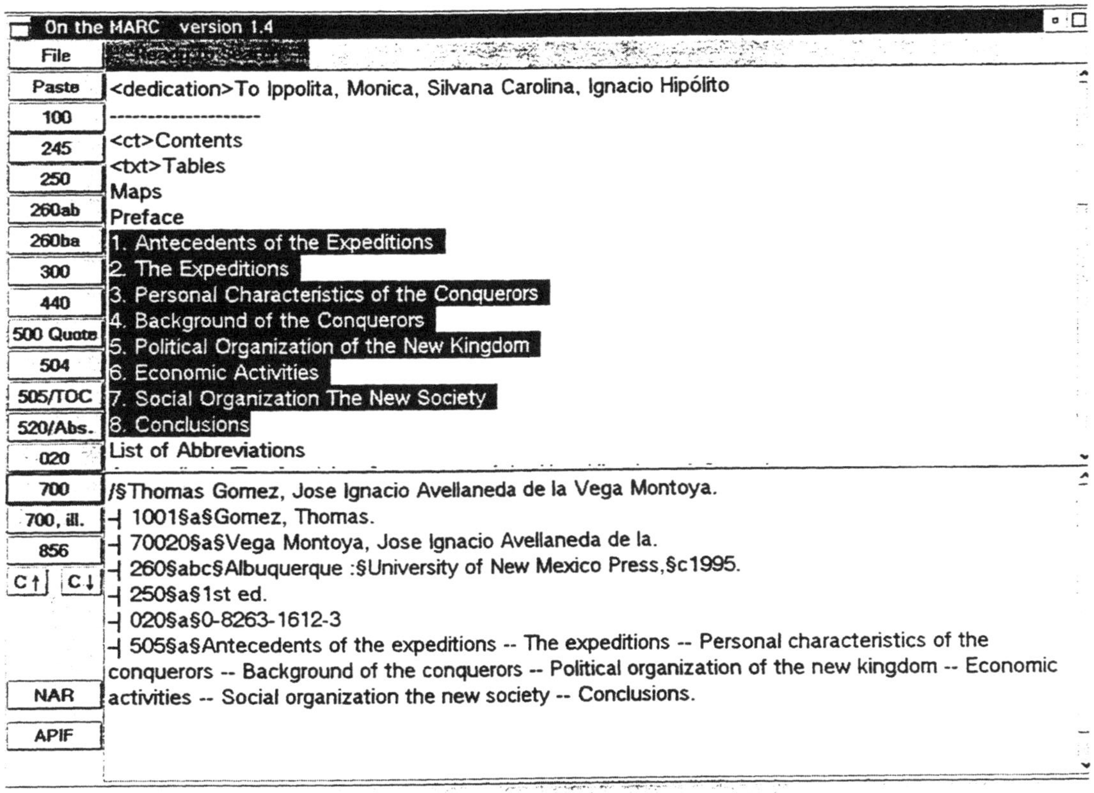
On the MARC version 1.4
File
Paste
100
245
250
260ab
260ba
300
440
500 Quote
504
505/TOC
520/Abs.
020
700
700, ill.
856
NAR
APIF
<dedication>To Ippolita, Monica, Silvana Carolina, Ignacio Hipólito
<ct>Contents
<txt>Tables
Maps
Preface
1. Antecedents of the Expeditions
2. The Expeditions
3. Personal Characteristics of the Conquerors
4. Background of the Conquerors
5. Political Organization of the New Kingdom
6. Economic Activities
7. Social Organization The New Society
8. Conclusions
List of Abbreviations
/§Thomas Gomez, Jose Ignacio Avellaneda de la Vega Montoya.
1001§a§Gomez, Thomas.
70020§a§Vega Montoya, Jose Ignacio Avellaneda de la.
260§abc§Albuquerque :§University of New Mexico Press,§c1995.
250§a§1st ed.
020§a§0-8263-1612-3
505§a§Antecedents of the expeditions -- The expeditions -- Personal characteristics of the conquerors -- Background of the conquerors -- Political organization of the new kingdom -- Economic activities -- Social organization the new society -- Conclusions.

record. After it inserts the fields, the operator checks the record, makes any adjustments, and then releases this version of the record. At that point the record is available in the LC database.

## *CREATING A NAME AUTHORITY RECORD*

Looking back at Figure 5 and the record that has been built from this file will reveal inclusion of a 700 added entry field. Notice that the name recorded has a multiple surname. To cause the program to start with a surname element other than the last element, the operator inserts an asterisk in the name where the program should start to formulate the name (in the example, the entry element would normally not be "Vega" but for demonstration purposes, "Vega" is used). When this field was created, the program performed a search against the LC database. Since the author's name used in the example is fictitious, no name authority record was found. In this case, it is necessary to create one for the heading. *On the MARC* is capable of generating a skeletal name authority record (NAR) *after* the 100, 245, and 260 fields have been created by the program (data needed for a NAR are in these three fields). To create a skeletal NAR, the operator clicks anywhere on the line containing the 100 or 700 fields to tell the program what heading needs an NAR. The operator then clicks on the NAR button to tell the program to make the NAR. Another window pops up on the screen as shown in Figure 7.

From this point, the operator can perform several functions. Notice that in the 670 field, both authors' names are given. This is intentional in case there is wording other than the name elements that the operator might want to include. The operator simply highlights the extraneous data and deletes it. If a reference structure is needed–as in the case in this name which has several surname elements, the operator clicks anywhere on the 100 field so that the cursor is blinking somewhere on that line. The operator then clicks on the "Ref" button at the top of the box and references are created automatically as shown in Figure 8.

Notice for the heading itself as well as for all references that the first indicator is properly set for single or multiple surnames. The program counts the number of words before the comma and assigns a value as appropriate. The program cannot distinguish surname

FIGURE 6

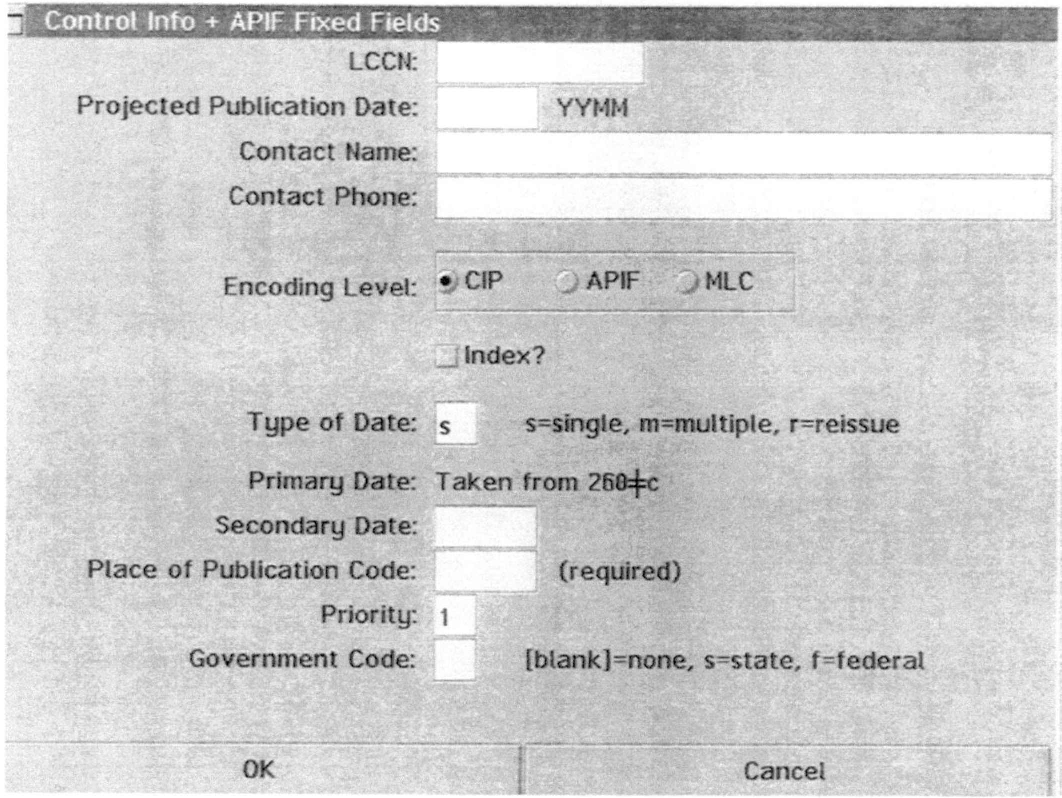
Control Info + APIF Fixed Fields
LCCN:
Projected Publication Date:
YYMM
Contact Name:
Contact Phone:
Encoding Level:
CIP
APIF
MLC
Index?
Type of Date:
s
s=single, m=multiple, r=reissue
Primary Date:
Taken from 260‡c
Secondary Date:
Place of Publication Code:
(required)
Priority:
1
Government Code:
[blank]=none, s=state, f=federal
OK
Cancel

FIGURE 7

Name Authority Creation Box : Sun, May 21 04:09

Ref Var Make NAR

┤ 10020§a§Vega Montoya, Jose Ignacio Avellaneda de la

┤ 670§ab§The conquerors of the new kingdom of ..., c1995:§CIP t.p. (Thomas Gomez, Jose Ignacio Avellaneda de la Vega Montoya) elements from particles so it may miscode a reference beginning with a particle.

The program created references from any element after the first element to the right of the comma. This resulted in an incorrect reference as highlighted above. The operator simply needs to highlight any unwanted reference and press the delete key. The program is not capable of distinguishing forenames from surnames, so it may occasionally generate bad references.

The operator can edit the text displayed in the NAR box. If a variant form of name is found in the electronic file, the operator can cite this form and create the reference structure needed. For example, if the name "Johnny Vega" is found in the preface, the operator can type this information into the 670, highlight the variant name, and then click on the "Var" button at the top of the screen. This operation will generate a new reference at the bottom of the box as seen in Figure 9.

If in turn a reference is also needed from this variant form, the operator will click on this variant reference as done above in the 100 field, and then would click on the "Ref" button, to generate all possible references from this entry automatically as well.

With this name authority more or less completed, the operator can click on the "Make NAR" button and the name authority record is sent to the LC name authority file.

## *AFTERWORD*

The Electronic CIP Experiment and *On the MARC* have shown that it is possible to create bibliographic records directly from electronic text. The manuscripts submitted for CIP cataloging are not intended for publication as electronic documents but rather as printed books. Nevertheless, this alternative to paper cataloging is proving to be efficient, accurate, and faster than traditional methods.

Other experiments involving Standard Generalized Markup Language (SGML) have demonstrated that bibliographic records can be created directly from electronic texts with little operator intervention. If a text were marked up to the MARC subfield level, a program could scan the text automatically and extract all of the data

FIGURE 8

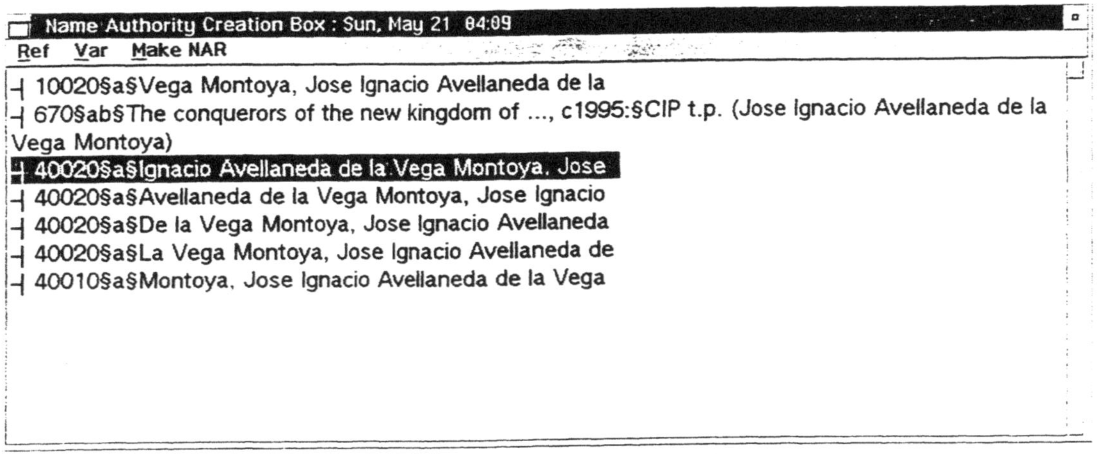
Name Authority Creation Box : Sun, May 21 04:09
Ref Var Make NAR
10020§a§Vega Montoya, Jose Ignacio Avellaneda de la
670§ab§The conquerors of the new kingdom of ..., c1995:§CIP t.p. (Jose Ignacio Avellaneda de la Vega Montoya)
40020§a§Ignacio Avellaneda de la Vega Montoya, Jose
40020§a§Avellaneda de la Vega Montoya, Jose Ignacio
40020§a§De la Vega Montoya, Jose Ignacio Avellaneda
40020§a§La Vega Montoya, Jose Ignacio Avellaneda de
40010§a§Montoya, Jose Ignacio Avellaneda de la Vega

FIGURE 9

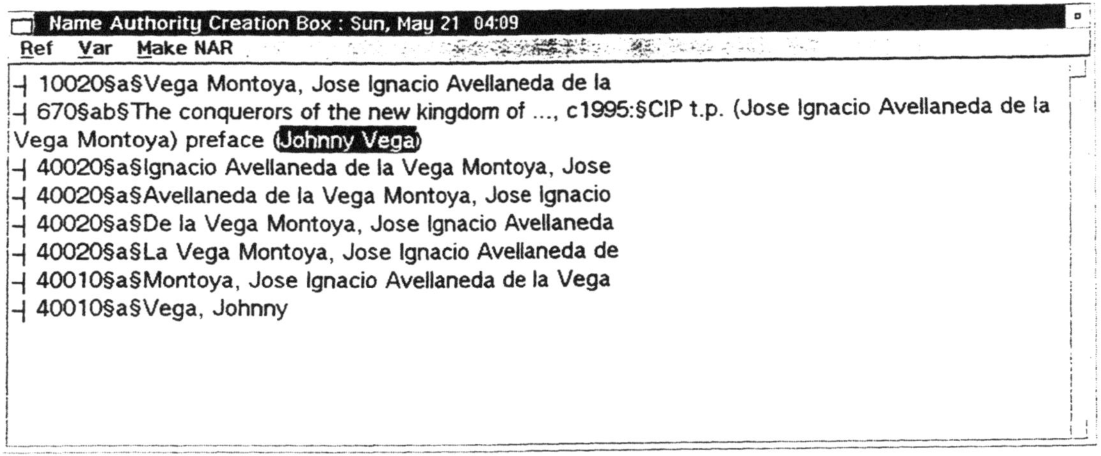
Name Authority Creation Box : Sun, May 21 04:09
Ref Var Make NAR
10020§a§Vega Montoya, Jose Ignacio Avellaneda de la
670§ab§The conquerors of the new kingdom of ..., c1995:§CIP t.p. (Jose Ignacio Avellaneda de la Vega Montoya) preface (Johnny Vega)
40020§a§Ignacio Avellaneda de la Vega Montoya, Jose
40020§a§Avellaneda de la Vega Montoya, Jose Ignacio
40020§a§De la Vega Montoya, Jose Ignacio Avellaneda
40020§a§La Vega Montoya, Jose Ignacio Avellaneda de
40010§a§Montoya, Jose Ignacio Avellaneda de la Vega
40010§a§Vega, Johnny

elements needed for the descriptive portion of the bibliographic record. However, in the absence of a single markup scheme, an SGML to MARC record conversion program would have to be modified for each flavor of SGML coding being used. It would therefore appear that only if the publishing community agreed to one coding scheme mapped to MARC subfields would this type of approach become feasible.

Finally, *On the MARC* is a home-grown, cataloger-produced product. It is the first of several utilities being developed as part of the LC Cataloging Directorate's Text Capture and Electronic Conversion (TCEC) efforts. The TCEC team consists of Richard Thaxter, Robert August, and David Williamson with special assistance from Howard Sanner. These utilities are add-on products designed to automate many aspects of the cataloging process. These products operate outside of the LC mainframe system but use the mainframe system to extract data (automated searches, data needed to start NARs) and to send data into the LC files (E-CIP records, computer generated NARs). *On the MARC* and the other TCEC applications represent LC's first steps toward the intelligent workstation.

The implications of these programs are significant for catalogers as well as the publishing community. With a program such as *On the MARC*, catalogers are freed from much of the rekeying of data that is instead transmitted electronically. From just one FTP'd file, the CIP cataloging record *and* the authority record can be derived. For descriptive catalogers in particular, the potential exists for them to devote almost their entire cataloging time to practicing and honing their professional judgment in determining the correct points of access, establishing and verifying headings, and creating authority records. For both descriptive and subject catalogers, automated searching speeds tasks, with *On the MARC* as the first step toward automatic authority verification. As a result, CIP cataloging records can be completed quickly and with diminished potential for simple typographical errors and omissions.

The advent of large numbers of digitized texts and images is an exciting time for the Cataloging Directorate at the Library of Congress. The challenges of cataloging digital materials and creating TCEC applications that are the building blocks of an intelligent cataloging workstation are enhancing professional facets of describing and classifying all types of materials. As a result of the large scale changes in the worlds of electronic texts and publishing, an environment flourishes at the Library of Congress in which many new learning experiences for catalogers and cataloging technicians have been created.

## AUTHOR NOTE

Beth Davis-Brown held public and technical services positions at academic and special libraries before coming to the Library of Congress as a subject cataloger in the Social Sciences Cataloging Division. Among other duties with the NDLP, she is working on finding aids and description of digital collections.

David Williamson's entire career at the Library has been in the Cataloging Directorate, and he currently holds a joint assignment to the Romance Languages Team, Social Sciences Cataloging Division and to the Regional and Cooperative Cataloging Division as a senior cooperative cataloger. David has always been involved in office automation projects at LC–instructing staff in several PC applications, developing software templates for various cataloging needs, providing graphics for presentations, and troubleshooting.

# Cataloging Internet Resources: The Convergence of Libraries and Internet Resources

Martin Dillon
Erik Jul

**SUMMARY.** This paper reviews issues related to the cataloging of Internet resources and considers short- and long-term directions for cataloging and the general provision of library services for remotely accessible, electronic information resources. The strengths and weakness of using a library catalog model to improve access to Internet resources are discussed and compared with a review of related efforts. Based on experience gained through two OCLC Internet cataloging projects, the authors recommend continued and vigorous application of library cataloging standards and methods for Internet resources with the expectation that catalogs, cataloging, and libraries in general will continue to evolve. *[Article copies available from The Haworth Document Delivery Service: 1-800-342-9678. E-mail address: getinfo@haworth.com]*

This paper reviews issues related to the cataloging of Internet resources and considers short- and long-term directions for cataloging and the general provision of library services for remotely acces-

---

Martin Dillon is Director of the Library Resources Management Division at OCLC. Erik Jul is Manager of the Custom Services at OCLC.

The authors gratefully acknowledge the grant support of the U.S. Department of Education, Office of Library Programs.

[Haworth co-indexing entry note]: "Cataloging Internet Resources: The Convergence of Libraries and Internet Resources." Dillon, Martin, and Erik Jul. Co-published simultaneously in *Cataloging & Classification Quarterly* (The Haworth Press, Inc.) Vol. 22, No. 3/4, 1996, pp. 197-238; and: *Electronic Resources: Selection and Bibliographic Control* (ed: Ling-yuh W. Pattie, and Bonnie Jean Cox) The Haworth Press, Inc., 1996, pp. 197-238. Single or multiple copies of this article are available from The Haworth Document Delivery Service [1-800-342-9678, 9:00 a.m. - 5:00 p.m. (EST). E-mail address: getinfo@haworth.com].

 

sible, electronic information resources. Section I provides an overview of the characteristics of Internet resources, their impact on cataloging, and the development of informal methods of network information discovery and retrieval to establish the broader environment in which libraries, catalogs, and catalogers now function. Section II examines the strengths and weaknesses of current cataloging standards and practices when applied to Internet resources and reviews related recent and current OCLC Internet cataloging projects. Section III surveys the impact of cataloging Internet resources on other library functions. Section IV presents conclusions; Section V proposes directions in which cataloging may fruitfully evolve, and next steps are suggested.

## *DEFINITION OF TERMS*

Throughout this paper, "Internet resources" is a convenient phrase that includes any electronic information resources accessible through a wide-area network. "Cataloging" refers to the creation of surrogate description and access records in accordance with formats, rules, and standards, including such functions as formal description, classification, subject analysis, and authority control.

## *PROBLEM STATEMENT*

The ability to discover, access, and use Internet resources has not kept pace with the explosive growth of these resources. A primary cause of this deficiency is the absence of a widespread application of library standards and practices to Internet resources which, for the most part, still lack the intellectual access provided by a typical library catalog.

In this paper, and in the projects carried out at OCLC that we will describe briefly below, we attempt to answer a simple question: can a library provide through its OPAC access to Internet resources that equals or exceeds the access it provides to the other information resources in its collection? Answering this question will occupy many of us for the next few years, and the answers will likely affect libraries and information professionals for years longer.

## *I. GENERAL CHARACTERISTICS OF INTERNET RESOURCES*

Information resources can be viewed from at least four distinct perspectives: (1) content, (2) format, (3) access, and (4) use. Examining each of these facets in the context of the Internet may help reveal characteristics that liken or distinguish Internet resources from other information resources and highlight which aspects of Internet resources can be addressed by existing library standards, methods, and systems, which could be accommodated by an extension of library systems, and which point toward new methods of organizing, accessing, and using information.

### *CONTENT*

Users seek traditional information objects such as books and articles because of their content, and this is no less true for Internet resources. Traditional library materials exist within a matrix of schemes that facilitate the expression and discovery of content: subject headings, classification, cumulative indexes, tables of contents, back-of-book indexes, and others. Internet resources also exist within a similar, though much less formal, milieu of subject access.

The methods of describing the content of Internet resources are closely related to the protocols and systems used for network information discovery. For example, at FTP sites (repositories of files accessible using the File Transfer Protocol), informal support tools–lists, directories, indexes, and README files, along with file and directory names of widely varying intelligibility and usefulness–may exist to describe the content of stored resources, but such methods of expressing information content suffer numerous deficiencies that diminish their usefulness.[1] The archie service is an example of how such names are used to provide access. It provides search access to an automatically collected index of file names at FTP sites, but access to content is still limited to information expressed in file names.[2]

Other Internet resources have adopted or invented rough-and-ready subject classification schemes. Usenet newsgroups, for example, are categorized using abbreviations such as .alt, .biz., .comp, .info, .misc, .rec, .soc, .talk, and others. These broad categories, in conjunction with a hierarchy of descriptive terms, form the actual newsgroup names, for example, rec.crafts.textiles.sewing. For each newsgroup, another document, the FAQ (Frequently Asked Questions), provides additional information. Actual newsgroup postings, however, are described only by the text in the subject line of the message header. Online information services such as DejaNews (http://www.dejanews.com) and The Open Text Web Index (http://opentext.uunet.ca:8080/omw.html) now provide keyword search access to a database of the full text of selected newsgroups, thus providing more direct access to the content of newsgroup messages.

At the University of Michigan School of Library and Information Studies, efforts to produce subject guides to Internet resources have led to the creation of the Clearinghouse for Subject-Oriented Internet Resource Guides (http://www.lib.umich.edu/chouse/chhome.html). Each subject guide, compiled by one or more editors, collates resources by broad subject disciplines and provides brief descriptions and hypertext links to the resources described. A search engine provides keyword access to the text of the subject guides.

The Dewey Decimal and Library of Congress classification schemes have also been used, more or less formally, to create searchable or browsable subject catalogs such as the Wolverhampton Web Library (http://www.scit.wlv.ac.uk/wwlib/newclass.html), Patrick's Catalog of Internet Resources (http://www.slac.stanford.edu/~clancey/dewey.html), the Dewey Decimal Hotlist (http://ivory.lm.com/~mundie/DDHC/DDH.html), the WWW Virtual Library (http://www.w3.org/hypertext/DataSources/bySubject/Overview.html), and OCLC NetFirst (http://www.oclc.org/netfirst). While these systems do employ classification systems to their benefit, they do not use or output MARC format records that could be exchanged among automated library systems. Continued experience with formal library catalogs will reveal the significance of that limitation.

Other methods have been developed to improve intellectual access to the content of Internet resources, and each distinguishes itself by its approach to network resource discovery. Some of the more important and popular systems: WAIS–full-text document indexing and iterative, ranked retrieval in a Z39.50-based client/server architecture; Gopher–access to hierarchical directory structures on remote machines; Veronica–automated collection and indexing of Gopher directory names; WWW–hyper-text links and transfer protocols; Harvest–distributed and shared information gathering and brokering; and, Yahoo–subject-oriented browsing and keyword searching.

Each of these systems has strengths and weaknesses, but only a few make full use of the subject analysis tools available in library science. Systems that have incorporated classification schemes vary widely in sophistication, and those using common library schemes lack other features that enhance subject access such as controlled vocabularies, uniform titles, and authority control for names. Ultimately, one fundamental question must be addressed: Can library methods and standards for subject access be used effectively to improve access to Internet resources? Because of the complexities of Internet resources and the networking environment, many of which are discussed elsewhere in this paper, more experience is needed before that question can be answered confidently.

## *FORMAT*

Until the advent of electronic information, information was recorded and transmitted using media that had form and shape. Computing, magnetic and optical storage, and wide-area networking technologies have created fundamentally new formats for information creation, storage, transmittal, display, and use. These new formats introduce problems for effective access. From the perspective of cataloging, the primary problem areas are (1) the ability for intellectually identical objects to exist in multiple formats, (2) the proliferation of format types, (3) the inherent mutability of electronic information, and (4) its replicability. Understanding each of these aspects will help clarify the implications for cataloging.

That identical content should exist in multiple formats is not a new cataloging problem. Books, for example, exist in hardback, paperback, large print, Braille, on tape, and in microform, and some of these manifestations require the use of supporting technologies such as a microform reader or cassette tape player. The problem of multiple formats is many times worsened in Internet resources because of the abundance of formal and quasi-formal standards: ASCII, PostScript, TeX, RTF, Adobe Acrobat, SGML, HTML, Word, Word Perfect, .gif, .tif, JPEG, MPEG, QuickTime, binary, and so on. How are these various file formats to be handled in a catalog record, and how are new formats to be accommodated as they are invented and gain ascendancy?

New formats also create fundamentally new object types. A Web page, for example, may consist of a short ASCII file containing text in HTML markup that, in turn, contains links to any combination of text, other Web pages, other types of servers, or image, sound, and video files. What, then, is the *format* of the Web page for cataloging purposes?

In a bibliographic record, Information about the format of a resource can be recorded in various 5XX fields such as 500, "General Note," 516, "Type of Computer File or Data Note," 520, "Summary, etc. Note." Figure 1 illustrates a variety of notes taken from bibliographic records for a wide variety of resources.

Even the few notes shown in Figure 1 reveal a wide variety of information formats that users and the systems they use must be able to interpret: text, marked-up text, plotter file, image, audio, and animation files. The ability for bibliographic records to capture and

FIGURE 1. Sample Notes Fields

| | |
|---|---|
| 500 | Text displays in color. Includes clickable map. |
| 516 | Electronic serial in ASCII format. |
| 516 | Electronic serial in ASCII, PostScript, and HTML formats. |
| 516 | Individual file in ASCII comma delimited format. |
| 516 | Conversion to TEI-conformant markup. |
| 516 | Test. |
| 516 | hypertext (electronic journal). |
| 516 | Main data file compressed. |
| 516 | Individual files in Wordperfect 5.1 format. |
| 520 | This report is a plotter-ready file in HPGL2 format. |
| 520 | Provides links to Internet resources . . . |
| 520 | . . . a multimedia hypertext environment consisting of linked test documents with graphics, animations and sounds. |
| 520 | . . . integrates clinical information with magnetic resonance (MR), x-ray tomography (CT) and nuclear medicine images. |
| 520 | This is a collection of movie clips . . . |
| 520 | . . . also has links to [. . .] departmental gophers. |

communicate this type of information is critical. Users must be able to identify, access, or obtain resources that are compatible with their computing environment.

A third characteristic of electronic information is its inherent mutability. Who has not enjoyed the changeability of a word-processing file? And who has not imagined what might happen to an electronic document once it has been made available on the Internet when, whether by accident or intent, data is changed in significant ways? While it is true that print materials are subject to mutilation, modification, or forgery, the skills and effort required to tamper with them exceed the capabilities of all but the most talented. With digital information, modification is generally a trivial act both for the author and for anyone with a copy. For traditional materials, matching a catalog record to the object described is nearly always sufficient for users to feel confident that the item obtained is authentic. For Internet resources this is no longer the case, and ensuring the authenticity of digital objects, therefore, is a critical issue. The impact of this fact on the use of Internet resources and on cataloging has not been determined.

Finally, digital objects can be replicated with great ease, a fact that potentially overcomes limitations of geography and space but introduces new considerations. Unlike physical materials, Internet resources can be available to multiple simultaneous users irrespective of their geographic location. If digital libraries, archives, or repositories are developed to ensure data integrity and access, then libraries do not need to maintain a local copy of every desired Internet resource. Today, resources are often "mirrored"; identical copies are maintained at multiple sites to achieve greater security through redundancy and to facilitate access by decreasing the network distance between a user and a given resource. What is the relationship between a bibliographic record and these mirror sites, and how does the record communicate to users which site might be preferred?

## *ACCESS*

Access may be viewed in at least two ways: access to information-bearing objects and access to their contents. Regardless of how orderly a collection of objects may be, each having benefited from formal description, classification, authority control, and subject analysis, access to individual objects is still reliant upon various aids that exist apart from the objects themselves. Ultimately, in a physical world, each object must rest in its place–both absolutely and, in a classified collection, relatively with respect to similar objects–and the catalog must direct users to that place. In a network environment, absolute location and collocation assume different characteristics. The place of storing a resource can be remote from the place of accessing it, and the physical collocation of resources is not necessary because they can be grouped on the fly as a result of searching or browsing irrespective of their actual storage locations.

For traditional materials, various cues in a catalog record may direct users to look for materials in the fiction section, for example, or the paperback section, the reserve shelf, or in a particular part of the library based on the shelving of classified materials. Such location indicators are relative; that is, they have meaning relative to some larger scheme such as the physical layout of a particular library or the intellectual ordering of a classifying scheme. They do not direct patrons to materials using absolute geospatial coordinates. To be accessible in a network environment, an object must be addressable. The address often comprises the IP (Internet Protocol) address of a host computer (for example, ftp.rsch.oclc.org) and, when applicable, the logical and physical location of the file or files that comprise the object (for example, /pub/internet_cataloging_project/manual.txt). Such an address pinpoints the location of a particular resource, and the ability to describe and exchange location information uniformly in these terms greatly facilitates access.

Both the Internet Engineering Task Force (IETF) Uniform Resource Locator (URL) scheme[3] and the USMARC field 856, "Electronic Location and Access," facilitate the encoding of Internet resource addresses.[4] By their nature, both schemes require absolute accuracy in the formulation of addresses because they are intended to be parsed and interpreted by machines. Slight errors in formulation or transcription render the address useless. Such direct addressing also fails if any element in the address is changed, and experience has demonstrated that this is not infrequent. File names, directory names or their structure, and machine addresses are all subject to change. Developing a method of addressing that remains viable despite changes in file names, directory names, or machine addresses is recognized by both the networking and library communities as an essential next step.

Having the address of an Internet resource, however, is not tantamount to access. A highly sophisticated and, for the average user, complicated system of computers, software applications, and network connections must be in place to access Internet resources. To be effective in the Internet world, the addressing function of library catalogs must enable users to locate and then directly access the Internet resources of interest. If immediate access is not possible or desired, then the catalog must provide the user with sufficient information to enable connection to selected resources at a later time or from another computer location. Cataloging records can record this type of information in various fields such as the 538 field, "System Requirements." Figure 2 shows examples taken from bibliographic records for a wide variety of Internet resources; each example is from a different record.

The information provided in these examples spans a wide range, from local requirements (PC, MAC, modem), to network connectivity (Internet), to protocol (electronic mail, FTP, gopher), to software application (Web browser). What cannot be determined from this list is whether such information is sufficient and useful.

Complexities deriving from the type of resource, its format, and any requisite ancillary computing applications, authorizations, passwords, or fees must be reflected in the catalog record, and the challenge of meeting those requirements exceeds the current capa-

FIGURE 2. Sample System Requirements Notes

| | |
|---|---|
| 538 | System requirements: PC; World Wide Web access. |
| 538 | Mode of access: World Wide Web. |
| 538 | Mode of access: Internet via the World Wide Web. |
| 538 | Mode of access: Internet resource via e-mail . . . |
| 538 | Mode of access: Internet. |
| 538 | Mode of access: Internet via gopher. |
| 538 | Mode of access: Electronic mail, FTP, gopher. |
| 538 | System requirements: PC with modem. |
| 538 | System requirements: PC with Web browser. |
| 538 | System requirements: PC or MAC with modem. |
| 538 | Mode of access: Gopher |

bilities of bibliographic description. The role and capability of catalog records in recording and expressing these complexities is not yet fully explored. Applying existing models repeatedly to an array of Internet resources will provide some answers to this uncertainty.

## *USE*

Content, format, and access all culminate in use, and libraries have traditionally provided additional resources that facilitate the use of materials in their collections such as tables, fiche readers, photocopiers, and computers. Using Internet resources is an increasingly complex proposition. Determining the fitness for use of any particular Internet resource is considerably more difficult than differentiating between a print and a microform version, for example, or between an English-language translation and a foreign-language original. *Fitness for use* is a composite measure of a resource's content, format, and manner of access *in conjunction with* a user's hardware, software and network environment, and is different from a user's actual *ability to use* any given resource, which is dependent upon training, experience, or pluck. Expressing in a bibliographic record how a particular Internet resource matches this matrix of needs is challenging. Such information may be recorded in various fields such as 500, "General Note," 516, "Type of Computer File or Data Note," or 520, "Summary, Etc. Note" (Figure 1). Using these fields for a wide variety of Internet resources will help determine the adequacy of this approach.

## *CONCLUSION*

Internet resources share fundamental characteristics with all information objects, and these characteristics influence the form and function of the systems that help manage physical and intellectual access. Digital and wide-area networking technologies create new problems and complexities of describing the content, format, manner of access, and use. How well bibliographic records can provide this essential information, and how cataloging and cataloging systems should evolve, will become clearer with experience.

## *TYPES OF INTERNET RESOURCES*

Historically, library cataloging has evolved along with information technologies, changing to accommodate new information formats as they emerge. The continued evolution of cataloging is not only natural in response to advances in digital and wide-area networking technologies, it is essential. Unlike the introduction of information technologies such as sound recordings, still and moving images, microforms, or compact discs, digital and networking technologies pose a host of new opportunities and problems for libraries. New types of information objects are emerging, and the rate with which new object types are introduced is quickening. Even a brief list such as the one in Table 1 shows the great diversity among Internet resources. Examining specific examples of Internet resources will provide some insight into the applicability of library methods and standards and indicate directions for further investigation or change.

Internet resources can be categorized as discrete files, databases, and servers, but not without some ambiguity. This general classification provides a framework for considering the various characteristics of Internet resources, which vary widely depending on the type of resource, and the effect of these characteristics on content, format, access, and use–key components of bibliographic description and access records.

TABLE 1. Internet Resource Types

| | | | |
|---|---|---|---|
| Audio file | Electronic journal | FTP site | Survey data |
| Bibliographic data | Electronic text | Graphic/image file | Video file |
| Census data | Electronic catalog | Gopher site | WWW site |
| Computer program | Electronic discussion group | Library catalog | |
| Database | Electronic newspaper | News group | |
| Electronic document | email discussion group | Numeric data | |

## *DISCRETE FILES*

Perhaps the Internet resource most analogous to traditional library material is the unitary, discrete text file. The bibliographic completeness of text files, in the sense of bearing information such as titles, authors, publishers, dates, or standard numbers, varies widely. Many text files contain little or no descriptive information, a troublesome fact that was borne out in a 1992 OCLC cataloging experiment.[5] Table 2 shows the frequency with the fields title, author, and publisher occurred in bibliographic records for a set of 300 discrete files obtained from the Internet. Half of the test collection comprised text files of all types. Title statements occurred frequently, although not universally, chiefly because catalogers are instructed to provide titles even when one cannot be determined from the chief source of information; a 245 field *must* appear in valid bibliographic records. That not all records contained 245 fields is attributed to technical difficulties that prevented catalogers from decompressing, decoding, or decrypting certain test files. Publication data, recorded in field 260, occurred less frequently, and author information occurred in a mere 18% of test records. The presence of these fields, however, does not indicate their completeness.

Some Internet text files, however, model the conventions of traditional book publishing and provide more complete descriptive information. Such wide variation in the amount of traditional bibliographic information present in electronic text files reflects a publishing continuum from casual and transient to formal and permanent. Materials at the low end of the continuum (casual, transient, incomplete bibliographic information) are not likely candidates for full cataloging. Resources at the high end of the continuum (formal, permanent, full bibliographic description) fall easily within the cat-

TABLE 2. Frequency of Title, Author, and Publisher Fields

| *Field* | **Name** | **% of Records** |
|---|---|---|
| 245 | Title Statement | 93 |
| 260 | Imprint | 73 |
| 100 | Main Entry Heading, Personal Name | 18 |

aloging model. The middle ground, even as with print materials, is more problematic, and cataloging these resources will certainly be governed by the needs and interests of libraries and their users and the relative value imputed to any given resource. The electronic nature of these resources, however, regardless of the manner of publication or the availability of bibliographic information, introduces new problems.

A significant number of discrete files accessible via the Internet are not text files. Earlier OCLC investigations found that 10% of the files available on 1,044 FTP sites could be automatically categorized as text files; 43% were computer source or system code and the remainder were an assortment of other digital file types such as data files, image files, or executable code.[6] That this information exists in discrete files does not simplify the cataloging process. The content, format, access methods, and use of these various file types present significant problems. Files may require decoding and decompression before they can be used, and they may need to be merged with other files before use, as when a large binary file is stored in multiple parts to facilitate storage or transport across the network. Files may require specific helper applications–or specific *versions* of helper applications–such as a viewer for images, an audio tool for playing sound files, or a spreadsheet or database program for viewing and manipulating data. The list of complexities goes on, and, to be most fully descriptive and useful, bibliographic records need to express sufficient information so that users can select from among numerous resources those that meet their requirements. Determining what information is salient and how to express it succinctly is a cataloging challenge.

Serial publications can be problematic in the print world, and they are no less so in the digital world. Serials comprise discrete units–articles, issues, volumes–but these components may not exist in electronic journals. Articles can be published independently or with other articles comprising an issue. Access can be through FTP, email, Gopher, WWW, proprietary systems or other methods, and, as always, files exist in various formats or require specific helper applications.

The journal, *Teaching English as a Second or Foreign Language: An Electronic Journal* (ISSN 1072-4303, OCLC #28945546) is typical of many e-journals. It is available via a Gopher site or Web home page, which is, in effect, what is cataloged. The Web version displays the journal's banner and lists available volumes and issues. At this point, the user has little information concerning the contents of the journal. Each issue provides a table of contents with links to individual articles. This method of article-level access is inadequate to begin with and fails rapidly as the list of volumes and issues lengthens.

Traditional library catalogs do not provide article-level access to serial publications. The emergence and growth of abstracting, indexing, and online information industries have been driven by the need for access to content not provided by catalogs. In a world of networked electronic resources, providing a bibliographic record for a journal title would certainly enhance the ability for users to discover it, but such records do not enhance access to the journal's content. It is unclear how best to exploit the capabilities of digital resources and wide-area networks to provide improved access to journal content, and the role of surrogate records and the cataloging model in future solutions deserves further investigation.

## *DATABASES*

Datasets can exist as discrete files, but *databases* are conventionally thought of as comprising both the data files and the database management systems that provide users the capability to access, obtain, or manipulate the data. Certainly, most large databases are intended to be *used*, not *acquired* as in the case of discrete files.

Bibliographic records must express myriad details concerning databases such as content (subject), format (e.g., text, image), manner of access, years of coverage, frequency of updating, functional capabilities of the database system, restrictions on use, and relation to other data. The following examples illustrate free-text descriptions that can be included in bibliographic records; examples were recorded in field 520, "Summary Note":

- *Monthly Energy Review (OCLC #31171632)*
  Contains data on energy production, consumption, stocks, prices, imports, and exports. Data are at the national level and

are monthly for up to 3 years for most series. Annual data are given back to 1973 for most series.

- *HIV Database (OCLC #32532680)*
  Human Retrovirus and AIDS Database collects, curates, analyzes, and publishes genetic sequences of the immunodeficiency virus (HIV) and related species.
- *The English Poetry Full-Text Database (OCLC #32714917)*
  This is a machine-readable full-text database encompassing the works of 1,350 poets from the Anglo-Saxon period to the end of the 19th century. The listed poets are found in: *The New Cambridge Bibliography of English Literature.*

Such notes in conjunction with other descriptive fields allow for rich description, and the continued application of cataloging standards to databases available via the Internet will provide the means to assess the adequacy of existing methods.

## *SERVERS*

This category is ambiguous. Gopher servers, for example, exhibit characteristics similar to a multipart work: they provide a hierarchical structure to facilitate access to a range of information, parts of which exist as complete entities. Cataloging a Gopher site, in effect, cataloging the main menu, can provide information that will help users discover and access the Gopher resource, but depending on the depth and breadth of information provided on a Gopher server at any particular site, providing a description of the contents of the site is problematic. The menus may function like a table of contents, but high-level menus may not be very expressive of the actual lower-level resources, and lower-level menus may be too numerous to include in a bibliographic record.

For Gophers dedicated to a limited, single purpose, such as the "Fish Biodiversity Gopher" (gopher://fowler.acnatsci.org:70/1, OCLC #32829527), high-level bibliographic access may be sufficient. Larger Gopher sites, such as the Bureau of Transportation Statistics (BTS) (gopher://gopher.bts.gov, OCLC #32399584), however, may contain documents that are themselves candidates for bibliographic description. In this example, the BTS Gopher contains the *Traffic Safety Facts Annual Report*, the bibliographic record for which would look and act quite differently from the record for the BTS Gopher. Similarly, the Congressional Quarterly Gopher (gopher://gopher.cqalert.com, OCLC #30912362) in an amalgam of information resources, including the current issue of *CQ Weekly Report*. The gopher is both more and less than the *CQ Weekly Report* itself; more, because ancillary information is provided; less, because only the current issue is available along with the full text of previous feature articles. Again, a bibliographic record for the Gopher would appear and function differently from a record for the serial *CQ Weekly Report*.

Some Gophers serve as information kiosks or campuswide information systems (CWIS) where content and function are closely aligned. The Gopher at the University of Milwaukee-Wisconsin (gopher://alpha1.csd.uwm.edu, OCLC #32908140) is a typical example. The Gopher provides access to information about the staff, programs, and services of the university. There are no serial publications lurking at lower levels of the Gopher menu structure, no technical reports awaiting description. Creating a catalog record for entries below the main menu seems unnecessary. Browsing or locally facilitated searching may be the best methods of guiding users to specific information resources accessible through the Gopher, a task for which the bibliographic record is less well suited.

These examples illustrate just a few of the difficulties that Internet resources can pose to catalogers: describing the content of hierarchically arranged resources is problematic; servers may be available through multiple modes of access, such as Gopher and WWW; and these modes of access may present different views of the data, provide access to more or less information, and provide different functionalities. The ability to express these complexities in bibliographic records warrants continued exploration.

## *CONCLUSION*

Digital technologies and wide-area networking enable the creation of new types of information resources whose characteristics can vary greatly. Regardless of the nature of the information resource, the need to express its content, describe its format, facilitate its access, and enable its use remains constant. Bibliographic records and the formats, rules, and methods of cataloging and classification provide a rich and well understood means of capturing and providing subsequent access to this type of information, and it should be expected that cataloging norms and the technologies that facilitate cataloging will continue to evolve to meet the new demands of information discovery.

## *SURVEY OF INTERNET DISCOVERY AND RETRIEVAL TOOLS*

Network information discovery and retrieval tools as currently conceived have been designed to provide users with a means for identifying, locating, and accessing Internet resources, and in many respects function as substitutes for formal cataloging systems. Understanding the capabilities, potentialities, and limitations of such systems will enable a more critical re-examination of cataloging systems.

The earliest tools for network information discovery and retrieval–lists of resources created by human compilers–were an improvement over nothing at all, and considerable, usually voluntary, effort went into their creation and maintenance. These earliest efforts suffered under their own weight and the burdens associated with collecting, verifying, editing, and producing useful lists. Several lists remain, most notably the Association of Research Libraries' publication, *Directory of Electronic Journals, Newsletters, and Academic Discussion Lists*, now in its fifth edition.[7]

## *ARCHIE*

Compiling and updating lists typically relies on human labor and does not exploit computing or network technologies for gathering information. Such exploitation arrived on the scene with the invention of archie, a service directed at providing improved access to resources available via FTP.[8] Archie comprises a searchable database of directory listings that have been obtained and indexed automatically. The archie database is updated by polling each publicly accessible FTP site periodically. Users can search for specific file names using exact matching techniques or regular expressions, but search precision is low because file names express limited information at best and, at worst, may bear no generally intelligible relation to the contents of associated files.

## *WAIS*

The WAIS Wide-Area Information Server introduced a client/server model that enables local system administrators to store textual information in WAIS servers.[9] The text objects are indexed, and the entire corpus of the database is searchable in this way. Retrieval is based upon weighted search results, and users can search iteratively, modifying searches based on previous results. Users must direct searches to specified servers, however, and determining which servers are likely to contain relevant information is difficult. A directory of servers intended to assist users in the selection of candidate databases suffers from its own imprecision, and the problem is worsened as the number of WAIS servers grows.

## *GOPHER*

Gopher systems and related protocols exploit hierarchical directory structures as a means of organizing, browsing, and accessing Internet resources.[10] The ease of mounting Gopher servers and maintaining local collections led to the rapid and widespread adoption of this solution. Browsing directories may be more intuitive than searching archie or WAIS servers, especially if the directory structure is descriptive and well organized. Some gopher sites adopt classification schemes as a method of organizing a hierarchy of menus. Before users can explore a Gopher's directory structure, however, they must learn which Gophers are likely to contain relevant information and their location, the difficulty of which often leaves users feeling as though they were burrowing about in some dark information space. Browsing itself, as a means of accessing information, can be inefficient and often fails completely when directory structures are complex.

## *VERONICA*

Veronica was invented to couple searching capabilities with Gopher hierarchical directories by building a searchable database of all Gopher directory names.[11,12,13] The weakness of this approach lies not in the concept so much as the practical reality that too many Gopher directory names provide too little useful information to conduct a precise search.

## *HARVEST*

More recent innovations such as Harvest are exploring sophisticated methods of sharing index information automatically gathered from "information brokers."[14] While tests prove the merits of this model in terms of the efficient use of storage and bandwidth, Harvest has not realized rapid and widespread adoption, and its real contributions to network information discovery have not been fully explored.

## *WORLD-WIDE WEB*

The introduction of the Hyper-Text Transfer Protocol (HTTP), the Hyper-Text Markup Language (HTML), and the development of graphical browser interfaces such as Mosaic and NetScape have led to the most recent Internet phenomenon, the World-Wide Web. Hyperlinked navigation is the key to the Web's success, along with the integration of tools for displaying text, graphics, audio, and video. Navigation (read "surfing" for those who think it is fun and "endless browsing" for those who have already spent a long time finding nothing) is easily accomplished by traversing embedded links within or among resources. Discovering the nature and whereabouts of Web resources is the province of yet another emerging industry, directories such as Yahoo, and InfoSeek. These directories, which couple browsing and searching capabilities, thus enabling users to discover Web resources of potential interest, are, in effect, the Web's version of archie. Much information about Web sites is gathered automatically or by human "net surfers" and transformed into a searchable, indexed database. In a continuing effort to differentiate themselves, directory services are now variously incorporating professionally prepared abstracts, rating systems, subject headings, classification information, and improved searching capabilities. The OCLC NetFirst service, for example, provides MARC-fielded records (although not full MARC-format records) that include traditional bibliographic data, professionally prepared abstracts, subject headings, Dewey classification numbers, and hot links to remote resources coupled with a powerful search engine that exploits the capabilities of fielded searches (http://www.oclc.org/netfirst).

A review of the characteristics of these various tools over against a library model may be useful (Table 3).

## *CONCLUSION*

The obvious need to discover, locate, and access Internet resources has prompted considerable innovative development, and each succeeding methodology has added to the array of tools available to Internet users and to the pool of knowledge and experience related to networked information discovery and retrieval. None of the systems described, however, fully exploits cataloging methods and standards, and none at this writing could be considered a substitute for a library catalog. Full-text, keyword searching has not proved to be a replacement for fielded searches of structured rec-

TABLE 3. Comparative Features of Resource Discovery and Retrieval Tools

| System | Search | Browse | Classification | Subject Analysis | Authority Control |
|---|---|---|---|---|---|
| Library Catalog | Yes | Yes | Yes | Yes | Yes |
| archie | Yes | No | No | No | No |
| WAIS | Yes | No | No | Sparse, uncontrolled | No |
| Gopher | No | Yes | Possible | No | No |
| Veronica | Yes | No | No | No | No |
| WWW | No | Yes | No | No | No |
| Yahoo | Yes | Yes | Yes | No | No |
| NetFirst | Yes | Yes | Yes | Yes | No |

ords, and no index has yet supplanted the catalog/surrogate record architecture.[15] Natural-language processing and iterative, weighted searching techniques do not make up for controlled vocabulary and authority control, and browsing, while highly desirable in some instances, is not a substitute for search precision. Current automated information gathering schemes have great promise but cannot as yet create a true bibliographic record equivalent.

Our view is that it is appropriate to apply the library catalog model to Internet resources and to continue to do so on a widespread basis until substitutes are provided that are demonstrably adequate. This approach will realize the immediate benefits of extending library services to selected Internet resources. Moreover, additional experience in the application of cataloging rules and standards will continue to bring problematic areas to light and ensure that the evolution of cataloging, library systems, and libraries in general will be based on empirical data.

## *II. CATALOGING INTERNET RESOURCES*

The preceding discussion reviews pertinent characteristics of Internet resources and the methods and systems that are being used in lieu of cataloging. This section discusses the application of formal cataloging methods to Internet resources and experiences gained through two OCLC projects.

### *OCLC INTERNET CATALOGING PROJECTS*

The 1991/92 OCLC Internet Resources project[16] and the 1994-96 OCLC Internet Cataloging project (http://www.oclc.org/oclc.man/catcall.htm), both of which were funded in part by grants from the U.S. Department of Education, Office of Library Programs, demonstrate the applicability of the USMARC format and AACR2 cataloging rules to the creation of description and access records for Internet resources. Although the results of a 1992 cataloging experiment indicated that catalogers had some difficulty determining basic information from a collection of test files, these difficulties were attributed to several factors, including (1) lack of experience cataloging computer files on the part of some participants, (2) lack of experience cataloging serials on the part of some participants, (3) unfamiliarity with or failure to adhere to the experiment's guidelines, and (4) technical problems.[17] The general conclusion of the experiment was that no deficiencies existed in either the USMARC format or the AACR2 cataloging rules that were significant enough to prohibit cataloging Internet resources, and the project's recommendations at that time were to:

1. Implement the creation of machine-readable cataloging records (MARC) for remotely accessible electronic information objects.
2. Monitor the use and effectiveness of records created for providing description and access information.
3. Extend cataloging rules and formats to include interactive network systems and services.

Despite the apparent suitability of cataloging methods, one glaring need remained: the ability to link bibliographic records directly with the remote resources they describe. In response to this need, OCLC and the Library of Congress jointly sponsored MARBI proposal 93-4, *Changes to the USMARC Bibliographic Format (Computer Files) to Accommodate Online Information Resource.*[18] This proposal included the recommendation to create a new MARC field, 856, "Electronic Location and Access." The 856 field expresses in bibliographic format what can now also be expressed in a URL, which itself was under development at about the same time by a Working Group of the Internet Engineering Task Force. The 856 field, however, accommodates the explicit encoding of additional electronic location and access information that cannot be expressed in a URL such as, for example, information related to dial-access, passwords, and logon instructions. The 856 field was approved by MARBI, implemented in the OCLC database, and is now being included in bibliographic records in the OCLC Online Union Catalog and local library catalogs.

Several recommendations in proposal 93-4 that required changes to AACR2 rules were not accepted. It was recommended that the list of descriptive terms available for use in field 256, "File Characteristics," namely, "computer data," "computer program," and "computer data and program," be expanded to enable fuller description of Internet resources. Currently, catalogers are expressing additional identifying vocabulary in a variety of 5XX note fields. Changes to the 256 field may still be warranted, and it is hoped that the broader experience gained through the current (1994-96) OCLC Internet Cataloging project will provide greater insight.

## *IMPLEMENTATION*

MARBI's action on the 856 field set the stage for new era in cataloging, but implementing the recommendations of the Internet Resources project on a large scale awaited the current (1994-96) Internet Cataloging project, "Building a Catalog of Internet Resources." At this writing, more than 3,000 bibliographic records for Internet resources have been created and contributed to the OCLC Online Union Catalog by more than 200 libraries worldwide. Records contributed by project participants must be in MARC format, comply with AACR2 cataloging rules, and contain one or more 856 fields as appropriate. To support the cataloging effort, OCLC published a manual of cataloging guidelines, which draws upon experience gained in the earlier OCLC project, the subsequent actions of MARBI, and a wider review by the cataloging community.[19] The records are the basis for the InterCat Catalog, which serves as a functional catalog of Internet resources, a testbed for experimentation, and a source of data for further research to assess the strengths and weaknesses of MARC/AACR2 cataloging for Internet resources.

The InterCat Catalog was implemented using OCLC SiteSearch and WebZ software, and is accessible throughout the project, ending March 31, 1996, without cost or special authorization to all Internet users at http://www.oclc.org:6990. Accessing the catalog requires an HTML form-compliant Web browser such as Mosaic or NetScape. The InterCat Catalog provides a full-featured search engine capable of simple or complex Boolean searches (AND, OR, NOT) with nested parentheses, right truncation, and wild card searches. Users can search or browse (view a list of index terms), and can direct searches to specific indexes for greater precision (basic, subject words, subject phrases, author, title words, title phrases, uniform titles, publisher, notes, electronic access, and OCLC number).

Search results are returned as brief records that display title, publication, and electronic access information. Clicking on a brief record displays a full record, which can be viewed in a labeled or MARC format. In both display formats, the 856 field is "hot," and clicking on it connects the user to the remote resource described in the record. Because all records in the InterCat Catalog are in MARC/AACR2 format, they are suitable for loading into local, regional, and national databases. Thus, the InterCat Catalog and the database of bibliographic records brings to Internet resources the power of fielded searching, the benefits of subject analysis, authority control, and other value-adding features of cataloging, and the point-and-click ease of accessing Internet resources, and it implements the library model for providing access to these resources.

## *THE 856 FIELD*

Familiarity with the characteristics of the 856 field will come with greater experience. An initial goal of the Internet Cataloging project was to demonstrate the capability of accessing Internet resources from a catalog. Since the inception of the project, several local systems vendors have announced or introduced the capability to access, whether locally or remotely, a local library catalog using a Web browser, search the integrated resources of the library's catalog, including records for Internet resources, and connect directly to the remote resource. This is exactly what was envisioned several years ago.

The 856 field shares a deficiency with the URL, however: each 856 (it is a repeatable field within records) points to exactly one network location. In the best of worlds, the resource described in the associated bibliographic record resides at the address in the 856 field, but this is a fragile relationship liable to a host of problems. Files or directories can be renamed or moved, host addresses or the mode of access can change, and host or intervening network computers are subject to failure. Any one of these possibilities breaks the connection between the bibliographic record and the remote resource, a fact many would argue is sufficient cause not to embed 856 fields (or URLs) in bibliographic records. Without any change to the status quo, it is hard to counter that position, and clearly the current situation is deficient. The problem persists, however, only if the world doesn't change.

The OCLC Internet Cataloging project considered the need to gain significant experience with the implementation and performance characteristics of the 856 field essential and worthwhile despite its inherent risks and limitations. All records created in association with the project, therefore, are required to contain an 856 field. Apart from providing access to the cataloged items through the InterCat Catalog, the 856 fields form a pool of data for further analysis.

Preliminary analyses of the 856 fields do reveal a number of predictable problems:

1. The field is coded incorrectly
2. The field lacks required data
3. The field contains typographical errors
4. The resource has moved
5. The address of the host computer has changed
6. The file/directory names do not match
7. The remote server restricts access to authorized users
8. The remote host was down
9. There was a transient network failure

Problems 1-3 are human errors, and problems 1 and 2 may be explained, at least in part, to inexperience. Problems 4-6 relate directly to the correspondence between the bibliographic record and the remote resource in the absence of cataloging errors. Such changes are beyond the control of the cataloger, as are problems 7-9. Problem 7 is not really a problem; limited access to certain resources is to be expected. In these cases, for unauthorized users the bibliographic record can and should provide additional contact information or instructions as appropriate. Problems 8 and 9 are beyond the control of both the cataloger and perhaps the resource provider as well. Resources that are cataloged are no more susceptible to these problems than any other Internet resource. Closer analyses of error reports related to the failure of 856 fields may reveal other types of errors and will show the frequency distribution of errors across the error types. Such analysis is just beginning at the time of this writing.

## CONCLUSION

The two OCLC projects described have sought to investigate systematically the problems and opportunities associated with cataloging Internet resources. As a proof-of-concept, the InterCat Catalog demonstrates that the standard practices of library science can be applied to Internet resources to good effect, and the newly implemented 856 field is an important first step in changing the relationship between bibliographic records and the items they describe.

At the time of this writing, findings from the 1994-96 project are still being collected and analyzed, and more will surely be learned through continued experience. Much is also yet to be learned of the impact of cataloging Internet resources on the workflow, staffing requirements, and training needs of individual libraries, and most libraries are only beginning to integrate bibliographic records for Internet resources into local catalogs or provide remote access from the catalog record.

Despite the benefits of cataloging Internet resources and the apparent suitability of MARC formats and AACR2 cataloging rules, weaknesses in the system are apparent, chief of which is the need to make more robust the access link between bibliographic records and Internet resources. At this juncture, however, gaining widespread experience and documenting problems encountered are preferable to inaction or premature acquiescence in the face of unproved alternatives to cataloging.

## III. CATALOGS AND COLLECTIONS

We would like now to consider other implications of cataloging Internet resources. It is a fundamental role of a library to provide a record of materials in its collection. For Internet resources, this basic library function is changing. The concept of "collection" is expanding to include materials owned *and* accessed by the library and its users, whether such resources are stored locally or at a remote site. Conceptually, libraries' boundaries are changing, and the role of cataloging is changing commensurably.

It is a common view today that library catalogs should present an integrated access point to the world of information. Such integration can be achieved in part by cataloging Internet resources and including the resultant records in local catalogs. Users approaching a library catalog that includes records for Internet resources will be able to cast their query across a much broader information space. Moreover, the system could return to users an integrated array of potentially relevant resources regardless of their format or manner of access, thus overcoming the current segregation of Internet resources to alternative finding schemes. Records for books, Web sites, or other Internet resources could be presented side by side. Finally, having located a desirable Internet resource, users could connect directly from the library catalog to the described resource.

Cataloging is the foundation for extending bibliographic access to Internet resources, but cataloging itself is only one function among the whole of library services. The following sections examine briefly the implications of cataloging Internet resources on other library functions.

## *REFERENCE*

Reference services are a mainstay of library operations whether references are obtained through the library catalog, through traditional reference sources specifically produced and arranged to facilitate quick access to information, or through the mediation of a reference librarian. Increasingly, the content, quality, and functionality of Internet resources warrant their selected inclusion in libraries' reference tools. To state the obvious, efficient access to Internet resources is essential and not to be left to surfing, casual lists, or even the hotlist or bookmark facilities of Web browsers, which themselves become unwieldy as they lengthen. Integrating bibliographic records for reference resources within the local catalog is likely to provide improved access for reference librarian and user alike.

## *SELECTING*

Libraries have never collected everything. Part of a library's value, in fact, derives from the informed selection of materials known or thought to be of interest and relevance to the library's service community, and applying selection criteria to Internet resources is no less reasonable than selecting among resources in other formats. Participants in the OCLC Internet Cataloging project are asked to exercise existing selection policies and procedures to determine their adequacy for Internet resources. Broad experience will quickly point out how well selection policies function and whether they may need to be revised or instituted anew, but evidence from other quarters already suggests that "the principles and practices of selection, when adapted coherently and systematically for networked information, amply serve to integrate this emerging electronic milieu into collection development strategies."[20]

## *ACQUIRING*

Libraries may never acquire most Internet resources in any traditional sense. Access is the key, and access may be free or for fee. Libraries that buy access to commercial database services or use document delivery are already familiar, if not completely comfortable, with the fact that their collections are a composite of locally owned and remotely accessible resources. Increasingly, libraries want to record in their local catalogs the full complement of services and information sources available to users–databases, journals available by subscription to full-text services, and Internet resources.

## *HOLDINGS*

Acquisition is tantamount to holdings in the world of physical objects, but this concept is recast in the world of Internet resources.

In the OCLC Online Union Catalog, "holdings" means that a library has used a bibliographic record for cataloging purposes, with the extended implication that the cataloging library also owns the item described in the record. Attaching holdings to records in a union catalog facilitates resource sharing by making known the collection of one library to potential borrowers, but Internet resources do not need to be borrowed, they need to be accessed. Nevertheless, if a library other than the cataloging library wants to represent a given resource in its local catalog, it is beneficial to preserve an environment of cooperative cataloging so that quality bibliographic records can be available to the library community. Attaching a holdings symbol may serve to indicate that the library provides access to the resource through its catalog, but it is unclear whether such information would be useful to other libraries that are themselves seeking to identify and select Internet resources. Automated record updating systems could take advantage of holdings symbols by propagating changes in records to all libraries with attached holdings. Answers to the question of holdings are likely to come with experience.

## *STORING*

Like three-dimensional, information-bearing objects, Internet resources require space, but their requirements are somewhat different. The "bookshelves" of Internet resources are the 6.6 million host computers that serve them up (Internet Domain Survey 1995, http://www.nw.com/WWW/report.html), and it is probably fair to say that these electronic bookshelves receive widely varying levels of administrative care and oversight. Plans and procedures for routine backup and data recovery and safeguards against catastrophic loss may not be in place or be supported by sufficient resources.

Libraries do not need to become data centers; such plants and the expertise to manage them already exist, but libraries are likely to continue developing new, synergistic relationships with computing centers. Such links are essential as society assumes the new challenge of collecting, storing, and providing intellectual access to the human record as committed to electronic media.

## ACCESSING

Much of this discussion has been on facilitating access to electronic resources. Both intellectual and logical access to Internet resources are essential. Failing at one is like failing at both. Libraries and computing centers represent the intellectual resources and the professional workforce necessary to ensure that access is protected, reliable, and efficient.

At this point, relying on automated systems to provide the level of intellectual access now achieved through cataloging seems dubious, and the application of library standards and methods to a selection of Internet resources would immediately provide improved access.

## CATALOG MAINTENANCE

Every catalog requires maintenance, and cataloging Internet resources introduces a new set of requirements and possibilities. As discussed, maintaining a link between a bibliographic record and the resource it describes is essential, but the volatility of Internet resources can make this difficult. Overcoming the volatility of resource availability must be a high priority for research and testing.

At the outset, it is fair to suggest that resources initially selected for cataloging are likely to be among the more stable by reason of their content and the commitment of the information provider. Emerging relationships between libraries, resource providers, and computing centers will bring a measure of stability to selected resources, and changes can be managed with the involvement of all cognizant parties. Methods of automating catalog maintenance must also be explored vigorously, even as such methods have been developed for the control of subject headings and authority records. Efforts to date by the Internet Engineering Task Force to develop a Uniform Resource Name (URN) scheme are directed at this problem, but solutions have not yet been forthcoming.

## PRESERVING

Preserving informational materials is a function libraries provide with more or less formality. Preserving electronic resources must be a concern of the communities that produce and rely upon them, and ongoing research in this area is needed. Libraries are assuming greater roles in the preservation of electronic resources, hastened by the view that the "content and historical value of thousands of records, databases and personal documents may be irretrievably lost to future generations if we do not take steps to preserve them now."[21]

The notion of depository libraries is certainly not new, and extending such capabilities to include electronic resources seems quite natural if not straightforward.[22] Determining the role of the library catalog within an electronic depository library is essential if such depositories are to be developed uniformly and offer a high level of access and confidence to their users. The fiscal, political, and organizational issues related to an electronic depository library system are apart from issues related to the actual preservation of digital data, and efforts on all fronts are warranted.

The Commission on Preservation and Access and The Research Libraries Group recently formed a Task Force on Archiving of Digital Information, which asserts that "Continued access indefinitely into the future of records stored in digital electronic form cannot under present circumstances be guaranteed within acceptable limits."[23] The report of this task force, which is forthcoming at this writing, will likely define the problems and issues more clearly and propose next steps, but it is unlikely to report solutions or recommend implementations.

## *SECTION III SUMMARY*

Cataloging is only one function within the fabric of library operations, and changes within integrated library functions affect the entire information management system. Cataloging as a function, the catalog as a tool, and catalogers as the practitioners of a specialized profession must all continue to evolve to provide access to Internet resources, but this evolution must be managed within the broader framework of related library functions. Such an approach will help ensure that Internet resources benefit more fully from library services, and that libraries themselves evolve harmoniously within themselves and in relation to the needs of users and the changing complexities of information management.

There is no reason to imagine that cataloging, as a fundamental library function, will be replaced anytime soon regardless of the format of the resources cataloged or their manner of access. The expectation is quite to the contrary: cataloging Internet resources makes sense now and is deserving of the significant and long-term commitment of the library community. Only such a commitment will ensure improved description and access to Internet resources, the integration of records for Internet resources within local catalogs, the extension of the full range of library services to electronic resources, and an evolutionary path that is guided by accumulated knowledge, enlightened current practice, and a wealth of experience.

## *IV. CONCLUSION*

In the past century or so, the library profession has developed a cataloging model appropriate for paper resources. We have been discussing the virtues of extending this model to Internet resources. What are the arguments against this approach? Three obvious ones come to mind: (1) more effective approaches exist; (2) although no other existing approach is clearly superior, cataloging won't work effectively, and we had better find another approach; and (3) libraries, suffering from budget shrinkages and scarce resources, can't afford to undertake this task. The first argument, that some other approach, clearly superior to cataloging in the traditional sense, is available for use, is manifestly mistaken. Or, stated differently, we are not aware of any comparable system. For example, none of the approaches outlined above that are gaining prominence in the Internet environment is likely to challenge cataloging as a tool for effective access. Indeed, they often resemble more a kind of proto or primitive cataloging than they do some new and more effective technique. Highly refined, they could look very much like cataloging.

The second argument, that cataloging in the traditional sense is guaranteed to fail, is harder to respond to. Although we are likely to experience substantial limitations in access using the cataloging model, these are not obvious at present. The approach recommended here is try it and see–carefully, reasonably, and systematically. Even if cataloging were to fail we would be able to see more clearly the proper route.

The third argument, that libraries are insufficiently funded to undertake this task, is more to the point. Numerous studies demonstrate the growing gap between library budgets and the information needs of library patrons. How will they be able to assume this new and rapidly growing responsibility when they are barely able to sustain themselves with the old? No simple answer is possible; in the next section we offer some suggestions.

## *V. NEXT STEPS*

We are experiencing very rapid growth in the availability of materials on the Internet, well beyond our capacity to catalog them effectively using current practices. It is clear that solutions to the problems of access will require major changes in the methods used by libraries and in the automated tools that support their efforts. We would now like to discuss some of these changes.

### *COMPUTER-ASSISTED CATALOGING*

Creating an original cataloging record for a selected Internet resource involves analysis, transcription, and formatting of data taken from the item, the addition of classification, subject headings, and the consultation or creation of authority records. Due to variations in source material, lack of familiarity and experience, and the complexities of adequately describing electronic objects, cataloging Internet resources often requires time and effort exceeding that required for traditional materials. Libraries, already struggling to stretch scarce resources to deal with the paper world will make little headway in this new world without substantial automated aids to leverage human skills and time.

Gathering information about Internet resources has already been automated to some extent. The archie service is an early example: information collected automatically from FTP archives is transformed into a searchable database. Other systems apply similar approaches to Gopher and Web sites. Typically, information extracted from resources obtained from these sites is indexed and searchable. The Open Text Web Index (http://opentext.uunet.ca:8080/omw.html) is a good example. The index recently contained 757 million words and 14,490,926 hyperlinks from 86,228 Web pages (http://opentext.uunet.ca:8080/omw-stats.html). The Web Index had recently "visited" 28,916 pages, removing 22,426 that were no longer on the Web, replacing 11,768 that had changed, and leaving 6,490 unchanged. Another example of this approach is the Harvest Information Discovery and Access System (http://harvest.cs.colorado.edu), which recently had a searchable index of 45,000 Web pages compiled using various methods. The index contains 27,276 objects from 13,845 Internet servers. Data collection occurs nightly at 3:21 a.m., and the system checks for expired objects every 12 hours. Index records returned contain the following fields: (1) http URL, (2) host, (3) path, (4) description, and (5) WAIS results (relevance score and length). The URLs are hot, and clicking on them connects to the remote resource. Such large-scale visitations to Internet resources are not possible without automation.

Methods used in archie, Open Text Web Index, Harvest, and others begin to exploit the automated collection and indexing of information about Internet resources. They do not yield records that approach the usefulness of the catalog record, nor could they be integrated into bibliographic catalogs, but they could serve as the starting point for such a record.

Spectrum, a project under way in the OCLC Office of Research that exploits the knowledge and energies of resource creators, is a second approach for creating minimal-level surrogates.[24] The general idea is to prompt authors at the point of adding a resource to the Internet for key fields of information-often referred to now as "metadata"–such as the author's name, a title, and selected key phrases to describe content, a function which itself will benefit from computer-assisted classification systems. Templates and forms have been proposed elsewhere, too; the CNI TopNode project (http://www.cni.org/projects/topnode) and the IIIR (Integration of Internet Information Resources) Working Group of the IETF have devised template schemes. The latter has been implemented in ALIWEB, a searchable database comprised of standardized resource registration forms (http://web.nexor.co.uk/public/aliweb/aliweb.html). The InterNIC Directory and Database Services (http://www.internic.net), funded in part by the National Science Foundation, and other information services also require the completion of a registration form to collect information about a resource.

The Text Encoding Initiative undertaken by the Center for Electronic Texts in the Humanities includes specifications for a document header.[25] Such an approach for expressing information about electronic texts bodes well for the automated creation of preliminary records; the rich TEI tagging schemes can capture discrete data elements that could be mapped into MARC or other record formats, a process already under investigation at OCLC.

The approaches described above result in surrogates that will have utility but are likely to be deficient, at least in comparison to records that result from full cataloging by experts. The expectation is that catalogers could select and enhance records for the more important items as their usefulness is demonstrated, either through their selection by librarians for inclusion in OPACs or feedback from patrons: just-in-time cataloging, rather than just-in-case. This follows a practice for authority control recommended by Jennifer Younger of The Ohio State University Libraries: provide minimal authority control for an item until it proves worthy of greater attention. (She doesn't explain, nor do we, how the circularity in this approach is to be overcome, that is, how one finds such a record despite what may be deficiencies in its surrogate.)

## *DYNAMIC RECORDS*

Digital and networking technologies provide new possibilities for bibliographic records. Even now, hypertext links expressed in 856 fields can be hot, enabling users to obtain or connect to a remote resource. This is a promising first step in expanding the functionality of bibliographic records, and within an object-oriented universe, a bibliographic record could be considerably more than a static storehouse of bibliographic information. A record may, for example, have associated files–software, image, video, sound, multimedia–that would provide users with additional information about the described resource. Such information could be a "click" away from the bibliographic record.

Managing the dynamic nature of Internet resources is a significant problem. Proposed solutions such as the IETF's Universal Resource Name (URN) are grappling with the problem of persistent, location-independent naming schemes and the associated architecture that would enable Internet resources to be locatable by name regardless of their physical network location. Such a solution would eliminate a weakness in the current use of the URL and the 856 field. One might well extend this notion, however, and invent an environment in which bibliographic records and their associated objects had some "knowledge" of each other: modifications to a resource are automatically transmitted to and recorded in the associated record, for example. The limits of an object-oriented architecture for enhancing surrogate record functionality are unknown but deserving of exploration.

## *BEYOND THE CATALOG*

But are we begging the question here? Is the practice of cataloging–where access is achieved for an object through a surrogate–no longer an approach worth applying or refining? Is there some evolutionary step we are missing, some new generation of access tool that no longer requires the kind of finicky extraction of descriptive properties from an object, and the formation from these extractions of a discrete record that, with added indicators of content, is then manipulated through a "catalog"? Is there a paradigmatic shift waiting in the wings that will rescue catalogers from their labor intensive practice? We can suggest two possibilities here, both of which bear promise and are worth study and experimentation. They are related and depend on the transformations that are occurring in the forms of knowledge as much as changes in packaging. The first is the knowledge base; the second is the knowbot.

### *Knowledge Bases*

At the Laboratory for Applied Research in Academic Information, and more recently at the Center for Knowledge Management at the

University of California at San Francisco, work is underway that may point the way toward new techniques for organizing, managing, and distributing knowledge.[26,27] Initially applied to the primary data and supporting documentation of the Human Genome Project, the approach has since been extended to internal medicine. Although the central focus of knowledge management as depicted by Lucier is a process, one major product exemplifies why it is important here: the Genome Data Base (GDB). "The primary data in GDB are gene locus and marker information with links to the literature and other source material, e.g., personal communications, proceedings and abstracts, and other related databases, such as GenBank."[28] In other words, the GDB combines knowledge, primary data, informal publications, and the mechanisms to access and use them. The knowledge base, as construed here, replaces the combination of library shelves and catalog, providing both the materials and the means of access to the material. It is a prototype of what could emerge in a fully electronic environment as a tool for managing the knowledge evolution process and the artifacts that result from the process.

### *Knowbots*

A second innovation that intimates the changes to come is the "knowbot."[29] A knowbot is a personal search engine that is capable of receiving and storing instructions about what kind of information its owner requires and has the wherewithal to carry out searches across the Internet. It is mentioned here as a prototype of a patron facility that is capable of bypassing or replacing the cataloging operation. Rather than working with document surrogates (though there is no reason that knowbots cannot be designed to operate on bibliographic databases and perhaps be more effective in this mode), the knowbot works directly with information objects, roving from site to site seeking only those objects that fit the instructions provided by the patron. It is an assistant that enters a warehouse of materials and exhaustively assesses each item for its relevance without benefit of catalog or ordered shelving.

Both the knowledge base and the knowbot offer alternatives to human cataloging. The knowledge base imbeds the information object in an architecture that combines with navigational aids to enable the user to locate what is being sought; the knowbot operates directly on information objects without the need for a surrogate, using its knowledge of what is needed to identify and carry back appropriate pieces of information. Each creates a challenge to traditional cataloging.

## A FINAL WORD

Cataloging, in theory and in practice, is in a state of flux. In our lifetimes, we are likely to see a transformation in its underpinnings equivalent to what occurred in the nineteenth century under Dewey and Cutter. Indeed, we are awaiting the appearance of their like today. Will they come from library schools (however renamed or refashioned)? Or from other sectors of the information world? A strong argument for the latter is available in the creative energy being applied in the many efforts outlined above and in the relentless thrust of the Internet protocol groups such as the IETF. If it is from such a quarter that we can expect a solution, we are likely to see the eclipse of professional librarianship and its replacement by information professionals drawn from computer science and other disciplines that deal with electronic information. Library schools, or their modern equivalents, may still contribute to the solutions of these problems through efforts like those undertaken at the University of Michigan; or in the recently rejuvenated school at the University of California at Berkeley.

OCLC will continue to experiment with new and alternative ways of achieving the traditional results. Through the direct cataloging of Internet resources by its membership, we will soon have a sufficiently rich and diverse database of catalog records to obtain conclusions about their effectiveness in this new environment. OCLC's Spectrum project will provide insight into the usefulness of author supplied records as a starting point for full records, and advances in automated or computer-assisted classification can be expected. Explorations into the usefulness of the knowledge base and its role in representing and delivering information to users will no doubt play an important role in the immediate future. Likewise, access mechanisms that work directly with objects, such as the knowbot, rather than surrogates must be investigated. These latter two approaches would no doubt achieve superior results if based exclusively on catalog records of professional quality. It remains to be seen how effectively either will be in bypassing the cataloging operation or in employing unproven substitutes for the richness of bibliographic description. By any measure there is much to do.

## REFERENCES

1. Martin Dillon [and others], *Assessing Information on the Internet: Toward Providing Library Services for Computer-Mediated Communication* (Dublin, Ohio: OCLC, 1993).

2. Peter Deutsch, "Resource discovery in an internet environment: The archie approach," *Electronic Networking: Research, Applications and Policy* 2, no. 1 (1992): 45-51.

3. T. Berners-Lee, L. Masinter, and M. McCahill, *Uniform Resource Locators* (URL), Internet Engineering Task Force Request for Comments #1738, ([Reston, Va.]: IETF, 1994). Available at http://ds.internic.net/ds/dspg1intdoc.html.

4. Library of Congress. Network Development and MARC Standards Office, *Guidelines for the Use of Field 856* (Washington, D.C.: Library of Congress,1995). Available at gopher://marvel.loc.00/.listarch/usmarc/856_guidelines.

5. Dillon [and others], op. cit.

6. Ibid.

7. Ann Okerson, ed., *Directory of Electronic Journals, Newsletters, and Academic Discussion Lists*, 5th ed. (Washington, D.C.: Association of Research Libraries, 1995).

8. Deutch, op. cit., *see also* http://www.sura.net/archie/Archie-Usage.html.

9. Brewster Kahle and Art Medlar, "An information system for corporte users: Wide area information servers," *Online* 15, no. 5 (1991): 56-60.

10. F. Anklesaria [and others], *The Internet Gopher Protocol: A Distributed Document Search and Retrieval Protocol*, Internet Engineering Task Force Request for Comments #1436, ([Reston, Va.]: IETF, 1993). Available at http://ds.internic.net/ds/dspg1intdoc.html.

11. Kevin M. Savetz, "Veronica in cyberspace," *Online Access* 10, no. 4 (1995): 50. *See also* gopher://veronica.scs.unr.edu/00/veronica/veronica-faq.

12. J. Mardikian, "How to use Veronica to find information on the Internet," *The Reference Librarian* 41/41 (1994): 37.

13. L. McGillis, "Gopher searching using Veronica," *The Reference Librarian* 41/42 (1994): 25.

14. C. Bowman [and others], *Harvest: A Scalable, Customizable Discovery and Access System*, Technical report no. CU-CS-732-94 (Boulder, Colo.: University of Colorado-Boulder, Department of Computer Science, 1995). *See also* http://harvest.cs.colorado.edu.

15. David C. Blair, *Language Representation in Information Retrieval* (New York: Elsevier Science Publishers, 1990).

16. Dillon, op. cit.

17. Ibid, 24-34.
18. Ibid, A:1-A:24.
19. Nancy B. Olson, ed., *Cataloging Internet Resources: A Manual and Practical Guide* (Dublin, Ohio: OCLC, 1995). Available at http://www.oclc.org/oclc/man/9256cat/toc/htm.
20. Samuel Demas, Peter McDonald, and Gregory Lawrence, "The Internet and collection development: Mainstreaming selection of Internet resources," *Library Resources and Technical Services* 39, no. 3 (1995): 275. For a more reserved view, see Dan C. Hazen, "Collection development policies in the information age," *College and Research Libraries* 56, no. 1 (1995): 29-31.
21. Jeff Rothenberg, "Ensuring the longevity of digital documents," *Scientific American* (January 1995): 42.
22. Diane H. Smith, "Depository libraries in the 1990s: Wither, or wither depositories?" *Government Publications Review* 17 (1990): 301-24.
23. The Commission on Preservation and Access and The Research Libraries Group, *Task Force on Archiving of Digital Information Proposed Charge* (n.p.: The Commission on Preservation and Access and The Research Libraries Group, n.d.). Available at http://www.oclc.org:5046/~weibel/archtf.html.
24. Diane Vizine-Goetz, "Cataloging productivity tools," in *Annual Review of OCLC Research*: 1994, Bradley C. Watson and Joanne Murphy, eds., 15-18 (Dublin, Ohio: OCLC, 1995).
25. Richard Giordano, "The documentation of electronic texts using Text Encoding Iniative headers: An introduction," *Library Resources and Technical Services* 38, no. 4 (1994): 389-401. *See also* Nancy Ide and Jean Veronis, eds., *Text Encoding Initiative: Background and Contents* (Boston: Kluwer Academic Publishers, 1995).
26. Richard Lucier, "Knowledge management: Refining roles in scientific communication," *Educom Review* 25, no. 3 (1990): 21-27.
27.________, "Embedding the library into scientific and scholarly communication through knowledge management," in *Designing Information: New Roles for Librarians*, Linda C. Smith and Prudence W. Dalrymple, eds., 5-18 (Urbana-Champaign: University of Illinois at Urbana-Champaign, Graduate School of Library and Information Science, 1992).
28.________, op. cit., 1990, 24.
29. Vinton G. Cerf, "Where libraries and the Internet meet," *Information Standards Quarterly* 2, no. 4 (1990): 3-6. *See also* G. Kessler and S. Shepard, *A Primer on Internet and TCP/IP Tools*, Internet Engineering Task Force Request for Comments #1739 ([Reston, Va.]: IETF: 1994). Available at http://ds.internic.net/ds/dspg1intdoc.html.

## SELECTED BIBLIOGRAPHY

Buck, Michael. 1989. Problems in cataloging computer files. *International Cataloging and Bibliographic Control* 18(4): 60-63.

Caplan, Priscilla. 1994. Controlling e-journals: The internet resources project, cataloging guidelines, and USMARC. *The Serials Librarian* 24(3/4): 103-11.

Cochenous, Donnice. 1994. Linking remote users and information: Cataloging internet publications. *Colorado Libraries* 20(3): 20.

Corbin, John. 1992. Technical services for the electronic library. *Library Administration and Management* (spring): 86-90.

Demas, Samuel, Peter McDonald, and Gregory Lawrence. 1995. The Internet and collection development: Mainstreaming selection of Internet resources. *Library Resources and Technical Services* 39(3): 275-90.

Dodge, Chris, Beate Marx, and Hans Pfeiffenberger. 1995. Web cataloging through cache exploitation and steps toward consistency maintenance. *Computer Networks and ISDN Systems* 27:1003-1008.

Dougherty, William et al. 1991. *Report of the task force on the electronic journal.* Blacksburg, VA: Virginia Polytechnic Institute and State University, University Libraries.

Duranceau, Ellen Finnieed. 1994. Naming and describing networked electronic resources: The role of uniform resources identifiers. *Serials Review* 20(4): 31-44.

Flannery, Melindar Reagor. 1995. Cataloging internet resources. *Bulletin of the Medical Library Association* 83(2): 211-15.

Hardy, Darren R., and Michael F. Schwartz. 1994. *Customized information extraction as a basis for resource discovery.* Report no. Cu-CS-707-94. Boulder: University of Colorado at Boulder, Department of Computer Science.

Harrison, A.D., F.A. Roos, and R.E. Thomas. (Semi) automatic capturing of bibliographic information from journal contents pages for inclusion in on-line library catalogues: The RIDDLE project. *The Electronic Library* 13(1): 15-19.

Intner, Sheila 1992. Our electronic heritage–Here today, gone tomorrow? *Technicalities* 12(3): 9-12.

Jacobson, Robert L. 1995. Taming the Internet: Librarians seek better indexing, subject by subject, but task is daunting. *The Chronicle of Higher Education* (April 21): A29-31.

Kleiner, K. 1994. What a tangled web they wove. *New Scientist* 143 (1994): 35-39.

Law, Derek. 1994. How microwaved is your poodle? *Catalogue & Index* 114 (winter): 1-6.

Leahy, Sheila and Richard J. Smith. 1992. A suggested guide and comments for cataloging electronic files. *Technicalities* 12(10): 8-11.

Litchfield, Charles. 1991. Local storage and retrieval of electronic journals: Training issues for technical services personal. *Serials Review* (winter): 83-84.

Lucier, Richard. 1990. Knowledge management: Refining roles in scientific communication. *Educom Review* 25(3): 21-27.

_______. 1992. Embedding the library into scientific and scholarly communication through knowledge management. In *Designing Information: New Roles for Librarians*, ed. Linda C. Smith and Prudence W. Dalrymple, 5-18. Urbana-Champaign: University of Illinois at Urbana-Champaign, Graduate School of Library and Information Science.

Lynch, Clifford A. and Cecilia M. Preston. 1992. Describing and classifying networked information resources. *Electronic Networking: Research, Applications and Policy* 2(1): 13-23.

McCoy, Patricia Sagre. 1995. Technical services and the Internet. *Wilson Library Bulletin* (March): 37-40.

McMillan, Gail. 1991a. Embracing the electric journal: One library's plan. *Serials Librarian* 21(2/3): 97-108.

_______. 1991b. Technical services for electronic journals today. *Serials Review* (winter): 84-86.

_______. 1992. Technical processing of electronic journals. *Library Resources and Technical Services* 36(4): 470-77.

Raitt, David 1994. The future of libraries in the face of the Internet. *The Electronic Library* 12(5): 275-76.

Rosenfeld, Louis B. 1994. Guides, clearing houses, and value-aded repackaging: Some thoughts on how Librarians can improve the Internet. *Reference Services Review* 22(4): 1-16.

Taylor, Arlene G. 1994. The information universe: Will we have chaos or control? *American Libraries* 25 (July/Aug.): 629-31.

Thornburn, Colleen. 1992. Cataloging remote electronic journals and databases. *The Serials Librarian* 23(1/2): 11-23.

Treloar, Andrew Edward. 1994. Classifying internet access tools: A user-centered approach. *Resource Sharing and Information Networks* 9(2): 19-37.

Weibel, Stuart L. 1995. The world wide web and emerging Intnernet resource discovery standards for scholarly literature. *Library Trends* 43(4): 627-44.

Woodward, Hazel and Cliff Mcknight. 1995. Electronic journals: Issues of access and bibliographic control. *Serials Review* (summer): 71-78.

# Index

Page numbers in *italics* indicate figures; page numbers followed by "t" indicate tables.



 

For Product Safety Concerns and Information please contact our EU
representative GPSR@taylorandfrancis.com
Taylor & Francis Verlag GmbH, Kaufingerstraße 24, 80331 München, Germany

www.ingramcontent.com/pod-product-compliance
Ingram Content Group UK Ltd.
Pitfield, Milton Keynes, MK11 3LW, UK
UKHW040102200926
475702UK00001B/6
* 9 7 8 1 5 6 0 2 4 8 4 7 7 *